T0155639

Machine Learning for Economics and Finance in TensorFlow 2

Deep Learning Models for Research and Industry

Isaiah Hull

APress®

Machine Learning for Economics and Finance in TensorFlow 2:
Deep Learning Models for Research and Industry

Isaiah Hull
Nacka, Sweden

ISBN-13 (pbk): 978-1-4842-6372-3   ISBN-13 (electronic): 978-1-4842-6373-0
https://doi.org/10.1007/978-1-4842-6373-0

Managing Director, Apress Media LLC: Welmoed Spahr
Acquisitions Editor: Aaron Black
Development Editor: James Markham
Coordinating Editor: Jessica Vakili

Distributed to the book trade worldwide by Springer Science+Business Media New York, 233 Spring Street, 6th Floor, New York, NY 10013. Phone 1-800-SPRINGER, fax (201) 348-4505, e-mail orders-ny@springer-sbm.com, or visit www.springeronline.com. Apress Media, LLC is a California LLC and the sole member (owner) is Springer Science + Business Media Finance Inc (SSBM Finance Inc). SSBM Finance Inc is a **Delaware** corporation.

For information on translations, please e-mail booktranslations@springernature.com; for reprint, paperback, or audio rights, please e-mail bookpermissions@springernature.com.

Apress titles may be purchased in bulk for academic, corporate, or promotional use. eBook versions and licenses are also available for most titles. For more information, reference our Print and eBook Bulk Sales web page at http://www.apress.com/bulk-sales.

Any source code or other supplementary material referenced by the author in this book is available to readers on GitHub via the book's product page, located at www.apress.com/978-1-4842-6372-3. For more detailed information, please visit http://www.apress.com/source-code.

Printed on acid-free paper

For my wife, Jamie; my son, Moses;
and my parents, James and Gale

Table of Contents

About the Author

Isaiah Hull is a senior economist at the Research Division of Sweden's Central Bank. He holds a PhD in economics from Boston College and conducts research on computational economics, machine learning, macro-finance, and fintech. He also teaches courses on the DataCamp platform, including Introduction to TensorFlow in Python, and is working on an interdisciplinary research project to introduce quantum computing and quantum money to the economics discipline.

About the Technical Reviewer

Vishwesh Ravi Shrimali graduated from BITS Pilani in 2018, where he studied mechanical engineering. Since then, he has worked with Big Vision LLC on deep learning and computer vision and was involved in creating official OpenCV AI courses. Currently, he is working at Mercedes Benz Research and Development India Pvt. Ltd. He has a keen interest in programming and AI and has applied that interest in mechanical engineering projects. He has also written multiple blogs about OpenCV and deep learning on Learn OpenCV, a leading blog on computer vision. He has also coauthored *Machine Learning for OpenCV 4* (second edition) by Packt. When he is not writing blogs or working on projects, he likes to go on long walks or play his acoustic guitar.

CHAPTER 1

TensorFlow 2

TensorFlow is an open source library for machine learning produced by the Google Brain Team. It was originally released to the public in 2015 and quickly became one of the most popular libraries for deep learning. In 2019, Google released TensorFlow 2, which was a substantial departure from TensorFlow 1. In this chapter, we will introduce TensorFlow 2, explain how it can be used in economics and finance, and then review preliminary material that will be necessary for understanding the material in later chapters. If you did not use TensorFlow 1, you may want to skip the "Changes in TensorFlow 2" section.

Installing TensorFlow

In order to use TensorFlow 2, you will need to install Python. Since Python 2 is no longer supported as of January 1, 2020, I recommend installing Python 3 via Anaconda, which bundles Python with 7,500+ commonly used modules for data science: `www.anaconda.com/distribution/`. Once you have installed Anaconda, you can configure a virtual environment from the command line in your operating system. The following code will install an Anaconda virtual environment with Python 3.7.4 named `tfecon`, which is what we will use in this book:

```
conda create -n tfecon python==3.7.4
```

© Isaiah Hull 2021
I. Hull, *Machine Learning for Economics and Finance in TensorFlow 2*,
https://doi.org/10.1007/978-1-4842-6373-0_1

You can activate the environment using the following command:

```
conda activate tfecon
```

Within the environment, you can install TensorFlow using the following command:

```
(tfecon) pip install tensorflow==2.3.0
```

When you want to deactivate your virtual environment, you can do so using the following command:

```
conda deactivate
```

We will use TensorFlow 2.3 and Python 3.7.4 throughout the book. To ensure compatibility with the examples, you should configure your virtual environment accordingly.

Changes in TensorFlow 2

TensorFlow 1 was structured around static graphs. In order to perform a computation, you needed to first define a set of tensors and a sequence of operations. This formed the computational graph, which was fixed at runtime. Static graphs provided an ideal environment for constructing optimized production code, but also discouraged experimentation and increased the difficulty of debugging.

In Listing 1-1, we provide an example of the construction and execution of a static computational graph in TensorFlow 1. We will consider the familiar case where we want to use a set of regressors (features), X, to predict a dependent variable, Y, using an ordinary least squares (OLS) regression. The solution to this problem is the vector of coefficients, ß, which minimizes the sum of the squared regression residuals. Its analytical expression is given in Equation 1-1.

Equation 1-1. The solution to the least squares problem.

$$\beta = \left(X'X\right)^{-1}X'Y$$

Listing 1-1. Implement OLS in TensorFlow 1

```
import tensorflow as tf

print(tf.__version__)
'1.15.2'

# Define the data as constants.
X = tf.constant([[1, 0], [1, 2]], tf.float32)
Y = tf.constant([[2], [4]], tf.float32)

# Matrix multiply X by X's transpose and invert.
beta_0 = tf.linalg.inv(tf.matmul(tf.transpose(X), X))

# Matrix multiply beta_0 by X's transpose.
beta_1 = tf.matmul(beta_0, tf.transpose(X))

# Matrix multiply beta_1 by Y.
beta = tf.matmul(beta_1, Y)

# Perform computation in context of session.
with tf.Session() as sess:
        sess.run(beta)
        print(beta.eval())

[[2.]
[1.]]
```

TensorFlow 1's syntax is cumbersome, which is why we have broken up the computation of the coefficient vector into multiple steps to maintain readability. Additionally, we must perform the computation by building the graph and then executing it within the context of a tf.Session(). We must also print the elements of the coefficient vector within a session. Otherwise, printing beta will simply return the object's name, shape, and data type.

Listing 1-2 repeats the same exercise, but for TensorFlow 2.

Listing 1-2. Implement OLS in TensorFlow 2

```
import tensorflow as tf

print(tf.__version__)
'2.3.0

# Define the data as constants.
X = tf.constant([[1, 0], [1, 2]], tf.float32)
Y = tf.constant([[2], [4]], tf.float32)

# Matrix multiply X by X's transpose and invert.
beta_0 = tf.linalg.inv(tf.matmul(tf.transpose(X), X))

# Matrix multiply beta_0 by X's transpose.
beta_1 = tf.matmul(beta_0, tf.transpose(X))

# Matrix multiply beta_1 by Y.
beta = tf.matmul(beta_1, Y)

# Print coefficient vector.
print(beta.numpy())

[[2.]
 [1.]]
```

While it is not immediately evident from the code, TensorFlow 2 uses imperative programming, which means that operations are executed as they are called by Python. This means that beta_0, for instance, is not an operation that will be executed in a static graph, but is actually the output of that computation. We can see this by printing the same objects in both the TensorFlow 1 and TensorFlow 2 code, as we do in Listings 1-3 and 1-4.

Listing 1-3. Print tensors in TensorFlow 1

```
# Print the feature matrix.
print(X)

tf.Tensor("Const_11:0", shape=(2, 2), dtype=float32)

# Print the coefficient vector.
print(beta)

tf.Tensor("MatMul_20:0", shape=(2, 1), dtype=float32)
```

In TensorFlow 1 (Listing 1-3), X is an operation that defines a constant tensor and beta is an operation that performs matrix multiplication. Printing returns the operation type and the shape and data type of the output. In TensorFlow 2 (Listing 1-4), printing X or beta will return a tf.Tensor() object, which consists of the output value, contained in an array, and its shape and data type. In order to retrieve the output values of operations in TensorFlow 1, we would have to apply the eval() method in the context of a session.

Listing 1-4. Print tensors in TensorFlow 2

```
# Print the feature matrix.
print(X)

tf.Tensor(
[[1. 0.]
```

```
[1. 2.]], shape=(2, 2), dtype=float32)
# Print the coefficient vector.
print(beta.numpy())

[[2.]
 [1.]]
```

While TensorFlow 1 was originally built around the construction and execution of static graphs, it later introduced the possibility of performing computations imperatively through the use of Eager Execution, which was released in October of 2017.[1] TensorFlow 2 moved further along this development path by enabling Eager Execution by default. This is why we do not need to execute computations within a session.

One consequence of the shift to Eager Execution is that TensorFlow 2 no longer builds static computational graphs by default. In TensorFlow 1, such graphs could readily be obtained from logs, such as those generated in Listing 1-5, and then visualized using TensorBoard. Figure 1-1 shows the graph for the OLS problem. The nodes represent operations, such as matrix multiplication and transposition, and the creation of tf.Tensor() objects. The edges of the graph indicate the shape of the tensor being passed between operations.

Listing 1-5. Generate logs for a TensorBoard visualization in TensorFlow 1

```
# Export static graph to log file.
with tf.Session() as sess:
        tf.summary.FileWriter('/logs', sess.graph)
```

---

[1]The Google Brain Team introduced Eager Execution through a post on the Google AI Blog: https://ai.googleblog.com/2017/10/eager-execution-imperative-define-by.html.

Another change in TensorFlow 2, which you may have noticed in Listings 1-1 and 1-2, is that we no longer need to evaluate tensors to expose their elements. We can do this by applying the numpy() method, which, as the name suggests, extracts the elements of a tf.Tensor() object as a numpy array.

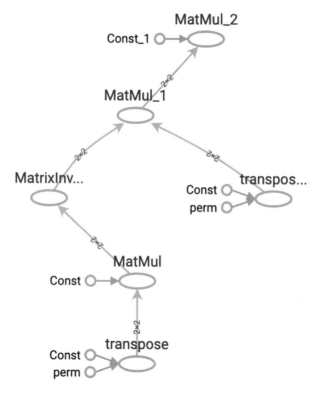

Figure 1-1. *The computational graph for OLS as generated by TensorBoard*

While TensorFlow 2 no longer uses static graphs by default, it does provide users with the option to construct them through the use of @tf.function. This decorator can be used to incorporate static graphs into code in a way that fundamentally differs from TensorFlow 1. Rather than explicitly constructing a graph and then executing it using tf.Session(), we can instead convert functions into static graphs by including the @tf.function decorator before them.

The primary advantage to using @tf.function to generate static graphs is that the function will be compiled and may run faster on a GPU or TPU. Furthermore, any functions called within a function defined under a @tf.function decorator will also be compiled. Listing 1-6 gives an example of the use of static graphs in TensorFlow 2. Here, we return to our OLS example and define a function to make predictions based on the feature matrix, X, and our estimated coefficient vector, beta. Note the use of @tf.function above the definition of ols_predict().

Listing 1-6. Generate OLS predictions with static graphs in TensorFlow 2

```
# Define OLS predict function as static graph.
@tf.function
def ols_predict(X, beta):
        y_hat = tf.matmul(X, beta)
        return y_hat

# Predict Y using X and beta.
predictions = ols_predict(X, beta)
```

In addition to what we have mentioned so far, TensorFlow 2 also introduces substantial namespace changes. This was an attempt to clean up TensorFlow 1, which had many redundant endpoints. TensorFlow 2 also eliminates the tf.contrib() namespace, which was used to house miscellaneous operations that were not yet fully supported in TensorFlow 1. In TensorFlow 2, this code has now been relocated to various relevant namespaces, making it easier to find.[2]

---

[2]For an overview of the namespace design decisions that went into the transition of TensorFlow 1 to TensorFlow 2, see <RefSource>https://github.com/tensorflow/community/blob/master/rfcs/20180827-api-names.md.

Finally, TensorFlow 2 is reoriented around a number of high-level APIs. In particular, greater emphasis has been placed on the Keras and Estimators APIs. Keras simplifies the construction and training of neural network models. And Estimators provides a limited set of models that can be defined with a small set of parameters and then deployed to any environment. In particular, Estimators models can be trained in multi-server settings, and on TPUs and GPUs without modifying the code.

In Listing 1-7, we show the process for defining and training an OLS model in Keras. We do the same in Listing 1-8 using the Estimators library. Notice that both Keras and Estimators require fewer lines of code to define and train an OLS model. However, contrary to the low-level TensorFlow example given in Listing 1-2, they solve the model by minimizing the sum of squared errors numerically, rather than making use of its analytical solution.

Listing 1-7. Solve an OLS model with tf.keras()

```
# Define sequential model.
ols = tf.keras.Sequential()

# Add dense layer with linear activation.
ols.add(tf.keras.layers.Dense(1, input_shape = (2,),
        use_bias = False, activation = 'linear'))

# Set optimizer and loss.
ols.compile(optimizer = 'SGD', loss = 'mse')

# Train model for 500 epochs.
ols.fit(X, Y, epochs = 500)

# Print parameter estimates.
print(ols.weights[0].numpy())

[[1.9754077]
 [1.0151987]]
```

Using the Keras approach, we first defined a sequential neural network model using `tf.keras.Sequential()`. A sequential model can be used to build and train a neural network by (1) stacking layers on top of each other in sequence; (2) compiling the model by specifying options, such as the optimizer, loss, and learning rate; (3) and applying the `fit()` method. Note that the model consists of a single dense layer with a linear activation, since we are performing a linear regression. Additionally, `use_bias` is set to `False`, since the first column of X is a vector of ones, which we use to estimate the constant (bias) term. We used the mean squared error loss when we compiled the model, since we are using ordinary least squares, which should minimize the sum of the squared errors. Finally, we set `epochs` – the number of times we pass over the full sample – to 500. Once the model has been trained, we can print the parameter estimates, which are available as a list in the `ols.weights` attribute. In this case, the list contains a single object, the model parameters, which we'll recover using the `numpy()` method.

Listing 1-8. Solve an OLS model with tf.estimator()

```
# Define feature columns.
features = [
tf.feature_column.numeric_column("constant"),
tf.feature_column.numeric_column("x1")
]

# Define model.
ols = tf.estimator.LinearRegressor(features)

# Define function to feed data to model.
def train_input_fn():
        features = {"constant": [1, 1], "x1": [0, 2]}
        target = [2, 4]
        return features, target

# Train OLS model.
ols.train(train_input_fn, steps = 100)
```

Using the Estimators approach, we first define feature columns, along with their names and types. In the example given in Listing 1-8, we had two features, one of which was the constant term (or "bias" in machine learning). We then defined the model by passing the feature columns to a LinearRegressor() model from tf.estimator. Finally, we defined a function that feeds the data to the model and then applied the train() method, specifying train_input_fn as the first argument and the number of epochs as the second.

To make predictions with tf.estimator, we can use the predict() method of the model we've defined, ols. Similar to the training routine, we'll need to define a function that generates the input dataset, which we'll call test_input_fn(), as shown in Listing 1-9. Passing that to ols.predict() will yield a generator function for model predictions. We can then collect all of the predictions using a list comprehension that iterates over all the generator outputs using next().

Listing 1-9. Make predictions with an OLS model with tf.estimator()

```
# Define feature columns.
def test_input_fn():
        features = {"constant": [1, 1], "x1": [3, 5]}
        return features

# Define prediction generator.
predict_gen = ols.predict(input_fn=test_input_fn)

# Generate predictions.
predictions = [next(predict_gen) for j in range(2)]

# Print predictions.
print(predictions)

[{'predictions': array([5.0000067], dtype=float32)},
 {'predictions': array([7.000059], dtype=float32)}]
```

TensorFlow for Economics and Finance

If you're unfamiliar with machine learning, you might wonder why it makes sense to learn it through the use of TensorFlow. Wouldn't it be easier to use MATLAB, which now offers machine learning toolboxes? Couldn't some supervised learning methods be performed using Stata or SAS? And doesn't TensorFlow have a reputation for being challenging, even among machine learning frameworks? We will explore those questions in this section and will discuss what both TensorFlow and machine learning can offer to economists.

We'll start with the argument for learning TensorFlow, rather than using more familiar tools or other machine learning frameworks. One benefit of using TensorFlow is that it is an open source library that can be used in Python and is maintained by Google. This means that there are no licensing costs, that it benefits from the large community of Python developers, and that it is likely to be well-maintained, since it is the tool of choice for one of the commercial leaders in machine learning. Another benefit of using TensorFlow is that it has consistently been one of the most popular frameworks for machine learning since its release.

Figure 1-2 shows the number of GitHub stars that the nine most popular machine learning frameworks have received. The figure indicates that TensorFlow is approximately four times as popular as the next most popular framework by this measure. In general, this will make it easier to find user-created libraries, code samples, and pretrained models for your projects. Finally, while TensorFlow 1 was challenging relative to other machine learning frameworks, TensorFlow 2 is considerably simpler. Much of the challenge comes from the flexibility that TensorFlow offers, which will provide substantial advantages relative to more limited frameworks.

There are at least two ways in which TensorFlow can be used in economics and finance applications. The first is related to machine learning, which is just beginning to gain widespread use in economics and finance. TensorFlow is ideally suited to this application, since it is a machine learning framework. The second way in which TensorFlow can be used is to solve theoretical economic and financial models. Relative to other machine learning libraries, TensorFlow has the advantage of allowing the use of both high- and low-level APIs. The low-level APIs can be used to construct and solve any arbitrary economic or financial model. In the remainder of this section, we will provide an overview of those two use cases.

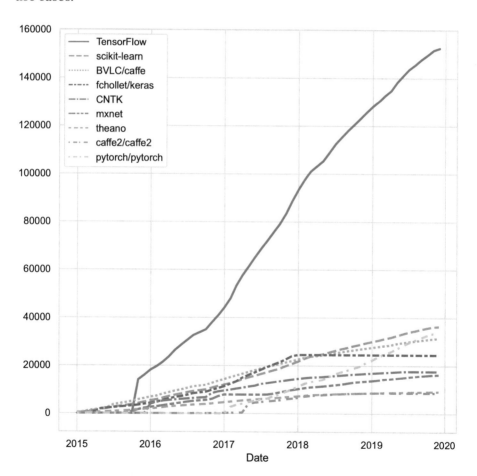

Figure 1-2. *GitHub stars by machine learning framework (2015–2019). Sources: GitHub and Perrault et al. (2019)*

Machine Learning

Economists initially resisted the adoption of methods from machine learning but have since come to embrace them. Part of this reluctance stemmed from the difference in orientation between econometrics and machine learning. Whereas econometrics is centered around causal inference in parsimonious linear models, machine learning is centered around prediction using non-linear models with many parameters.

There is, however, some degree of overlap between economics and machine learning. Economic and financial forecasting, for instance, have the same objective as machine learning: accurate out-of-sample prediction. Additionally, many of the linear models commonly used in econometrics are also used in machine learning. There is, however, substantially more potential for machine learning to be used in economics, which we will discuss in detail in Chapter 2.

What specifically does TensorFlow have to offer when it comes to machine learning applications in economics? There are at least five advantages of TensorFlow that are likely to be beneficial for economics and finance applications: (1) flexibility, (2) distributed training, (3) production quality, (4) high-quality documentation, and (5) extensions.

Flexibility

As we will discuss in detail in Chapter 2, many applications of machine learning in economics will not permit the use of off-the-shelf routines (Athey, 2019). Consequently, it will be useful to develop a familiarity with a machine learning framework that allows for flexibility. This, of course, comes at a cost. For many off-the-shelf applications, simpler and more rigid frameworks, such as `sklearn` or `keras`, will typically allow for faster and less error-prone development. However, for work that combines causal inference with machine learning or requires non-standard model architecture, there will be no option other than to develop in a flexible machine learning framework. TensorFlow is particularly well-suited to this task because it allows for development in a mix of high- and low-level APIs. We can, for instance, construct an algorithm that nests a deep neural network (DNN) within an econometric estimation routine using `tensorflow`, where the DNN is handled using the high-level `keras` API in `tensorflow` and the outer algorithm is constructed using low-level `tensorflow` operations.

Distributed Training

Many machine learning applications in economics do not require the use of a distributed training process. For instance, CPU training is typically sufficient for penalized linear regression models with a few hundred regressors and a few tens of thousands of observations. If, however, you want to fine-tune a ResNet model to predict trade flows from satellite images of ship traffic, you will want to make use of distributed training. TensorFlow 2 detects graphics processing units (GPUs) and tensor processing units (TPUs) automatically and can make use of them in the training process. Listing 1-10 provides an example of the process by which we may list all available devices and select one, such as the GPU or CPU, for use in training.

In some cases, you will want to distribute computations over both the cores of a device, such as GPU or TPU, and across multiple devices. You might, for instance, have access to a workstation with two GPUs. If you aren't using TensorFlow or another framework that provides functionality for distributed computing, you will not be able to efficiently make use of both GPUs. Alternatively, you might want to distribute a computation across multiple GPUs in the cloud to circumvent memory bottlenecks. Or, if you work in industry, you may have an application that must perform classification using a large model in real time and return the information to a user. Again, distributed computing over multiple GPUs or TPUs may be the only option for achieving this while keeping latency low.

TensorFlow provides an interface for multi-device distributed computing through `tf.distribute.Strategy()`. The advantage of TensorFlow's approach is that it is simple and performs well without modification. Rather than deciding how the computation should be distributed down to the low-level details, you can simply specify the devices that will be used and a strategy for distribution. TensorFlow allows for both synchronous strategies, which maintain the same parameter values and gradient across device, and asynchronous strategies, which allow for local updating on individual devices.

Listing 1-10. List all available devices, select CPU, and then switch to GPU

```
import tensorflow as tf

# Print list of devices.
devices = tf.config.list_physical_devices()
print(devices)

[PhysicalDevice(name='physical:device:CPU_0',
Device_type='CPU'),
PhysicalDevice(name='physical_device:XLA_CPU:0',
Device_type='XLA_CPU'),
PhysicalDevice(name='physical_device:XLA_GPU:0',
Device_type='XLA_GPU'),
PhysicalDevice(name='physical_device:GPU:0',
Device_type='GPU')

# Set device to CPU.
tf.config.experimental.set_visible_devices(
        devices[0], 'CPU')

# Change device to GPU.
tf.config.experimental.set_visible_devices(
        devices[3], 'GPU')
```

Production Quality

For economists working in industry and using machine learning to create products or provide services, it is essential that code eventually moves from an "experimental" or "developmental" stage to production quality. This reduces the likelihood that end users will encounter bugs or issues with stability. Another advantage of TensorFlow is that it offers functionality for producing and serving production-quality code.

For the creation of production-quality code, TensorFlow offers the high-level Estimators API. This can be used, for instance, to train a neural network in an environment that enforces best practices and removes error-prone parts of the development process. The Estimators API allows developers to both make use of pre-made models, where the model architecture can be fully specified with a handful of parameters, and also to develop their own.

In addition to the Estimators API, which is used to develop models, TensorFlow Serving can be used to develop and deploy production-quality applications to end users. Using TensorFlow Serving, we can, for instance, allow users to submit queries in the form of data, text, or images that will then be input into a model, yielding a classification or prediction for the user.

High-Quality Documentation

TensorFlow 1 initially had opaque and incomplete documentation, which is part of what made it intimidating for newcomers. This is especially true for economists who often use well-documented commercial offerings for econometrics and computation, such as MATLAB, Stata, and SAS. This changed, however, when Google began work on TensorFlow 2. It has since transitioned to high-quality and detailed documentation, which is now one of its primary assets as a machine learning framework.

One advantage of TensorFlow's documentation is that it is often paired with a Google Colaboratory (Colab) notebook. If you are unfamiliar with Google Colab, it is a free service for hosted Jupyter notebooks. It also allows users to execute notebooks on Google's servers using GPUs and TPUs for free. Pairing documentation with a Colab notebook enables users to immediately launch a minimal example of the code, modify it if desired, and execute it on state-of-the-art hardware.

Extensions

Another advantage of using TensorFlow for economic and financial applications of machine learning is that it has many extensions. We will highlight just four such extensions in the following subsections, but there are several others that may be of interest to economists.

TensorFlow Hub

Located at `https://tfhub.dev/`, TensorFlow Hub provides a searchable library of pretrained models that can be imported into TensorFlow, and then either used as is for classification and regression tasks or fine-tuned for related tasks. You could, for instance, use TensorFlow Hub to import an EfficientNet model trained on the ImageNet dataset, drop the classification head, and then train the model to perform a different classification task using an alternative dataset.

TensorFlow Probability

Designed for statisticians and machine learning researchers, TensorFlow probability offers an expanded set of probability distributions and tools for developing probabilistic models, including probabilistic layers in neural network models. It also provides support for variational inference, Markov chain Monte Carlo (MCMC), and an expanded set of optimizers commonly used in econometrics, such as BFGS. For academic economists who wish to perform causal inference with machine learning models, TensorFlow probability will be an indispensable tool.

TensorFlow Federated

In some cases, the data needed to train a model will be decentralized, making the task infeasible with standard methods. For academic and public sector economists, this issue often arises when legal or privacy concerns prevent data sharing. For industry economists, this may occur when the data is distributed across user devices, such as mobile phones, but cannot be centralized. In all of the preceding cases, federated learning offers the possibility of training a model without centralizing the data. This can be done using the TensorFlow Federated extension.

TensorFlow Lite

Economists working in industry often train models using multiple GPUs or TPUs, only to deploy them to an environment with severe computational resource constraints. TensorFlow Lite can be used in such situations to avoid resource constraints and improve performance. It works by converting a TensorFlow model to an alternative format, compressing the weights, and then outputting a .tflite file, which can be deployed to a mobile environment.

Theoretical Models

While TensorFlow was designed primarily for constructing and solving deep learning models, it offers a wide variety of computational tools that can be used to solve any arbitrary model. This differs from narrower machine learning frameworks, which are not sufficiently flexible to construct models outside of a well-defined family.

In particular, TensorFlow can be used to solve theoretical models in economics and finance. This can be done by (1) defining a computational graph that represents the model and (2) defining the associated loss function. We may then apply a standard optimization routine in TensorFlow, such as stochastic gradient descent (SGD), to minimize the loss function.

TensorFlow's state-of-the-art automatic differentiation libraries, along with the ease of performing parallel and distributed computation, make it a formidable alternative to existing software for solving theoretical models in economics and finance. We will discuss this issue in detail in Chapter 10.

Introduction to Tensors

TensorFlow was primarily designed for the purpose of performing deep learning with neural networks. Since neural networks consist of operations performed on tensors by tensors, TensorFlow was a natural choice for the name.

While tensors have specific mathematical definitions in certain contexts, such as physics, we will adopt the one that is most relevant to machine learning, taken from *Deep Learning* (Goodfellow, Bengio, and Courville, 2016):

> *In the general case, an array of numbers arranged on a regular grid with a variable number of axes is known as a tensor.*

In practice, we will often describe a tensor by its rank and shape. A rectangular array with k indices, $Y_{i_1 \ldots i_k}$, is said to be of rank-k. You may alternatively see such an array described as having order or dimension k. The shape of a tensor is specified by the length of each of its dimensions.

Consider, for example, the OLS problem we described in Listing 1-2, where we made use of three tensors: X, Y, and β. These were the feature matrix, the target vector, and the coefficient vector, respectively. In a regression problem with m features and n observations, X is a rank-2 tensor with shape (n, m), Y is a rank-1 tensor with shape n, and β is a rank-1 tensor of shape m.

More generally, a rank-0 tensor is a scalar, a rank-1 tensor is a vector, and a rank-2 tensor is a matrix. We will refer to tensors of rank-k, where $k \geq 3$, as k-tensors. Figure 1-3 illustrates these definitions for a batch of images that have three color channels.

At the top left of Figure 1-3, we have a single pixel from the blue color channel, which would be represented by a single integer. This is a scalar or rank-0 tensor. To the right, we have a collection of pixels, which form the border of the green color channel of an image. These constitute a rank-1 tensor or vector. If we take the entire red color channel itself, this is a matrix or rank-2 tensor. Furthermore, if we combine the three color channels, this forms a color image, which is a 3-tensor; and if we stack multiple images into a training batch, we get a 4-tensor.

It is worth emphasizing that definitions of tensors often assume rectangularity. That is, if we're working with a batch of images, each image is expected to have the same length, width, and number of color channels. If each image had a different shape, it isn't obvious how we would specify the shape of the batch tensor. Furthermore, many machine learning frameworks will not be able to process non-rectangular tensors in a way that fully exploits the parallelization capabilities of a GPU or TPU.

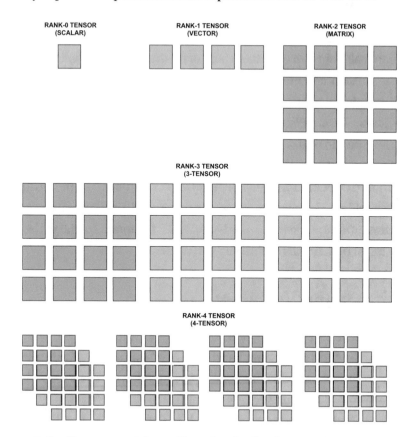

Figure 1-3. *Decomposition of batch of color images into tensors*

For most problems that we consider in this book, the data will either naturally be rectangular or can be reshaped to be rectangular without a substantial loss in performance. There are, however, cases in which it cannot. Fortunately, TensorFlow offers a data structure called a "ragged tensor," which is available as `tf.ragged`, that is compatible with more than 100 TensorFlow operations. There is also a new generation of convolutional neural networks (CNNs) that make use of masking, a process which identifies the important parts of images, allowing for the use of variable input shape images.

Linear Algebra and Calculus in TensorFlow

Similar to econometric routines, machine learning algorithms make extensive use of linear algebra and calculus. Much of this, however, remains hidden from users in standard machine learning frameworks. To the contrary, TensorFlow allows users to construct models from both high- and low-level APIs. With low-level APIs, they can build, for instance, a non-linear least squares estimation routine or an algorithm to train a neural network at the level of linear algebra and calculus operations. In this section, we will discuss how common operations in linear algebra and calculus can be performed using TensorFlow. However, before we do that, we will start with a discussion of constants and variables in TensorFlow, which are fundamental to the description of both linear algebra and calculus operations.

Constants and Variables

TensorFlow divides tensor objects into constants and variables. The meaning of the terms "constant" and "variable" coincide with standard usage in programming. That is, a constant is fixed, whereas a variable may change over time. To illustrate this, we return to the OLS example in Listing 1-11. Rather than solving the problem analytically, we'll simply compute a residual term, which could be used to construct a loss function.

The feature matrix, X, and the target, Y, are defined as constant tensors, since they do not change as the model is trained. The parameter vector, beta, is defined as a variable using tf.Variable(), since it will be varied by the optimization algorithm to try to minimize a transformation of the residuals.[3]

Listing 1-11. Define constants and variables for OLS

```
import tensorflow as tf

# Define the data as constants.
X = tf.constant([[1, 0], [1, 2]], tf.float32)
Y = tf.constant([[2], [4]], tf.float32)

# Initialize beta.
beta = tf.Variable([[0.01],[0.01]], tf.float32)

# Compute the residual.
residuals = Y - tf.matmul(X, beta)
```

In general, we will use constant tensors for both input data and intermediate data produced by the model, such as the residuals. We will also use constant tensors to capture model hyperparameters. For neural networks and penalized regression models, for instance, we will select regularization parameters outside of the training process and will use tf.constant() to define them.

In general, we will use tf.Variable() to initialize trainable model parameters. This includes, for example, the weights in a neural network, the coefficient vector for a linear regression, or an intermediate step in a model that involves a linear transformation using a matrix of parameters.

---

[3]If you're running the listings in this chapter consecutively in a Jupyter Notebook, you can avoid runtime errors by executing listings in separate Python sessions. In particular, you may wish to initiate a new session after running tf.estimator listings.

Linear Algebra

Since TensorFlow is centered around deep learning models – which make use of tensor inputs, produce tensor outputs, and apply linear transformations – it was designed with considerable capacity to perform linear algebra computations and to distribute those computations over GPUs and TPUs. In this section, we will discuss how common operations in linear algebra can be performed using TensorFlow.

Scalar Addition and Multiplication

Although scalars can be considered to be rank-0 tensors and are defined as tensor objects in TensorFlow, we will often use them for different purposes than vectors, matrices, and k-tensors. Furthermore, certain operations that can be performed on vectors and matrices cannot be performed on scalars.

In Listing 1-12, we examine how to perform scalar addition and multiplication in TensorFlow. We'll do this using two scalars, s1 and s2, which we will define using tf.constant(). If we wanted these scalars to be trainable parameters in a model, we would instead use tf.Variable(). Notice that we first perform addition using tf.add() and multiplication using tf.multiply(). We then make use of operator overloading and perform the same operations using + and *. Finally, we print the sum and product we computed. Note that both are tf.Tensor() objects of type float32, since we defined each constant as a tf.float32.

Tensor Addition

We next examine tensor addition, since it takes only one form and generalizes to k-tensors. For 0-tensors (scalars), we saw that the tf.add() operation could be applied and that it summed the two scalars taken as arguments. If we extend this to rank-1 tensors (vectors), addition works as in Equation 1-2: that is, we sum the corresponding elements in each vector.

24

Equation 1-2. Example of vector addition.

$$\begin{bmatrix} a_0 \\ a_1 \\ a_2 \end{bmatrix} + \begin{bmatrix} b_0 \\ b_1 \\ b_2 \end{bmatrix} = \begin{bmatrix} a_0 + b_0 \\ a_1 + b_1 \\ a_2 + b_2 \end{bmatrix}$$

Listing 1-12. Perform scalar addition and multiplication in TensorFlow

```
import tensorflow as tf

# Define two scalars as constants.
s1 = tf.constant(5, tf.float32)
s2 = tf.constant(15, tf.float32)

# Add and multiply using tf.add() and tf.multiply().
s1s2_sum = tf.add(s1, s2)
s1s2_product = tf.multiply(s1, s2)

# Add and multiply using operator overloading.
s1s2_sum = s1+s2
s1s2_product = s1*s2

# Print sum.
print(s1s2_sum)

tf.Tensor(20.0, shape=(), dtype=float32)

# Print product.
print(s1s2_product)

tf.Tensor(75.0, shape=(), dtype=float32)
```

Furthermore, we may extend this to rank-2 tensors (matrices), as shown in Equation 1-3, as well as rank-k tensors, where $k>2$. In all cases, the operation is performed the same way: the elements in the same positions in the two tensors are summed.

Equation 1-3. Example of matrix addition.

$$
\begin{bmatrix} a_{00} & \cdots & a_{0n} \\ \vdots & \ddots & \vdots \\ a_{m0} & \cdots & a_{mn} \end{bmatrix} + \begin{bmatrix} b_{00} & \cdots & b_{0n} \\ \vdots & \ddots & \vdots \\ b_{m0} & \cdots & b_{mn} \end{bmatrix} = \begin{bmatrix} a_{00} + b_{00} & \cdots & a_{0n} + b_{0n} \\ \vdots & \ddots & \vdots \\ a_{m0} + b_{m0} & \cdots & a_{mn} + b_{mn} \end{bmatrix}
$$

Notice that tensor addition can only be performed using two tensors of the same shape.[4] Two tensors with different shapes will not always have two elements defined in the same positions. Additionally, note that tensor addition trivially satisfies the commutative and associative laws.[5]

In Listing 1-13, we demonstrate how to perform tensor addition with rank-4 tensors. We will use two 4-tensors, images and transform, which have been imported as numpy arrays. The images tensor is a batch of 32 color images, and the transform tensor is an additive transformation.

We first print the shapes of both images and transform to check that that they are the same, as is required for tensor addition. We can see that both objects have the shape (32, 64, 64, 3). That is, they consist of a batch of 32 images, which are 64x64, with three color channels. Next, we convert both numpy arrays into TensorFlow constant objects using tf.constant(). We then apply the additive transformation using tf.add() and the overloaded + operator separately. Note that the + operator will perform the computation in TensorFlow, since we converted both tensors into constant objects in TensorFlow.

---

[4]As we'll discuss later in the chapter, there are two types of exceptions to this rule: broadcasting and scalar-tensor addition.

[5]Let A, B, and C be rank-k tensors. The commutative law states that $A + B = B + A$, and the associative law states that $(A + B) + C = A + (B + C)$.

Listing 1-13. Perform tensor addition in TensorFlow

```
import tensorflow as tf

# Print the shapes of the two tensors.
print(images.shape)
(32, 64, 64, 3)
print(transform.shape)
(32, 64, 64, 3)

# Convert numpy arrays into tensorflow constants.
images = tf.constant(images, tf.float32)
transform = tf.constant(transform, tf.float32)

# Perform tensor addition with tf.add().
images = tf.add(images, transform)

# Perform tensor addition with operator overloading.
images = images+transform
```

Tensor Multiplication

In contrast to tensor addition, where we only considered elementwise operations, performed on two tensors of identical shape, we will consider three different types of tensor multiplication:

- Elementwise multiplication

- Dot products

- Matrix multiplication

Elementwise Multiplication

As with tensor addition, elementwise multiplication is only defined for tensors with identical dimensions. If, for instance, we have two rank-3 tensors, A and B, each with indices i, j, and r, where $i \in \{1, ..., I\}, j \in \{1, ..., J\}$, and $r \in \{1, ..., R\}$, then their elementwise product is the tensor C, where each element, C_{ijr}, is defined as in Equation 1-4.

Equation 1-4. Elementwise tensor multiplication.

$$C_{ijr} = A_{ijr} * B_{ijr}$$

Equation 1-5 provides an example of elementwise tensor multiplication for two matrices. Note that $\odot$ represents elementwise multiplication.

Equation 1-5. Elementwise tensor multiplication.

$$\begin{bmatrix} a_{00} & a_{01} \\ a_{10} & a_{11} \end{bmatrix} \odot \begin{bmatrix} b_{00} & b_{01} \\ b_{10} & b_{11} \end{bmatrix} = \begin{bmatrix} a_{00} * b_{00} & a_{01} * b_{01} \\ a_{10} * b_{10} & a_{11} * b_{11} \end{bmatrix} = \begin{bmatrix} c_{00} & c_{01} \\ c_{10} & c_{11} \end{bmatrix}$$

The TensorFlow implementation of elementwise tensor multiplication is given in Listing 1-14. We'll multiply two 6-tensors, A and B, which we generate by drawing from a normal distribution. The list of integers we provide to `tf.random.normal()` is the shape of the 6-tensor. Notice that both A and B were 6-tensors of shape (5, 10, 7, 3, 2, 15). In order to perform elementwise multiplication, both tensors must have the same shape. Furthermore, we can use either the TensorFlow multiplication operator, `tf.multiply()`, or the overloaded multiplication operator, *, to perform elementwise multiplication, since we generated both A and B using TensorFlow operations.

Dot Product

A dot product can be performed between two vectors, A and B, with the same number of elements, n. It is the sum of the products of the corresponding elements in A and B. Let $A = [a_0...a_n]$ and $B = [b_0...b_n]$. Their dot product, c, is denoted $c = A \cdot B$ and is defined in Equation 1-6.

Equation 1-6. Dot product of vectors.

$$c = \sum_{i=0}^{n} a_i b_i$$

Listing 1-14. Perform elementwise multiplication in TensorFlow

```
import tensorflow as tf

# Generate 6-tensors from normal distribution draws.
A = tf.random.normal([5, 10, 7, 3, 2, 15])
B = tf.random.normal([5, 10, 7, 3, 2, 15])

# Perform elementwise multiplication.
C = tf.multiply(A, B)
C = A*B
```

Notice that a dot product transforms the two vectors into a scalar, c. Listing 1-15 demonstrates how to perform a dot product in TensorFlow. We start by defining two vectors, A and B, each of which has 200 elements. We then apply the tf.tensordot() operation, which takes the two tensors the parameter axes as arguments. To compute the dot products of two vectors, we will use 1 for the axes parameter. Finally, we extract the numpy attribute of c, which gives a numpy array of the constant object. Printing it, we can see that the output of the dot product is, indeed, a scalar.[6]

Listing 1-15. Perform dot product in TensorFlow

```
import tensorflow as tf

# Set random seed to generate reproducible results.
tf.random.set_seed(1)
```

---

[6]The reason we specify an axes arugment when using tf.tensordot() is because we are actually performing an operation called a "tensor contraction," which is more general than a dot product. A tensor contraction takes two tensors of arbitrary rank, A and B, as well as dimension indices, i and j, in A and B. It then contracts A and B by performing elementwise multiplication over the specified dimensions and then summing the products.

```
# Use normal distribution draws to generate tensors.
A = tf.random.normal([200])
B = tf.random.normal([200])

# Perform dot product.
c = tf.tensordot(A, B, axes = 1)

# Print numpy argument of c.
print(c.numpy())
```

-15.284362

Matrix Multiplication

We next consider matrix multiplication, which we will exclusively discuss for the case of rank-2 tensors. This is because we will only apply this operation to matrices. In the case where we are performing matrix multiplication with k-tensors for k>2, we will actually be performing "batch" matrix multiplication. This is used, for instance, in training and prediction tasks with convolutional neural networks (CNNs), where we might want to multiply the same set of weights by all of the images in a batch of images.

Let's again consider the case where we have two tensors, A and B, but this time, they do not need to have the same shape, but do need to be matrices. If we wish to matrix multiply A by B, then the number of columns of A must be equal to the number of rows of B. The shape of the product of A and B will be equal to the number of rows in A by the number of columns in B.

Now, if we let $A_{i:}$ represent row i in matrix A, $B_{:j}$ represent column j in matrix B, and C denote the product of A and B, then matrix multiplication is defined for all rows, $j \in \{1, .., J\}$ in C, as in Equation 1-7.

Equation 1-7. Matrix multiplication.

$$C_{ij} = A_{i:} \cdot B_{:j}$$

That is, each element, C_{ij}, is computed as the dot product of row i of matrix A and column j of matrix B. Equation 1-8 provides an example of this for 2x2 matrices. Additionally, Listing 1-16 demonstrates how to perform matrix multiplication in TensorFlow.

Equation 1-8. Matrix multiplication example.

$$C = \begin{bmatrix} a_{00} & a_{01} \\ a_{10} & a_{11} \end{bmatrix} \begin{bmatrix} b_{00} & b_{01} \\ b_{10} & b_{11} \end{bmatrix} = \begin{bmatrix} a_{00}b_{00} + a_{01}b_{10} & a_{00}b_{01} + a_{01}b_{11} \\ a_{10}b_{00} + a_{11}b_{11} & a_{10}b_{01} + a_{11}b_{11} \end{bmatrix}$$

We first generate two matrices using random draws from a normal distribution. Matrix A has the shape (200, 50), and matrix B has the shape (50, 10). We then use tf.matmul() to multiply A by B, assigning the result to C, which has a shape of (200, 10).

What would happen if we instead multiplied B by A? We can see from the shapes of A and B that this is not possible, since the number of columns in B is 50 and the number of rows in A is 200. Indeed, matrix multiplication is not commutative, but it is associative.[7]

Listing 1-16. Perform matrix multiplication in TensorFlow

```
import tensorflow as tf

# Use normal distribution draws to generate tensors.
A = tf.random.normal([200, 50])
B = tf.random.normal([50, 10])

# Perform matrix multiplication.
C = tf.matmul(A, B)

# Print shape of C.
print(C.shape)

(200, 10)
```

---

[7]Assume we have three matrices: X, Y, and Z. The shape of the matrices is such that XY is defined and YZ is defined. It will not generally be the case that XY = YX and YX may not be defined. It is, however, the case that (XY)Z = X(YZ).

Broadcasting

In some circumstances, you will want to want to make use of broadcasting, which involves performing linear algebraic operations with two tensors that do not have compatible shapes. This will most commonly occur when you want to add a scalar to a tensor, multiply a scalar by a tensor, or perform batch multiplication. We will consider each of these cases.

Scalar-Tensor Addition and Multiplication

When manipulating image data, it is common to apply scalar transformations to matrices, 3-tensors, and 4-tensors. We'll start with the definition of scalar-tensor addition and scalar-tensor multiplication. In both cases, we'll assume we have a scalar, γ, and a rank-k tensor, A. Equation 1-9 defines scalar-tensor addition, and Equation 1-10 defines scalar-tensor multiplication.

Equation 1-9. Scalar-tensor addition.

$$C_{i_1 \ldots i_k} = \gamma + A_{i_1 \ldots i_k}$$

Equation 1-10. Scalar-tensor multiplication.

$$C_{i_1 \ldots i_k} = \gamma A_{i_1 \ldots i_k}$$

Scalar-tensor addition is performed by adding the scalar term to each of the elements in the tensor. Similarly, scalar-tensor multiplication is performed by multiplying the scalar by each element in the tensor. That is, we repeat the operations specified in Equations 1-9 and 1-10 for all $i_1 \in \{1, \ldots, I_1\}$, $i_2 \in \{1, \ldots, 2\}$, ..., $i_k \in \{1, \ldots, I_k\}$. Listing 1-17 provides the TensorFlow implementation of both scalar-tensor addition and multiplication for a 4-tensor of images of shape (64, 256, 256, 3) called images.

We first define two constants, gamma and mu, which are the scalars we will use in the addition and multiplication operations. Since we have defined them using tf.constant(), we can make use of the overloaded operators * and +, rather than tf.multiply() and tf.add(). We have now transformed the elements in a batch of 64 images from integers in the [0, 255] interval to real numbers in the [–1, 1] interval.

Listing 1-17. Perform scalar-tensor addition and multiplication

```
import tensorflow as tf

# Define scalar term as a constant.
gamma = tf.constant(1/255.0)
mu = tf.constant(-0.50)

# Perform tensor-scalar multiplication.
images = gamma*images

# Perform tensor-scalar addition.
images = mu+images
```

Batch Matrix Multiplication

A final instance of broadcasting we'll consider is batch matrix multiplication. Consider the case where we have a 3-tensor batch of grayscale images of shape (64, 256, 256) named images and want to apply the same linear transformation of shape (256, 256) named transform to each of them. For the sake of illustration, we'll use randomly generated tensors for images and transformation, which are defined in Listing 1-18.

Listing 1-18. Define random tensors

```
import tensorflow as tf

# Define random 3-tensor of images.
images = tf.random.uniform((64, 256, 256))

# Define random 2-tensor image transformation.
transform = tf.random.normal((256, 256))
```

Listing 1-19 demonstrates how we can perform batch matrix multiplication in TensorFlow using the 3-tensor and 2-tensor we've defined.

Listing 1-19. Perform batch matrix multiplication

```
# Perform batch matrix multiplication.
batch_matmul = tf.matmul(images, transform)

# Perform batch elementwise multiplication.
batch_elementwise = tf.multiply(images, transform)
```

We used `tf.matmul()` to perform batch matrix multiplication. It is also possible to perform batch elementwise multiplication, too, as we showed in Listing 1-19.

Differential Calculus

Both economics and machine learning make extensive use of differential calculus. In economics, differential calculus is used to solve analytical models, estimate econometric models, and solve computational models that are structured as systems of differential equations. In machine learning, differential calculus is typically used in routines that are applied to train models. Stochastic gradient descent (SGD) and its many variants rely on the computation of gradients, which are vectors of derivatives.

Virtually all applications of differential calculus in economics and machine learning are done with the same intention: to find an optimum – that is, a maximum or minimum. In this section, we'll discuss differential calculus, its use in machine learning, and its implementation in TensorFlow.

First and Second Derivatives

Differential calculus is centered around the computation of derivatives. A derivative tells us how much a variable, Y, changes in response to a change in another variable, X. If the relationship between X and Y is linear, then the derivative of Y with respect to X is simply the slope of a line, which is trivial to compute. Consider, for instance, a deterministic linear model with one independent variable, β, which takes the form of Equation 1-11.

Equation 1-11. A linear model with one regressor.

$$Y = \alpha + X\beta$$

What is the derivative of Y with respect to X in this model? It's the change in Y, ΔY, with respect to a change in X, ΔX. For a linear function, we can compute this using two points (X_1, Y_1) and (X_2, Y_2), as in Equation 1-12.

Equation 1-12. Calculating the change in Y with respect to a change in X.

$$Y_2 - Y_1 = \left(\alpha + X_2\beta\right) - \left(\alpha + X_1\beta\right)$$

$$= \Delta Y = \Delta X\beta$$

Dividing both sides of the equation by ΔX yields the expression for the change in Y with respect to a change in X. This is just the derivative X, which is shown in Equation 1-13.

Equation 1-13. The derivative of Y with respect to X.

$$\frac{\Delta Y}{\Delta X} = \beta$$

This, of course, is just the slope of a linear function, as depicted in Figure 1-4. Notice that the points we select do not matter. Irrespective of the choice of (X_1, Y_1) and (X_2, Y_2), the derivative (or slope) will always be the same. This is a property of linear functions.

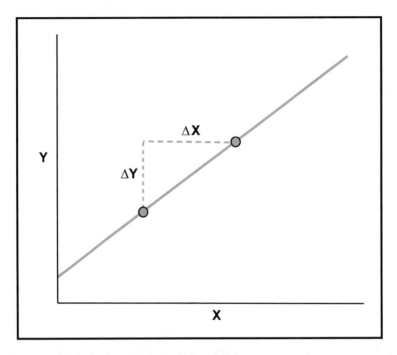

Figure 1-4. *The slope of a linear function*

But what if we have a non-linear relationship? Figure 1-5 shows examples of two such functions. We can see that the approach we used to recover the derivative of X doesn't quite work for X^2 or $X^2 - X$.

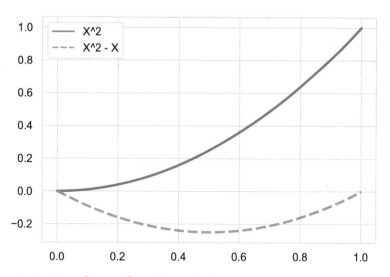

Figure 1-5. *Non-linear functions of X*

Why not? Because the slopes of X^2 and $X^2 - X$ are not constant. The slope of X^2 is increasing in X. The slope of $X^2 - X$ is initially decreasing, followed by an increase when the X^2 term begins to dominate. Irrespective of the choices of (X_1, Y_1) and (X_2, Y_2), the derivative of Y with respect to X will always vary over the interval over which it is calculated. In fact, it will only be constant if we calculate it at a point, rather than over an interval, which is precisely what differential calculus tells us how to do.

Equation 1-14 provides a definition for the derivative of any general function of one variable, $f(X)$, including non-linear functions. Since the derivative itself depends on where we evaluate it, we will denote it using a function, $f'(X)$.

Equation 1-14. Definition of derivative of f(X) with respect to X.

$$f'(X) = \lim_{h \to 0} \frac{f(X+h) - f(X)}{(X+h) - X} = \lim_{h \to 0} \frac{f(X+h) - f(X)}{h}$$

Notice the similarity between this definition and the one we used earlier for the derivative (slope) of a linear function. We can see that $\Delta X = h$ and $\Delta Y = f(X + h) - f(X)$. The only thing that has changed is the addition of the limit term, which we have not defined.

Informally, a limit tells us how a function behaves as we approach some value for one of its arguments. In this case, we are shrinking the interval, h, over which we compute the derivative. That is, we're moving X_1 and X_2 closer together.

In Figure 1-5, one of the functions we plotted was $Y = X^2$. We'll plug that into our definition of a derivative for a general function in Equation 1-15.

Equation 1-15. Example of a derivative for $Y = X^2$.

$$f'(X) = \lim_{h \to 0} \frac{(X + h)^2 - X^2}{h}$$

$$= \lim_{h \to 0} 2X + h$$

$$= 2X$$

How did we compute the limit of $2X + h$ as h approaches 0? Since we no longer have an expression for $f'(X)$ that is undefined at $h = 0$, such as the original expression, which contained h in the denominator, we may simply plug $h = 0$ into the expression, yielding $2X$.

And what did we learn? The derivative of $Y = X^2$ is $2X$, which is also a function of X. You might already have the intuition that the slope of X^2 is increasing in X. Computing the derivative tells you precisely how much it increases: that is, a one unit increase in X increases the slope of $f(X)$ by two units. Additionally, we may evaluate the slope at a point. At $X = 10$, for instance, the slope is 20.

We can now compute the slope at any point of our choosing, but what can we do with this? Let's return to Figure 1-5. This time, we'll look at the function $f(X) = X^2 - X$. We can see that the curve in the plot is bowl-shaped over the interval. In mathematical optimization, such functions are said to be "convex," which means that any arbitrary line segment drawn through two points on their graph will always lie either above or on the graph itself.

As we can see from the derivative in Equation 1-16 and also from Figure 1-5, the slope of the function is initially negative, but eventually becomes positive as we move from 0 to 1 over the [0, 1] interval. The point at which the derivative changes from negative to positive is the minimum value of $f(X)$ over the interval. As the plot indicates visually, the slope of the function is zero at the minimum.

Equation 1-16. Example of a derivative for Y = X² - X.

$$f'(X) = \lim_{h \to 0} \frac{\left[(X+h)^2 - (X+h)\right] - \left(X^2 - X\right)}{h}$$

$$= \lim_{h \to 0} 2X + h - 1$$

$$= 2X - 1$$

This hints at another important property of derivatives: we can use them to find the minimum value of a function. In particular, we know that $f'(X) = 0$ at the minimum. We can exploit this, as in Equation 1-17, to identify points that could be minimums – that is, "candidate" minima.

Equation 1-17. Finding a candidate minimum of Y = X² - X.

$$0 = 2X - 1$$

$$\rightarrow X = 0.5$$

Computing the derivative, setting it to zero, and then solving for X yields a candidate value for the minimum: 0.5. Why is it only a candidate minimum, rather than just the minimum? There are two reasons. First, the derivative will also be zero at the maximum value. And second, there may be many local minima and maxima. Thus, it might be the lowest value in the [0, 1] interval, which would be a "local minimum," but it is unclear whether it is the lowest value over the domain of interest for our function, which could be the real numbers. Such a minimum is called a "global minimum."

For the preceding reasons, we'll call the requirement that the derivative be zero the first-order condition (FOC) for a local optimum. We will always have a derivative that is zero at the minimum value of the function, but both the global maximum and local optima will also have a derivative of zero. Thus, it is also said to be a necessary, but not sufficient condition for a minimum.

We will deal the insufficiency problem by making use of what's called a second-order condition (SOC), which involves the computation of a second derivative. So far, we have computed two derivatives, both of which were "first derivatives." That is, they were the derivatives of some function. If we take the derivatives of those derivatives, we get "second derivatives," denoted $f''(X)$. A positive second derivative indicates that a function's derivative is increasing at the point at which it is evaluated. In Equation 1-18, we compute the second derivative of $Y = X^2 - X$.

Equation 1-18. Example of a second derivative for $Y = X^2 - X$.

$$f''(X) = \lim_{h \to 0} \frac{\left[2(X+h)-1\right] - \left[2X - 1\right]}{h} = 2$$

In this case, the second derivative is constant. That is, it is always two, irrespective of where we evaluate it. This means that the derivative is also increasing at $X = 0.5$, which is the candidate local minimum, where we have demonstrated the derivative is zero. If the derivative is both zero and increasing, then it must be a local minimum. This is because we're at the lowest point in the neighborhood of $X = 0.5$, and for $X > 0.5$, we know that $f(X)$ is increasing and, therefore, will not yield values below that of $f(0.5)$.

We may now provide a formal statement of the necessary and sufficient conditions for a local minimum. Namely, a candidate local minimum, X^*, satisfies the necessary and sufficient conditions for being a local minimum if the statements in Equation 1-19 are true.

Equation 1-19. Necessary and sufficient conditions for local minimum.

$$f'(X^*) = 0$$

$$f''(X^*) > 0$$

Similarly, the conditions for a local maximum are satisfied if the statements in Equation 1-20 are true.

Equation 1-20. Necessary and sufficient conditions for local maximum.

$$f'(X^*) = 0$$

$$f''(X^*) < 0$$

In general, we may convert maximization problems into minimization problems by minimizing over $-f(X)$. For this reason, it is sufficient to discuss the minimization of functions.

We've now covered first derivatives, second derivatives, and their use in optimization, which is primarily how we will encounter them in economics and machine learning. In the next section, we'll provide an overview of how to compute derivatives for common functions of one variable.

Common Derivatives of Polynomials

In the previous section, we introduced the concept of first and second derivatives. We also gave examples of the computation of derivatives, but performed the computation in a relatively inconvenient way. In each instance, we computed the change in $f(X)$ over the change in X, as the change in X went to zero in the limit. For the two examples we consider, this was straightforward; however, for more complicated expressions, such an approach could become quite cumbersome. Additionally, since we haven't introduced the concept of limits formally, we are likely to encounter problems when we can't simply evaluate the expression at its limit value.

Fortunately, derivatives take predictable forms, which makes it possible to compute them using simple rules, rather than evaluating limits. You may have already noticed a few such rules, which applied to the derivatives we've computed earlier. Recall that we took four derivatives (first and second order), which are given in Equation 1-21.

Equation 1-21. Examples of derivatives.

$$f(X) = X^2 \rightarrow f'(X) = 2X$$

$$f(X) = 2X \rightarrow f'(X) = 2$$

$$f(X) = X^2 - X \rightarrow f'(X) = 2X - 1$$

$$f(X) = 2X - 1 \rightarrow f'(X) = 2$$

What are the common relationships between the functions and derivatives in Equation 1-21? The first is called the power rule: $f(X) = X^n \rightarrow f'(X) = nX^{n-1}$. We can see this, for example, in the following transformation: $f(X) = X^2 \rightarrow f'(X) = 2X$. Another is the multiplication rule. That is, if we have a variable raised to a power and multiplied by a constant, the derivative is just the derivative of the variable raised to a power, multiplied by the constant: $f(X) = 2X \rightarrow f'(X) = 2$. We can also see that each term of the polynomial is differentiated independently: $f(X) = X^2 - X \rightarrow f'(X) = 2x - 1$. This is a consequence of the linearity of differentiation and is called the sum or difference rule, depending on whether it is addition or subtraction.

For the sake of brevity, we'll list these rules in Table 1-1 for the derivative of polynomials with one variable. Note that there are several different forms of notation that can be used for differentiation. So far, we have used $f'(X)$ to indicate that we are taking the derivative of $f(X)$ with respect to X. We may also express differentiation as df/dx. And if we have an expression, such as $X^2 - X$, we may use $d/dx\, X^2 - X$ to denote its derivative. For the purpose of the table, we will use $f(X)$ and $g(X)$ to indicate two different functions of the variable X and c to represent a constant term.

Table 1-1. *Differentiation rules for polynomials*

Constant Rule	$\dfrac{d}{dx}c = 0$
Multiplication Rule	$\dfrac{d}{dx}cX = c$
Power Rule	$\dfrac{d}{dx}X^n = nX^{n-1}$
Sum Rule	$\dfrac{d}{dx}f(X)+g(X) = f'(X)+g'(X)$
Product Rule	$\dfrac{d}{dx}f(X)g(X) = f'(X)g(X)+f(X)g'(X)$
Chain Rule	$\dfrac{d}{dx}f(g(X)) = f'(g(X))g'(X)$
Reciprocal Rule	$\dfrac{d}{dx}\dfrac{1}{f(X)} = -\dfrac{f'(X)}{(f(X))^2}$
Quotient Rule	$\dfrac{d}{dx}\dfrac{f(X)}{g(X)} = \dfrac{f'(X)g(X)-g'(X)f(X)}{g(X)^2}$

Memorization of the preceding rules will equip you to compute the analytical derivatives for nearly any function of a single variable. In some cases, however, a function will be transcendental, which means that it cannot be expressed algebraically. In the following section, we will consider those cases.

Transcendental Functions

Taking the derivatives of polynomials initially appeared daunting and cumbersome, but ultimately boiled down to memorizing eight simple rules. The same is true for transcendental functions, such as sin(X), which cannot be expressed algebraically. Table 1-2 provides rules for four transcendental functions we will encounter regularly.

***Table 1-2.** Differentiation rules for transcendental functions*

Exponential Rule	$\dfrac{d}{dx} e^{cx} = ce^{cx}$
Natural Log Rule	$\dfrac{d}{dx} \ln(X) = \dfrac{1}{X}$
Sine Rule	$\dfrac{d}{dx} \sin(X) = \cos(X)$
Cosine Rule	$\dfrac{d}{dx} \cos(X) = -\sin(X)$

Notice that all the differentiation we have done thus far has been with functions of a single variable, which are sometimes called "univariate" functions. In both machine learning and economics, we will rarely encounter problems with a single variable. In the next section, we'll discuss the extension of univariate rules for differentiation to the multivariate objects we will typically encounter in machine learning.

Multidimensional Derivatives

You might wonder what, exactly, qualifies as a "variable" in economics and machine learning. The answer is that it depends on the problem under consideration. When we solve a regression problem by employing OLS, which minimizes the sum of the squared errors, the variables will be the regression coefficients and the input data can be treated as constants. Similarly, when we train a neural network, the weights in the network will be variables and the data will be constants.

It is not difficult to see that virtually all problems we'll encounter in economics and machine learning will be inherently multivariate. Solving a model, estimating a regression equation, and training a neural network all entail finding the set of variable values that minimizes or maximizes the objective function. In this section, we will discuss some of the multivariate objects we'll encounter when doing this.

Gradient

Gradients are the multivariate extension of the concept of derivatives. And we need a multivariate extension of derivatives because most problems we encounter will have many variables. Take, for instance, the case where we want to estimate an econometric model. We'll do this by minimizing some loss function, which will typically be a transformation of variables (model parameters) and constants (data). Let $L(X_1, ..., X_n)$ denote the loss function and $X_1, ..., X_n$ denote the n parameter values of interest. In this setting, the gradient, denoted $\nabla L(X_1, ..., X_n)$, is defined as a vector-valued function, which takes $X_1, ..., X_n$ as inputs and outputs a vector of n derivatives, as is shown in Equation 1-22.

Equation 1-22. Gradient of n-variable loss function.

$$\nabla L\left(X_1, ..., X_n\right) = \left[\frac{\partial L}{\partial X_1}, ..., \frac{\partial L}{\partial X_n}\right]$$

Notice that we're using the notation $\partial L/\partial X_i$ to denote the "partial" derivative of L with respect to X_i. That is, we take the derivative of L with respect to X_i, treating all other variables as if they were constants. Computing the gradient is no different than computing all partial derivatives of the loss function and then stacking them into a vector.

The reason why we attach special significance to the gradient in economics and machine learning is because it is employed in many optimization routines. Algorithms such as stochastic gradient descent (SGD) include the following gradient-related steps:

1. Compute the gradient of the loss function, $\nabla L(X_1, ..., X_n)$.

2. Update the values of the variables, $X_j = X_{j-1} - \alpha \nabla L(X_1, ..., X_n)$.

In the preceding steps, X_j is the iteration number and α is the "step size." The routine is repeated until convergence: that is, until we reach a j where $|X_j - X_{j-1}|$ is smaller than some tolerance parameter. If we want to move slowly to avoid passing the optimum, we can set α to be a small number.

Why do such algorithms work? Consider the one variable case for which we have clear intuition. To have a candidate minimum, it must be the case that the derivative is zero. We can find a point where the derivative is zero by starting with a randomly drawn value of the variable and evaluating the derivative at that point. If it is negative, we step forward – that is, increase the value of X – since it will make the loss function more negative. If it is positive, we decrease X, since it will also lower the loss function. At some point, as we approach the minimum, the magnitude of the gradient will begin to decline, moving toward zero. If we approach it slowly enough, the near-zero gradient will result in very small updates to X_j, until they are so small that the tolerance isn't exceeded, terminating the algorithm.

In general, when we use gradient-based optimization methods, we'll extend the intuition behind these steps to hundreds, thousands, or even millions of variables.

Jacobian

The Jacobian extends the concept of a gradient to a system of n variables and m functions. The definition of the Jacobian matrix is given in Equation 1-23.

Equation 1-23. The Jacobian of m functions in n variables.

$$J = \begin{pmatrix} \dfrac{\partial f_1}{\partial X_1} & \cdots & \dfrac{\partial f_1}{\partial X_n} \\ \vdots & \ddots & \vdots \\ \dfrac{\partial f_m}{\partial X_1} & \cdots & \dfrac{\partial f_m}{\partial X_1} \end{pmatrix}$$

To make this concrete, let's calculate the Jacobian of two functions and two variables, which are given in Equation 1-24.

Equation 1-24. A system of two functions and two variables.

$$f_1(X_1, X_2) = 2X_1 X_2$$

$$f_2(X_1, X_2) = X_1^2 - X_2^2$$

Recall what we said earlier about computing partial derivatives: other than the variable with respect to which we are differentiating, all others can be treated as constants. If we want to compute $\partial f_1/\partial X_1$, for instance, then we may treat X_2 as a constant. The Jacobian for this system is given in Equation 1-25.

Equation 1-25. Example of a Jacobian for a 2x2 system.

$$J = \begin{pmatrix} 2X_2 & 2X_1 \\ 2X_1 & -2X_2 \end{pmatrix}$$

Jacobians will prove useful when solving systems of equations or optimizing vector-valued functions. In machine learning, for instance, a neural network with a categorical target variable can be viewed as a vector-valued function, since the network outputs predicted values for each class. To train such networks, we'll apply optimization algorithms that make use of Jacobian matrices.

Hessian

We previously discussed first and second derivatives and their role in optimization. We have extended the concept of first derivatives to gradients and Jacobian matrices. We will also extend the concept of second derivatives to multivariable, scalar-valued functions. We'll do this by arranging all such derivatives into a matrix called a Hessian, which is given in Equation 1-26.

Equation 1-26. The Hessian matrix for an n-variable function.

$$
Hf = \begin{pmatrix} \dfrac{\partial f}{\partial X_1^2} & \cdots & \dfrac{\partial f}{\partial X_1 X_n} \\ \vdots & \ddots & \vdots \\ \dfrac{\partial f}{\partial X_n X_1} & \cdots & \dfrac{\partial f}{\partial X_n^2} \end{pmatrix}
$$

There are two things worth noticing about the Hessian. First, it is computed on a scalar-valued function, similar to the gradient. And second, it consists of second partial derivatives. In the notation used, $\partial f / \partial X_i^2$ is the second partial derivative with respect to X_i, not the partial derivative with respect to X_i^2.

Finally, let's consider a Hessian for the two-variable function. The function is given in Equation 1-27, followed by its Hessian in Equation 1-28.

Equation 1-27. Example function for the computation of a Hessian matrix.

$$f(X_1, X_2) = X_1^2 X_2 - 2X_2^2$$

Equation 1-28. The Hessian matrix for a two-variable function.

$$\text{Hf} = \begin{pmatrix} 2X_2 & 2X_1 \\ 2X_1 & -4 \end{pmatrix}$$

In practice, we will encounter Hessian matrices in two places in machine learning. The first is to check optimality conditions. This requires some additional knowledge of the properties of matrices, so we will say relatively little about this. The other way in which Hessians will be used is to train models with optimization algorithms. In some cases, such algorithms will require us to approximate a function using first and second derivatives. The Hessian matrix will be a useful construct for organizing the second derivatives.

Differentiation in TensorFlow

TensorFlow computes derivatives using something called "automatic differentiation" (Abadi et al. 2015). This is a form of differentiation that is neither purely symbolic nor purely numerical and is particularly efficient in the context of training deep learning models. In this section, we'll discuss the concept of automatic differentiation and explain how it differs from symbolic and numerical differentiation. We'll then demonstrate how to compute a derivative in TensorFlow. Importantly, while TensorFlow does have this functionality, most non-research applications will not require users to explicitly program the computation of derivatives.

Automatic Differentiation

Let's say you want to compute the derivative of $f(g(x))$, where $f(y) = 5y^2$ and $g(x) = x^3$. You know from the previous section that this can be done with the chain rule, as in Equation 1-29.

Equation 1-29. Example of the chain rule.

$$\frac{d}{dx} f\left(g\left(x\right)\right) = f'\left(g\left(x\right)\right) g'\left(x\right) = 30x^5$$

What's shown in Equation 1-29 is called "symbolic" differentiation. Here, we perform differentiation either manually or computationally, ultimately yielding an exact, algebraic expression for the derivative.

While having tidy, exact expression for derivatives ensures efficient and accurate computations, computing symbolic derivatives can be quite challenging. First, if we do it manually, the process is likely to be time-consuming and error-prone, especially for neural networks with millions of parameters. And second, if we do it computationally, we are likely to encounter problems with the complexity of higher-order derivative expressions and the computation of derivatives that have no closed-form expression.

Numerical differentiation, which is commonly used as an alternative to symbolic differentiation in economics, relies on our original, limit-based definition of a derivative and is given in Equation 1-30.[8] The only difference is that we now use a small value of h in the numerical implementation, rather than evaluating the expression in the limit as h goes to zero.

---

[8]See Judd (1998) for a comprehensive overview of numerical differentiation methods.

Equation 1-30. Definition of numerical derivative using forward difference method.

$$f'(x) \approx \frac{f(x+h) - f(x)}{h}$$

There are, in fact, several ways to do this. The one we've used in Equation 1-30 is called the "forward difference" method, since we compute the difference between the function evaluated at x and then some value greater than x – namely, $x + h$. We can see two immediate implications of switching to numerical differentiation. First, we are no longer computing an exact, algebraic expression for the derivative. In fact, we're not even attempting to; rather, we're merely evaluating the function at different points. And second, the size of h will determine the quality of our approximation of $f'(x)$.

Equation 1-31 shows how the derivative would be computed for the example we used for symbolic differentiation.

Equation 1-31. Example of numerical derivative using forward difference method.

$$\frac{d}{dx} f(g(x)) \approx \frac{5(x+h)^6 - 5x^6}{h}$$

Automatic differentiation, in contrast, is neither fully symbolic nor fully numerical. Relative to numerical differentiation, it has the advantage of increased accuracy. It is also more stable than numerical differentiation in deep learning settings, where models often have thousands or even millions of parameters. Furthermore, it doesn't suffer from symbolic differentiation's requirement to provide a single expression for the derivative. This, again, will prove particularly useful in deep learning settings, where we must compute the derivative of the loss function with respect to parameters that are nested deep inside of a sequence of functions.

How does automatic differentiation improve this process? First, it compartmentalizes the symbolic computation of a derivative into its elementary parts. And second, it evaluates the derivative at a single point, sweeping either forward or backward through the chain of partial derivatives.

Let's revisit the nested function example again, where $f(y) = 5y^2$ and $g(x) = x^3$, and where we want to compute $d/dxf(g(x))$. We could use numerical differentiation by taking finite differences or compute a single expression for the derivative using symbol differentiation, but let's try using automatic differentiation instead.

We'll start by breaking the computation up into its elementary components. In this case, they are x, y, $\partial f/\partial y$, and $\partial y/\partial x$. We then compute expressions for the partial derivatives symbolically. That is, $\partial f/\partial y = 10y$ and $\partial y/\partial x = 3x^2$. Next, we construct the chain of partial derivatives, which is simply $\partial f/\partial y * \partial y/\partial x$. The chain rule tells us that this is $\partial f/\partial x$. Rather than actually performing the multiplication symbolically, we will sweep through the chain numerically.

We'll start with $\partial y/\partial x$ by setting $x = 2$, since we must perform automatic differentiation at a point. This immediately yields $\partial y/\partial x = 12$ and $y = 8$. We can now step through the chain, plugging in $y = 8$ to yield $\partial f/\partial y = 80$. This allows us to compute $\partial f/\partial x$ by simply multiplying through the chain of partial derivatives, yielding 960.

In this case, we've swept through the chain of partial derivatives by moving from the front (the input value) to the back (the output). For neural networks, we'll do the exact opposite: we'll move in reverse during the backpropagation step.

While we won't need to implement automatic differentiation algorithms ourselves, knowing how they work will give you a better sense of how TensorFlow works. For a survey of the literature on automatic differentiation, see Baydin et al. (2018).

Computing Derivatives in TensorFlow

Earlier in the section, we used an example of a nested function and demonstrated how to compute it using automatic differentiation. Let's do the same thing in TensorFlow and verify that our manual computations were correct. Listing 1-20 will provide the details.

We start, as usual, by importing tensorflow under the alias tf. Next, to match our example from earlier in the section, we define x as a tf. constant() object equal to two. We then define the nested function $f(g(x))$ within the context of a gradient tape instance. We start by applying the watch() method to x to indicate that GradientTape() should record what happens to x. By default, it will not, since x is a constant. Note that we could have defined x as a tf.Variable() object for the sake of simplicity; however, for this problem, we have been treating x as an input, so it would be defined as a constant.

Listing 1-20. Compute a derivative in TensorFlow

```
import tensorflow as tf

# Define x as a constant.
x = tf.constant(2.0)

# Define f(g(x)) within an instance of gradient tape.
with tf.GradientTape() as t:
        t.watch(x)
        y = x**3
        f = 5*y**2

# Compute gradient of f with respect to x.
df_dx = t.gradient(f, x)
print(df_dx.numpy())

960.0
```

Finally, we apply the gradient() method of GradientTape() to differentiate f with respect to x. We then print the result, applying the numpy() method to extract the value. Again, we find that it is 960, matching the automatic differentiation we performed manually earlier.

TensorFlow's automatic differentiation approach is fundamentally different from standard packages for computation in economics, which typically offer either numerical or symbolic computation of derivatives, but not automatic differentiation. This will provide us with an advantage when solving theoretical economic models.

Loading Data for Use in TensorFlow

In this chapter, we have introduced TensorFlow, discussed the differences between versions 1 and 2, and provided an extended overview of preliminary topics. We will end the chapter on a practical note by explaining how to load data for use in TensorFlow. If you are familiar with TensorFlow 1, you may remember that static graphs required all fixed input data to be imported as or transformed into a `tf.constant()`. Otherwise, the data would not be included in the computational graph.

Since TensorFlow 2 uses Eager Execution by default, it is no longer necessary to work within the restrictions of a static computational graph. One implication of this is that you may now directly make use of `numpy` arrays without first converting them to `tf.constant()` objects. This also means that we can use standard data importation and pre-processing pipelines in `numpy` and `pandas`.

Listing 1-21 provides a loading and pre-processing pipeline for a rank-4 image tensor input to a neural network. We will assume that the tensor has been stored in the npy format, which can be used to save arbitrary `numpy` arrays.

Notice that we transform the tensor by dividing each of its elements by 255. This is a common pre-processing step for image data, which, if given in red-green-blue (RGB) format, consists of a rank-3 tensor of integers between 0 and 255. Finally, we print the shape, yielding (32, 64, 64, 3), which suggests that we have a batch of 32 images of shape (64, 64, 3) in the tensor.

Note that the pre-processing step was performed using numpy. What if we instead want to perform it using TensorFlow? We can do this using the approach in either Listing 1-22 or Listing 1-23. Listing 1-23 transforms images into a tf.constant() object before performing division. Since one of the objects involved in the division is a TensorFlow object, the operation will be performed using TensorFlow.

Listing 1-21. Import image data with numpy

```python
import numpy as np

# Import image data using numpy.
images = np.load('images.npy')

# Normalize pixel values to [0,1] interval.
images = images / 255.0

# Print the tensor shape.
print(images.shape)

(32, 64, 64, 3)
```

In contrast, the approach in Listing 1-23 explicitly makes use of the TensorFlow operation tf.division(), rather than operation overloading with the division symbol, /. This is necessary because neither images nor 255.0 is a TensorFlow object. Since we are not working with a static graph, we did not have to specify this. However, if we are not careful, we will end up performing operations using numpy, rather than TensorFlow.

In many cases, we will want to load data in a flat format, such as a table of features, which may be stored in a csv file. As in Listing 1-24, we can do this using the read_csv() function from pandas. However, before we can use the data in TensorFlow operations, we must first convert it to either a numpy array or a tf.constant() object.

Listing 1-22. Perform division in TensorFlow using constant tensors

```
import tensorflow as tf

# Import image data using numpy.
images = np.load('images.npy')

# Convert the numpy array into a TensorFlow constant.
images = tf.constant(images)

# Normalize pixel values to [0,1] interval.
images = images / 255.0
```

Listing 1-23. Perform division in TensorFlow using the division operation

```
import tensorflow as tf

# Import image data using numpy.
images = np.load('images.npy')

# Normalize pixel values to [0,1] interval.
images = tf.division(images, 255.0)
```

To reiterate, there are two things to remember about loading data for use in TensorFlow. The first is that you may use whichever module you prefer to load the data, including numpy and pandas. TensorFlow also offers functionality for importing data. And second, once the data has been imported, it must be converted to either a numpy array or a TensorFlow object, such as a constant or variable, before you can include it in TensorFlow operations. Furthermore, if you would prefer to use operator overloading, such as the division symbol, rather than `tf.division()`, at least one of the objects must be a TensorFlow tensor.

Listing 1-24. Load data in pandas for use in TensorFlow

```
import pandas as pd

# Import data using pandas.
data = np.load('data.csv')

# Convert data to a TensorFlow constant.
data_tensorflow = tf.constant(data)

# Convert data to a numpy array.
data_numpy = np.array(data)
```

Summary

This chapter served as a broad introduction to TensorFlow 2, covering not just the basics of TensorFlow itself, including how to load and prepare data, but also a mathematical description of calculus and linear algebra operations commonly applied in machine learning algorithms. We also explained that TensorFlow is a useful tool for applying machine learning routines to economic problems and can also be used to solve theoretical economic models, making it an ideal choice for economists. Additionally, we discussed how it offers a high level of flexibility, distributed training options, and a deep library of useful extensions.

Bibliography

Abadi, M. et al. 2015. "TensorFlow: Large-Scale Machine Learning on Heterogeneous Distributed Systems." Preliminary White Paper.

Athey, S. 2019. "The Impact of Machine Learning on Economics." In *The Economics of Artificial Intelligence: An Agenda*, by Joshua gans and Avi Goldfarb Ajay Agrawal. University of Chicago Press.

Baydin, A.G., B.A. Pearlmutter, A.A. Radul, and J.M. Siskind. 2018. "Automatic Differentiation in Machine Learning: A Survey." *The Journal of Machine Learning Research* 18 (153): 1–43.

Goodfellow, I., Y. Bengio, and A. Courville. 2016. *Deep Learning*. MIT Press.

Judd, K.L. 1998. *Numerical Methods in Economics*. Cambridge, Massachusetts: The MIT Press.

Perrault, R., Y. Shoham, E. Brynjolfsson, J. Clark, J. Etchemendy, B. Grosz, T. Lyons, J. Manyika, S. Mishra, and J.C. Niebles. 2019. *The AI Index 2019 Annual Report*. AI Index Steering Committee, Human-Centered AI Institute, Stanford, CA: Stanford University.

CHAPTER 2

Machine Learning and Economics

Machine learning is primarily oriented toward prediction, whereas much of economics is concerned with causality and equilibrium. While the two disciplines have a shared interest in forecasting, they often approach it with different preferences and objectives. The economics discipline tends to favor forecasting models that are explicable, parsimonious, and stable, whereas machine learning uses an empirical process for determining what is included in a model, prioritizing feature selection, regularization, and testing over intuition.

As a consequence of these seemingly intractable differences, the economics discipline was initially slow in adopting methods from machine learning. It has since become clear that economics can benefit from integrating the models, methods, and conventions of machine learning. In this chapter, we will examine work that has argued in favor of introducing elements of machine learning into economics and finance. This research not only identifies where machine learning can be fruitfully employed to solve problems in economics but also determines where there are genuine conflicts between the two disciplines that are unlikely to be reconcilable.

© Isaiah Hull 2021
I. Hull, *Machine Learning for Economics and Finance in TensorFlow 2*,
https://doi.org/10.1007/978-1-4842-6373-0_2

While this book centers around building, training, and testing models using TensorFlow, this chapter has a different objective: to build a strong conceptual understanding of the relationship between economics and machine learning. We will do this by stepping through the landmark papers in economics and finance that discuss machine learning and its role in the discipline.

"Big Data: New Tricks for Econometrics" (Varian 2014)

Varian (2014) made one of the earliest attempts to introduce methods from machine learning to economists in a paper entitled "Big Data: New Tricks for Econometrics." Among other things, he argues that economists could benefit from developing a better understanding of ML's approach to model uncertainty and validation.

He points out that economists typically use a single model that is assumed to be the "true" one, whereas machine learning scientists often average over many small models. With respect to validation, he explains how machine learning methods for cross-validation could be used. For instance, k-fold cross-validation, which is depicted in Figure 2-1, divides a dataset into k folds or subsets of equal size. It then uses a different fold as the validation set in each of k training iterations. He argues that k-fold validation and other ML cross-validation techniques could provide an alternative to goodness-of-fit measures, such as R^2, which are commonly used in econometrics.

In addition to high-level insights, Varian (2014) also discusses common methods in machine learning that could be employed in econometrics. This includes the use of classification and regression trees; random forests; variable selection techniques, such as LASSO and spike-and-slab regression; and methods for combining models into ensembles, such as bagging, boosting, and bootstrapping.

Varian (2014) also provides a number of concrete examples of how machine learning could be used in economics. He applies tree-based estimators to measure the impact of racial discrimination on mortgage lending decisions, making use of the Home Mortgage Disclosure Act (HMDA) data. He argues that such estimators could provide an alternative to more commonly used methods for binary classification in economics, such as the logit and probit models.

Varian also uses models that incorporate feature selection, including LASSO and a spike and slab, to examine the importance of different determinants of economic growth. He does this using a dataset that consists of 72 countries and 42 potential determinants of growth, originally introduced by Sala-i-Martín (1997).

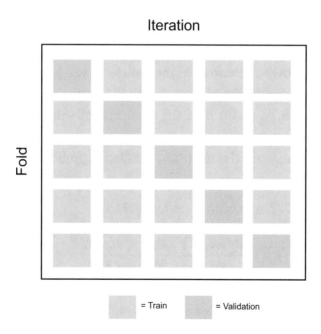

Figure 2-1. *A diagram of k-fold cross-validation for k = 5*

"Prediction Policy Problems" (Kleinberg et al. 2015)

Kleinberg et al. (2015) discuss the concept of "prediction policy problems," where the generation of accurate predictions is more important than a causal inference assessment. They argue that machine learning, which is organized around the generation of accurate predictions, has an advantage over traditional econometric methods in such applications.

Kleinberg et al. (2015) provide an illustrative comparison between two types of policy problems. In the first, a policymaker is confronted with a drought and is deciding whether to use a technology, such as cloud seeding, to increase rainfall. In the second, an individual is deciding whether to take an umbrella on a commute to work to avoid becoming wet if it rains. In the first case, the policymaker is concerned with causality, since the effectiveness of the policy will depend on whether cloud seeding causes rainfall. In the second case, the individual will only be concerned with predicting the likelihood of rain and will be uninterested in causal inference. In both cases, the intensity of the rainfall will affect the policy outcome of interest.

The authors summarize the policy prediction problem in general terms in Equation 2-1.

Equation 2-1. The prediction policy problem.

$$\frac{d\pi(X_0, Y)}{dX_0} = \frac{\partial \pi}{\partial X_0} Y + \frac{\partial \pi}{\partial Y} \frac{\partial Y}{\partial X_0}$$

Here, π is the payoff function, X_0 is the policy adopted, and Y is the outcome variable. In the umbrella choice example, π is the extent to which the person is wet after commuting, Y is the intensity with which it rained, and X_0 is the policy adopted (umbrella or not). In the drought example, π

measures the impact of the drought, Y is the intensity with which it rained, and X_0 is the policy adopted (cloud seeding or not).

If we select the umbrella as our policy option, then we know that $\partial Y / \partial X_0 = 0$, since the umbrella does not stop the rain from falling. This reduces the problem to an evaluation of $\partial \pi / \partial X_0$ and Y, that is, the impact of the umbrella on the payoff function and the intensity of rainfall. Since the impact of the umbrella on preventing wetness is known, we only need to predict Y. Thus, the policy problem itself reduces to a prediction problem.

Notice that this is not the case in the drought example, where we try to increase rainfall through the use of cloud seeding. Here, we must estimate the effect of the method itself on rainfall, $\partial Y / \partial X_0$. The two cases are illustrated in a causality diagram, which is shown in Figure 2-2.

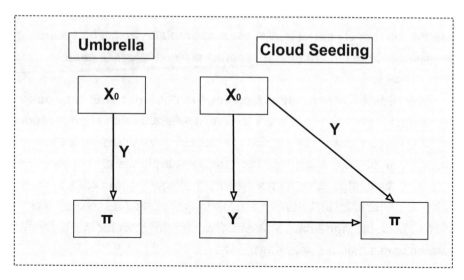

Figure 2-2. *Illustration of policy prediction problems from Kleinberg et al. (2017)*

Kleinberg et al. (2015) suggest that important policy problems can sometimes be resolved by predicting Y itself, rather than performing causal inference. This opened up a subfield of problems in economics for which machine learning is particularly well-suited to solve. This also has useful implications for practitioners, including public and private sector economists: identifying problems where a policy can be determined purely through prediction allows you to use off-the-shelf ML techniques without further modification.[1]

"Machine Learning: An Applied Econometric Approach" (Mullainathan and Spiess 2017)

Mullainathan and Spiess (2017) examine how supervised machine learning methods could be applied to economics. They argue that problems in economics are typically centered around recovering estimates of model parameters, $\hat{\beta}$, whereas problems in machine learning are typically centered around the recovery of fitted values or model predictions, $\hat{y}$.

While this difference may initially seem trivial, it turns out to be quite important for two reasons. First, it leads to a different orientation in model building and estimation that typically results in inconsistent parameter estimates in machine learning. That is, as the sample size grows, the parameter estimates, $\hat{\beta}$, won't necessarily converge in probability to the true parameter values, β, in machine learning models. And second, it is often difficult or impossible to construct a standard error for any individual parameter in a machine learning model.

Despite these substantial differences, Mullainathan and Spiess (2017) argue that machine learning can still be useful for economics, as long as economists exploit its advantages. That is, rather than using machine learning to do parameter estimation and hypothesis testing, they argue

---

[1]See Kleinberg et al. (2017) for an example of a policy prediction problem involving bail decisions.

that economists should instead consider tasks where prediction itself is important. They identify three such cases for economists:

1. **Measuring economic activity**: This could be done, for instance, using image or text datasets. Model parameters do not need to be consistently estimated, as long as the model returns an accurate prediction of economic activity.

2. **Inference tasks that have a prediction step**: Certain inference tasks, such as instrumental variables (IV) regression, involve intermediate steps where fitted values are generated. Since biases in parameter estimates arise from overfitting in the intermediate steps, making use of machine learning techniques, such as regularization, could reduce bias in IV estimates. Figure 2-3 illustrates the case where we have a regressor of interest, X; a confounder, C; a dependent variable, Y; and a set of instruments, Z. We then use ML to transform Z into fitted values for X.

3. **Policy applications**: The objective of policy work in economics is ultimately to offer recommendations to policymakers. For instance, a school may be deciding whether to hire an additional teacher or a criminal justice system may be deciding when to give bail to those who have been arrested. Making a recommendation ultimately involves making a prediction. Machine learning models are better suited to this task than simple linear models.

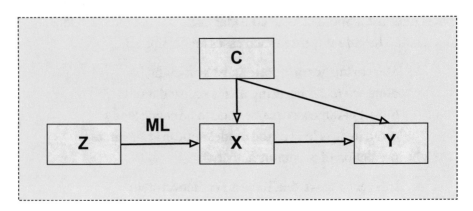

Figure 2-3. *Illustration of instrumental variables regression using ML*

Mullainathan and Spiess (2017) also conduct an empirical application in the paper to evaluate the usefulness of machine learning in improving fit. The exercise involves the prediction of the natural logarithm of house prices from a random sample of 10,000 houses drawn from the American Housing Survey. They make use of 150 features and evaluate the results using R^2. Comparing OLS, a regression tree, LASSO regression, a random forest, and an ensemble of models, they find that ML methods are, in general, able to deliver improvements in R^2 over OLS. Furthermore, there is heterogeneity in those improvements: for certain house price quintiles, the gains are large, whereas they are small or even negative in other quintiles.

Finally, Mullainathan and Spiess (2017) argue that ML offers value added to economics along two additional dimensions. First, it provides an alternative process for estimating or training models, which is centered around regularization to prevent overfitting and tuning based on empirical feedback. And second, it can be used to test theories about predictability. The Efficient Markets Hypothesis (EMH), for instance, implies that risk-adjusted excess returns should not be predictable. Consequently, using ML models to demonstrate predictability has implications for the theory, even if all parameters used in the prediction are inconsistently estimated.

"The Impact of Machine Learning on Economics" (Athey 2019)

Similar to Mullainathan and Spiess (2017), Athey (2019) reviews the impact of machine learning on economics and makes predictions about likely future developments. Her work centers on a comparison between machine learning and traditional econometric methods, an evaluation of off-the-shelf machine learning routines for use in economics, and a review of policy prediction problems of the variety discussed in Kleinberg et al. (2015).

Machine Learning and Traditional Econometric Methods

Athey (2019) argues that machine learning tools are not suitable for performing causal inference, which is the objective of most econometric exercises. They are, however, useful for improving semi-parametric methods and do enable researchers to make use of a large number of covariates. Given the parsimony of econometric models and the increasing availability of "big data," it seems likely that there will be substantial value in adopting methods and models from machine learning, which are generally better suited to processing and modeling large volumes of data.

Another area of strength Athey identifies is the use of flexible functional forms. The econometrics literature has broadly specialized around producing tools for a single narrow task: performing causal inference in a linear regression model. In many cases, however, there are good reasons to believe that such models fail to capture important non-linearities. Machine learning offers a rich variety of models that allow for non-linearities between features, and between features and the target, something that is usually absent from econometric models.

In addition to causal inference, Athey also compares the processes for performing empirical analysis, selecting a model, and computing confidence intervals on parameter values. The conclusions she reaches about machine learning are covered in the following subsections.

Empirical Analysis

Athey (2019) highlights an important contrast between economics and machine learning, which is most visible in their differing approach to empirical analysis. Economists typically select a model using some set of principles and determine its functional form through the use of theory. They then estimate the model once.

Machine learning takes a different approach to empirical analysis – namely, an iterative one. Rather than starting with a model determined by principles and theory, machine learning starts with a standard model architecture and/or set of hyperparameters. It then trains the model, evaluates performance using a form of cross-validation, and then tunes the hyperparameters and model architecture to improve performance. The training process is then repeated.

Athey argues that tuning and cross-validation are some of the most useful tools that machine learning offers to econometricians. Reorienting empirical analysis in economics around an iterative and empirical process could lead to substantial improvements in explaining variation in the data.

Model Selection

While Athey (2019) argues that the empirical tuning process in machine learning could offer benefits to certain applications in economics, she also cautions that it is less likely to be helpful for causal inference. This is because machine learning applications typically involve cases where the evaluation of performance is simple and measurable. For instance, in machine learning, we may want a high rate of accuracy in the validation sample or we might want a low mean squared error. In fact, when we estimate regression models in economics, we are also, of course, minimizing some loss function, such as the sum of the squared errors. We may also look at performance metrics, such as measures of out-of-sample forecast errors, as is illustrated in Figure 2-4.

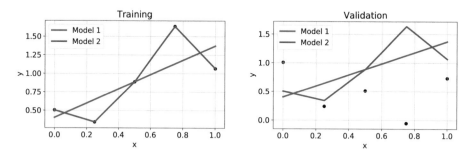

Figure 2-4. *Illustration of model evaluation process in machine learning*

What we can't do, however, is measure "causality" and train our models to maximize it. This is a serious challenge, whether we are using econometric tools or machine learning tools; however, it is particularly important to point it out for machine learning tools, since this is a reason to believe that they will not help us to improve along the causality dimension.

Confidence Intervals

One drawback of using machine learning methods in economics is that such models typically do not produce valid confidence intervals. In fact, confidence intervals are not usually an object of interest in machine learning, since models often contain thousands of parameters. Athey (2019) argues that this is a challenge for research in economics, which typically involves hypothesis testing that is centered around the statistical significance of individual parameters. It is, however, possible to overcome this restriction in certain settings, but it requires the use of advanced, recently developed methods in economics and statistics, which are not typically available with off-the-shelf ML routines.

Off-the-Shelf ML Routines

Athey (2019) evaluates a broad set of off-the-shelf routines to consider how they would perform if applied to tasks in economics and finance. She argues that unsupervised machine learning methods, such as clustering algorithms and topic modeling, could play a valuable role in economics. They have the benefit of not generating spurious relationships, since there is no dependent variable, and can, themselves, be used to generate a dependent variable.

She then evaluates supervised machine learning methods, classifying such methods according to their widespread adoption in the social sciences. Neural networks, for instance, have been used in various applications in the social sciences in the past, but have only recently gained widespread use and acceptance. As such, Athey (2019) would classify such models as "machine learning models." The same cannot be said, for instance, for OLS or the logit model, which have long been used in economics and finance.

Athey (2019) identifies the following models which can be classified as "machine learning models" under this scheme: regularized regression, including LASSO, ridge, and elastic net; random forests and regression trees; support vector machine (SVM) models; neural networks; and matrix averaging.

The standard trade-off inherent in using such models, as originally argued by Mullainathan and Spiess (2017), is expressiveness versus overfitting. Using more features, allowing for more flexible functional forms, and reducing regularization penalties come at the cost of a higher probability of overfitting.

Athey argues that this approach has many advantages in settings where there are a high number of covariates. It is, however, necessary to employ non-standard routines to compute confidence intervals. It is also important to evaluate whether results are spurious.

Policy Analysis

In addition to causal inference, economics is also concerned with prediction for its own sake. An accurate economic forecasting model, for instance, will still be useful for planning purposes, even if the accuracy arises as a result of non-causal associations between variables. As discussed previously in the review of Kleinberg et al. (2015), this concept also applies to policy problems. Governments and organizations trying to decide whether to take a specific action will often do so under two different sets of circumstances. In the first set of circumstances, there is uncertainty about the efficacy of the policy they will adopt. In the second, the uncertainty is about some external event.

Consider, for instance, a small bank deciding whether or not to build a larger capital buffer to prepare for a financial crisis. They might construct a model that indicates the targeted size of their buffer conditional on the state of the world. This would involve constructing and estimating a model that produces a policy prediction. Importantly, causality is irrelevant in this model, since the small bank does not influence the state of the financial sector to any appreciable extent. Rather, it simply needs to be able to predict a crisis in advance, so it can adopt the correct policy.

Athey (2019) conducts a review of the related policy prediction problem literature. She argues that there are several topics of interest within this literature that remain critically important for economists to evaluate:

1. **Model interpretability**: Economic models tend to be simple and interpretable, making the origin of the policy prescription understandable. This is not the case for many ML models.

2. **Fairness and non-discrimination**: The complexity of machine learning models often makes it difficult to determine the origin of unfair or discriminative policy prescriptions. As such, transitioning to ML models will necessitate an evaluation of how fairness and non-discrimination can be preserved.

3. **Stability**: Given the complexity of machine learning models, it is not clear whether relationships estimated for one population will tend to hold for others. Additional work will be needed to evaluate the generalizability of results.

4. **Manipulability**: The size and complexity of ML models, along with their low level of interpretability, opens up the possibility of manipulation. This is already a problem in economic models, but it is compounded by the complexity and black-box nature of many ML models.

These remain both interesting topics of research and also important considerations for practitioners. Both public and private sector economists will need to evaluate the interpretability, fairness, stability, and manipulability of the predictions that arise from the use of ML models in economics.

Active Research and Predictions

Athey (2019) concludes with an exhaustive review of active lines of ML research in economics, as well as predictions for the future. Interested readers should refer to the manuscript itself for details. We will, however, highlight some of the areas of active research and predictions about future developments.

Active lines of research include (1) the use of ML to estimate average treatment effects,[2] (2) the estimation of optimal policy under heterogeneous treatment effects,[3] (3) the use of ML to perform supplementary analyses that evaluate the extent of the confoundedness problem in causal inference,[4] and (4) the use of ML in panel and difference-in-difference methods.[5]

Athey includes an extensive list of predictions for ML's adoption and spread within economics, starting with increased use of off-the-shelf methods, initially employed for their intended purpose within ML. From there, ML is likely to be localized to perform tasks that are of particular interest to economists and social scientists. She predicts that the impact on causal inference in economics will be small, but the overall impact will be large, necessitating increased interdisciplinary work, coordination with private businesses, and a revival of stale literatures focused on economic measurement.

"Machine Learning Methods Economists Should Know About" (Athey and Imbens 2019)

Separately, Athey and Imbens made substantial contributions to the advancement of machine learning methods in economics through multiple works. In Athey and Imbens (2019), they provide an overview of methods in machine learning that are useful for economists.

---

[2]See Chernozhukov et al. (2015), Athey et al. (2016), and Chernozhukov et al. (2017).

[3]See Athey and Imbens (2017), Wager and Athey (2018), and Athey et al. (2019).

[4]See Athey and Imbens (2017).

[5]See Doudchenko and Imbens (2016).

They start with a discussion of the integration of ML into economics, the initial resistance it faced, and the reasons underlying that resistance. The most serious initial objection was that ML models failed to produce valid confidence intervals off the shelf. While not important for ML itself, this was a substantial hindrance for the use of ML in traditional problems in economics.

Athey and Imbens (2019) explain that the literature has since approached this problem by producing modified versions of machine learning models. In particular, they argue that it is often necessary to modify ML models to exploit the structure of specific economic problems. This might include issues related to causality, endogeneity, monotonicity of demand, or theoretically motivated restrictions.

The paper itself is intended as a brief introduction to each of these methods. In particular, they identify the following families of models and methods that they deem essential for those who want to use ML to explore traditional problems in economics:

1. Local linear forests

2. Neural networks

3. Boosting

4. Classification trees and forests

5. Unsupervised learning with k-means clustering and GANs

6. Average treatment effects under the confoundedness assumption

7. Orthogonalization and cross-fitting

8. Heterogeneous treatment effects

9. Experimental design and reinforcement learning

10. Matrix completion and recommender systems

11. Synthetic control methods

12. Text analysis

Interested readers should consult Athey and Imbens (2019) for the details of how each method can be integrated into economic analysis. We will return to some of these methods in detail later in the book and will delay a detailed discussion to those chapters.

"Text as Data" (Gentzkow et al. 2019)

In contrast to the other surveys we have covered, Gentzkow et al. (2019) are narrowly focused on a single topic: text analysis. They provide a comprehensive survey of text analysis methods used in economics, as well as an introduction to methods that are not currently used in economics, but which they argue would be useful if adopted.

The paper is divided into three sections: (1) representing text as data, (2) statistical methods, and (3) applications. Since we will cover text analysis in Chapter 6, including extended coverage of Gentzkow et al. (2019), we will limit ourselves to a brief overview here.

Representing Text As Data

The paper starts with an extended discussion of standard pre-processing routines for text datasets. For most economists, such routines will be unfamiliar, but learning how to perform them is essential for conducting text analysis. These routines involve the transformation of text documents into a numerical format that is usable in models. This usually starts with a cleaning process, followed by a feature selection process. Common features include words and phrases. We will cover this process in detail in Chapter 6.

Statistical Methods

The authors point out that most text analysis done in economics makes use of dictionary-based methods. Dictionary-based methods fall into the category of unsupervised learning methods. Rather than training a model to learn the relationship between features and a target, you instead specify a dictionary in advance, which is then applied to a document, yielding a measure of some feature of the text.

One common form of dictionary-based method measures the sentiment of documents. Sentiment tells us the extent to which the text in a document is positive or negative. Such dictionaries were originally created for purposes unrelated to economics. However, early work in economics produced dictionaries that were designed to extract features specific to economics. Figure 2-5 illustrates the application of a general sentiment dictionary to the first paragraph of a Federal Open Market Committee (FOMC) announcement.[6] Positive words are highlighted in green and negative words in red. We can see that the sentiment of certain words is not correctly identified given the context in which they are used.

September 18, 2019

Federal Reserve issues FOMC statement

For release at 2:00 p.m. EDT

Share →

Information received since the Federal Open Market Committee met in July indicates that the labor market remains strong and that economic activity has been rising at a moderate rate. Job gains have been solid, on average, in recent months, and the unemployment rate has remained low. Although household spending has been rising at a strong pace, business fixed investment and exports have weakened. On a 12-month basis, overall inflation and inflation for items other than food and energy are running below 2 percent. Market-based measures of inflation compensation remain low; survey-based measures of longer-term inflation expectations are little changed.

Figure 2-5. *Application of general sentiment dictionary to FOMC statement*

---

[6]See the following link for the full FOMC statement: www.federalreserve.gov/ newsevents/pressreleases/monetary20190918a.htm.

The authors argue that Baker et al. (2016) is an ideal use of dictionary-based methods in economics. First, the feature they want to extract, uncertainty about economic policy, is unlikely to emerge from a topic model applied to newspaper articles. And second, the dictionary they used to extract the feature was tested against human readers and produced similar results. In such cases, a dictionary-based method is likely to be ideal. A plot of the EPU indices for selected countries is shown in Figure 2-6.[7]

They do, however, point out that economics currently relies heavily on dictionary-based methods and that the discipline could benefit from an expansion into other methods within text analysis. They cover a combination of different methods, some of which are unfamiliar to economists and others of which are familiar, but only when used in different contexts.

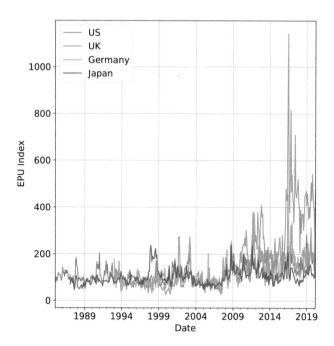

Figure 2-6. *EPU indices for US, UK, Germany, and Japan*

---

[7]The following link provides updated EPU indices for more than 20 countries: `www.policyuncertainty.com/`.

Their coverage includes text-based regression, penalized linear regression, dimensionality reduction, and non-linear text regression, including regression trees, deep learning, Bayesian regression methods, and support vector machines.

Finally, they also cover word embeddings, which are arguably underused in text analysis applications within economics. Word embeddings provide an alternative means of expressing features in text, which are continuous and retain the information content of words. This contrasts with commonly used approaches in economics, which typically involve treating words as one-hot encoded vectors, all of which are orthogonal to each other.

Applications

Gentzkow et al. (2019) end with an expansive literature review of text analysis methods in economics. Such applications include authorship identification, stock price prediction, central bank communication, nowcasting, policy uncertainty measurement, and media slant quantification. We will return to this literature and the details of the applications in question in Chapter 6.

"How is Machine Learning Useful for Macroeconomic Forecasting" (Coulombe et al. 2019)

Both the reviews of machine learning in economics and the methods that have been developed for machine learning in economics tend to neglect the field of macroeconomics. This is, perhaps, because macroeconomists typically work with nonstationary time series datasets, which contain relatively few observations. Consequently, macroeconomics is often seen as a poor candidate for benefitting from the adoption of machine learning methods, even though prediction (forecasting) is a common task among private and public sector macroeconomists.

Coulombe et al. (2019) examine whether this is truly the case by comparing machine learning methods to standard tools for macroeconometric analysis. They identify four areas in which ML could plausibly provide improvements for macroeconometric forecasting:

1. **Non-linearities**: Macroeconomics is inherently non-linear. Unemployment tends to decline slowly during economic expansions, only to spike suddenly when a recession occurs. Furthermore, if a downturn affects the financial sector, leading to a credit contraction, a recession might become considerably more severe and prolonged. Capturing such elements could be critical for producing accurate macroeconomic forecasts. At least in principle, ML provides a toolset that allows for flexible functional forms, including non-linearities, which could be used for such a purpose.

2. **Regularization**: In the era of big data, there are now many time series available for use in macroeconomic forecasting models. The St. Louis Federal Reserve Bank's FRED system, for instance, currently includes more than 700,000 time series. Given the low frequency of commonly forecasted series, such as GDP and inflation, traditional models will have too few observations to make use of the high number of covariates without overfitting. ML suggests that such problems can be resolved by the application of regularization techniques, which penalize the inclusion of additional variables.

3. **Cross-validation**: As with ML, the test of a good forecast model is its out-of-sample performance. However, unlike ML, this is not typically the only test of a good model. As such, less emphasis is placed on cross-validation techniques, which are generally better developed in the ML literature. It is possible that economics and finance could benefit by adopting both techniques and best practices.

4. **Alternative loss functions**: The uniformity of methods used in economics has resulted in the widespread adoption of the same loss functions for all problems. It is possible, however, that not all prediction errors should be weighted using the same scheme; and thus, there may be something to gain from examining the ML literature, where it is common to train models with exotic loss functions.

The authors perform the comparison exercise in a fixed effects regression setting. With respect to ML methods, they consider penalized regression and random forests. They also make use of hyperparameter tuning and loss function selection. They reach four broad conclusions about the use of ML in macroeconometric forecasting:

1. Having more data and exploiting non-linearities improve forecasting at long time horizons for real variables.

2. Factor models, which are already commonly in use in macroeconomics, are a suitable source of regularization.

3. K-fold cross-validation is as useful in evaluating overfitting as the Bayesian Information Criterion (BIC).

4.   The L_2 loss function, which is already common in macroeconomics, proved sufficient for their forecasting exercise.

Overall, the authors find that ML methods can improve macroeconomic forecasts; however, the gains, as we may have expected, might be small relative to other categories of problems within economics. Time series forecasts for financial series, for instance, might benefit considerably more than macroeconomic forecasts, since the data is often available at considerably higher frequencies.

Summary

In this chapter, we covered a conceptual overview of the landscape of ML methods and their use in economics. We examined how they have been used historically and how economists conducting research on ML believe they will be used in the future. We encountered several recurring themes, which we list as follows:

1.   Off-the-shelf machine learning methods, if applied to policy prediction problems or economic forecasting, can generate improvements over existing econometric methods.

2.   Off-the-shelf ML methods are unlikely to be useful for causal inference. Modifying ML algorithms to localize them for use in economics will be necessary.

3.   Unlike economics models, ML models don't typically yield valid confidence intervals for individual parameter values.

4. Whereas economics uses a theory-driven approach to modeling and performs estimation only once, ML is grounded in empirics and iterative improvement via tuning.

5. Big data, coupled with ML methods, such as regularization and cross-validation, is likely to have a substantial impact on which economic questions can be answered and how they are answered.

6. Machine learning is likely to be useful for measuring economic activity, performing inference with models that have a prediction step, and solving policy prediction problems.

In the coming chapters, we will focus primarily on applying the methods and strategies discussed in this chapter to economic and financial problems using TensorFlow.

Bibliography

Athey, S. 2019. "The Impact of Machine Learning on Economics." In *The Economics of Artificial Intelligence: An Agenda*, by Joshua gans, and Avi Goldfarb Ajay Agrawal. University of Chicago Press.

Athey, S., and G.W. Imbens. 2019. "Machine Learning Methods that Economists Should Know About." *Annual Review of Economics* 11: 685–725.

Athey, S., and G.W. Imbens. 2017. "The State of Applied Econometrics: Causality and Policy Evaluation." *Journal of Economic Perspectives* 31 (2): 3–32.

Athey, S., G.W. Imbens, and S. Wager. 2016. "Approximate Residual Balancing: De-Biased Inference of Average Treatment Effects in High Dimensions." *arXiv.*

Athey, S., J. Tibshirani, and S. Wager. 2019. "Generalized random forests." *The Annals of Statistics* 47 (2): 1148–1178.

Baker, S.R., N. Bloom, and S.J. and Davis. 2016. "Measuring Economic Policy Uncertainty." *The Quarterly Journal of Economics* 131 (4): 1593–1636.

Chernozhukov, V., C. Hansen, and M. Spindler. 2015. "Post-Selection and Post-Regularization Inference in Linear Models with Many Controls and Instruments." *American Economic Review: Papers & Proceedings* 105 (5): 486–490.

Chernozhukov, V., D. Chetverikov, M. Demirer, E. Duflo, C. Hansen, W. Newey, and J. Robins. 2017. "Double/debiased machine learning for treatment and structural parameters." *The Econometrics Journal* 21 (1).

Coulombe, P.G., M. Leroux, D. Stevanovic, and S. Surprenant. 2019. "How is Machine Learning Useful for Macroeconomic Forecasting?" *CIRANO Working Papers.*

Doudchenko, N., and G.W. Imbens. 2016. "Balancing, Regression, Difference-In-Difference and Synthetic Control Methods: A Synthesis." *NBER Working Papers 22791.*

Friedberg, R., J. Tibshirani, S. Athey, and S. Wager. 2018. "Local Linear Forests." *arXiv.*

Gentzkow, M., B. Kelly, and M. Taddy. 2019. "Text as Data." *Journal of Economic Literature* 57 (3): 535–574.

Glaeser, E.L., A. Hillis, S.D. Kominers, and M. Luca. 2016. "Crowdsourcing City Government: Using Tournaments to Improve Inspection Accuracy." *American Economic Review: Papers & Proceedings* 106 (5): 114–118.

Goodfellow, I., Y. Bengio, and A. Courville. 2016. *Deep Learning.* MIT Press.

Kleinberg, J, J. Ludwig, S. Mullainathan, and Z. Obermeyer. 2015. "Prediction Policy Problems." *American Economic Review: Papers & Proceedings* 105 (5): 491–495.

Kleinberg, J., H. Lakkaraju, J. Leskovec, J. Ludwig, and S. Mullainathan. 2017. "Human Decisions and Machine Predictions." *The Quarterly Journal of Economics* 133 (1): 237–293.

Mullainathan, S., and J. Spiess. 2017. "Machine Learning: An Applied Econometric Approach." (Journal of Economic Perspectives) 31 (2): 87–106.

Perrault, R., Y. Shoham, E. Brynjolfsson, J. Clark, J. Etchemendy, B. Grosz, T. Lyons, J. Manyika, S. Mishra, and J.C. Niebles. 2019. *The AI Index 2019 Annual Report*. AI Index Steering Committee, Human-Centered AI Institute, Stanford, CA: Stanford University.

Sala-i-Martín, Xavier. 1997. "I Just Ran Two Million Regressions." *American Economic Review* 87 (2): 178–183.

Varian, Hal R. 2014. "Big Data: New Tricks for Econometrics." *Journal of Economic Perspectives* 28 (2): 3–28.

Wager, S., and S. Athey. 2018. "Estimation and Inference of Heterogeneous Treatment Effects using Random Forests." *Journal of the American Statistical Association* 113 (532): 1228–1242.

CHAPTER 3

Regression

The term "regression" differs in common usage between econometrics and machine learning. In econometrics, a regression involves the estimation of parameter values that relate a dependent variable to independent variables. The most common form of regression in econometrics is multiple linear regression, which involves the estimation of a linear association between a continuous dependent variable and multiple independent variables. Within econometrics, however, the term also encompasses non-linear models and models where the dependent variable is discrete. To the contrary, a regression in machine learning refers to a linear or non-linear supervised learning model with a continuous dependent variable (target). Throughout this chapter, we will adopt the broader econometrics definition of regression, but will introduce methods commonly applied in machine learning.

Linear Regression

In this section, we'll introduce the concept of a "linear regression," which is the most commonly employed empirical method in econometrics. It is used when the dependent variable is continuous, and the true relationships between the dependent variable and the independent variables are assumed to be linear.

© Isaiah Hull 2021
I. Hull, *Machine Learning for Economics and Finance in TensorFlow 2*,
https://doi.org/10.1007/978-1-4842-6373-0_3

Overview

A linear regression models the relationship between a dependent variable, Y, and a set of independent variables, $\{X_0, ..., X_k\}$, under the assumption of linearity in the coefficients. Linearity requires that the relationship between each X_j and Y can be modeled as a constant slope, represented by a scalar coefficient, β_j. Equation 3-1 provides the general form for a linear model with k independent variables.

Equation 3-1. A linear model.

$$Y = \alpha + \beta_0 X_0 + ... + \beta_{k-1} X_{k-1}$$

In many cases, we will adopt the notation given in Equation 3-2, which explicitly specifies an index for each observation. Y_i, for instance, denotes the value of variable Y for entity i.

Equation 3-2. A linear model with entity indices.

$$Y_i = \alpha + \beta_0 X_{i0} + ... + \beta_{k-1} X_{ik-1}$$

In addition to entity indices, we will often use time indices in economic problems. In such cases, we will typically use a t subscript to indicate the time period in which the variable is observed, as we have done in Equation 3-3.

Equation 3-3. A linear model with entity and time indices.

$$Y_{it} = \alpha + \beta_0 X_{it0} + ... + \beta_{k-1} X_{itk-1}$$

In a linear regression, the model parameters, $\{\alpha, \beta_1, ..., \beta_k\}$, do not vary with time or by entity and, thus, are not indexed by either. Additionally, non-linear transformations of the parameters are not permitted. A dense neural network layer, for instance, has a similar functional form, but applies a non-linear transformation to the sum of coefficient-variable products, as shown in Equation 3-4, where σ represents the sigmoid function.

Equation 3-4. A dense layer of a neural network with a sigmoid activation function.

$$Y_{it} = \sigma\left(\alpha + \beta_0 X_{it0} + \ldots + \beta_{k-1} X_{itk-1}\right)$$

While linearity may appear to be a severe functional form restriction, it does not prevent us from applying transformations – including non-linear transformations – to the independent variables. We can, for instance, re-define X_0 as its natural logarithm and include it as an independent variable. Linear regressions also permit interactions between two variables, such as $X_0 * X_1$, or indicator variables, such as $1_{\{X_0 > x_0\}}$. Additionally, in time series and panel settings, we can include lags of variables, such as X_{t-1j} and X_{t-2j}.

Transforming and re-defining variables makes linear regression a flexible method that can be used to approximate non-linear functions to an arbitrarily high degree of precision. For instance, consider the case where the true relationship between X and Y is given by the exponential function in Equation 3-5.

Equation 3-5. An exponential model.

$$Y_i = exp\left(\alpha + \beta X_i\right)$$

If we take the natural logarithm of Y_i, we can perform the linear regression in Equation 3-6 to recover the model parameters, $\{\alpha, \beta\}$.

Equation 3-6. A transformed exponential model.

$$\ln\left(Y_i\right) = \alpha + \beta X_i$$

In most settings, we won't know the underlying data generating process (DGP). Furthermore, there will not be a deterministic relationship between the dependent variable and independent variables. Rather, there will be some noise, ϵ_i, associated with each observation, which could arise as the result of unobserved, random differences across entities or measurement error.

As an example of this, let's say that we have data drawn from a process that is known to be non-linear, but its exact functional form is unknown. Figure 3-1 shows a scatterplot of the data, along with plots of two linear regression models. The first is trained under the assumption that the relationship between X and Y is well-approximated over the [0, 10] interval using a single line, as in Equation 3-7. The second is trained under the assumption that five line segments are needed, as in Equation 3-8.

Equation 3-7. A linear approximation to a non-linear model.

$$Y_i = \alpha + \beta X_i + \epsilon_i$$

Equatio 3-8. A linear approximation to a non-linear relationship.

$$Y_i = \left[\alpha_0 + \beta_0 X_i\right]1_{\{0 \leq X_i < 2\}} + \ldots + \left[\alpha_0 + \beta_0\left(X_i - 8\right)\right]1_{\{8 \leq X_i \leq 10\}} + \epsilon_i$$

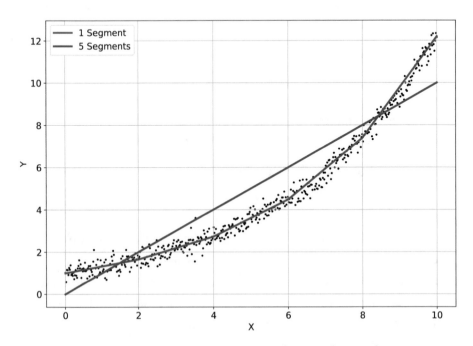

Figure 3-1. *Two linear approximations of a non-linear function*

Figure 3-1 suggests that using a linear regression model with a single slope and intercept was insufficient; however, using multiple line segments in the form of a piecewise polynomial spline was sufficient to approximate the non-linear function, even though we worked entirely within the framework of linear regression.

Ordinary Least Squares (OLS)

Linear regression, as we have seen, is a versatile method that can be used to model the relationship between a dependent variable and set of independent variables. Even when that relationship is non-linear, we saw that it was possible to approximate it in a linear model using indicator functions, variable interactions, or variable transformations. In some cases, we were even able to capture it exactly through a variable transformation.

In this section, we'll discuss how to implement a linear regression in TensorFlow. The way in which we do this will depend on our choice of loss function. In economics, the most common loss function is the sum or mean of the squared errors, which we will consider first. For the purpose of this example, we will stack all of the independent variables in an $n \times k$ matrix, X, where n is the number of observations and k is the number of independent variables, including the constant (bias) term.

We will let $\hat{\beta}$ denote the vector of estimated coefficients on the independent variables, which we distinguish from the true parameter values, β. The "error" term that we will use to construct our loss function is given in Equation 3-9. It will often be referred to by different names, such as error, residual, or disturbance term.

Equation 3-9. The disturbance term from a linear regression.

$$\epsilon = Y - \hat{\beta}X$$

Note that ϵ is an n-element column vector. This means that we can square and sum each element by pre-multiplying by its transpose, as in Equation 3-10, which gives us the sum of squared errors.

Equation 3-10. The sum of squared errors.

$$\epsilon'\epsilon = \left(Y - \hat{\beta}X\right)'\left(Y - \hat{\beta}X\right)$$

One of the benefits of using the sum of squared errors as a loss function – also called performing "ordinary least squares" (OLS) – is that it permits an analytical solution, as derived in Equation 3-11, which means that we do not need to use time-consuming and error-prone optimization algorithms. We obtain this solution by choosing $\hat{\beta}$ to minimize the sum of squared errors.

Equation 3-11. Minimizing the sum of squared errors.

$$\frac{\partial \epsilon'\epsilon}{\partial \hat{\beta}} = \frac{\partial}{\partial \hat{\beta}}\left(Y - \hat{\beta}X\right)'\left(Y - \hat{\beta}X\right) = 0$$

$$-2X'Y + 2X'X\,\hat{\beta} = 0$$

$$X'X\hat{\beta} = X'Y$$

$$\hat{\beta} = \left(X'X\right)^{-1}X'Y$$

The only thing left to check is whether $\hat{\beta}$ is a minimum or a maximum. It will be a minimum whenever X has "full rank." This will hold if no column of X is a linear combination of one or more other columns of X. Listing 3-1 provides a demonstration of how we can perform ordinary least squares (OLS) in TensorFlow for a toy problem.

Listing 3-1. Implementation of OLS in TensorFlow 2

```
import tensorflow as tf

# Define the data as constants.
X = tf.constant([[1, 0], [1, 2]], tf.float32)
Y = tf.constant([[2], [4]], tf.float32)

# Compute vector of parameters.
XT = tf.transpose(X)
XTX = tf.matmul(XT,X)
beta = tf.matmul(tf.matmul(tf.linalg.inv(XTX),XT),Y)
```

For convenience, we have defined the transpose of X as XT. We have also defined XTX as XT post-multiplied by X. We can compute $\hat{\beta}$ by inverting XTX, post-multiplying by XT, and then post-multiplying by Y again.

The parameter vector we've computed, $\hat{\beta}$, minimizes the sum of squared errors. While computing $\hat{\beta}$ was simple, it might be unclear why we would want to use TensorFlow for such a task. If we had instead used MATLAB, the syntax for writing the linear algebra operations would have been compact and readable. Alternatively, if we had used Stata or any statistics module in Python or R, we'd be able to automatically compute standard errors and confidence intervals for the vector of parameters, as well as measures of fit for the regression.

TensorFlow does, of course, have natural advantages if a task requires parallel or distributed computing; however, the need for this is likely to be minor when performing OLS analytically. The value of TensorFlow will become apparent when we want to minimize a loss function that doesn't have an analytical solution or when we cannot hold all of the data in memory.

Least Absolute Deviations (LAD)

While OLS is the most commonly used form of linear regression in economics and has many attractive properties, we will sometimes want to use an alternative loss function. We may, for instance, want to minimize the sum of the absolute values of the errors, rather than the sum of the squares. This form of linear regression is referred to as Least Absolute Deviations (LAD) or Least Absolute Errors (LAE).

For all models, including OLS and LAD, the sensitivity of parameter estimates to outliers is driven by the loss function. Since OLS minimizes the squares of errors, it places a high emphasis on setting parameter values to explain outliers. That is, OLS will place a greater emphasis on eliminating a single large error than it will on two errors half of its size. To the contrary, LAD would place equal weight on the large error and the two smaller errors.

Another difference between OLS and LAD is that we cannot express the solution to a LAD regression analytically, since the absolute value prevents us from obtaining a closed-form algebraic expression. This means we must search for the minimum by "training" or "estimating" the model.

While TensorFlow wasn't particularly useful for solving OLS, it has clear advantages when performing a LAD regression or training another type of model that has no analytical solution. We'll see how to do this in TensorFlow and also evaluate how accurately TensorFlow identifies the true parameter values at the same time. More specifically, we'll perform a Monte Carlo experiment, where we randomly generate data under certain assumed parameter values. We'll then use the data to estimate the model, allowing us to compare the true and estimated parameters.

Listing 3-2 shows how the data is generated. We start by defining the number of observations and number of samples. Since we want to evaluate TensorFlow's performance, we'll train the model parameters on 100 separate samples. We'll also use 10,000 observations to ensure that there is sufficient data to train the model.

Next, we define the true values of the model parameters, alpha and beta, which correspond to the constant (bias) term and the slope. We set the constant term to 1.0 and the slope to 3.0. Since these are the true values of the parameters and do not need to be trained, we will use tf.constant() to define them.

We now draw X and epsilon from normal distributions. For X, we use a standard normal distribution, which has a mean of 0 and a standard deviation of 1. These are the default parameter values for tf.random. normal(), so we do not need to specify anything beyond the number of samples and observations. For epsilon, we use a standard deviation of 0.25, which we specify using the stddev parameter. Finally, we compute the dependent variable, Y.

We can now use the generated data to train the model using LAD. There are a few steps we will need to complete, which are common to all model construction and training processes in TensorFlow. We'll first illustrate them using an example that makes use of only the first sample of randomly drawn data. We'll then repeat the process for each of the 100 samples.

Listing 3-2. Generate input data for a linear regression

```
import tensorflow as tf

# Set number of observations and samples
S = 100
N = 10000

# Set true values of parameters.
alpha = tf.constant([1.], tf.float32)
beta = tf.constant([3.], tf.float32)

# Draw independent variable and error.
X = tf.random.normal([N, S])
```

95

```
epsilon = tf.random.normal([N, S], stddev=0.25)

# Compute dependent variable.
Y = alpha + beta*X + epsilon
```

Listing 3-3 provides the code for the first step in the model training process in TensorFlow. We first draw values from a normal distribution with a mean of 0 and a standard deviation of 5.0 and then use them to initialize alphaHat and betaHat. The choice of 5.0 is arbitrary, but is intended to emulate a problem in which we have limited prior knowledge about the true parameter values. We use the suffix "Hat" to indicate that these are not the true values, but estimates. Since we want to train the parameters to minimize the loss function, we will define them using tf.Variable(), rather than tf.constant().

The next step is to define a function to compute the loss. A LAD regression minimizes the sum of absolute errors, which is equivalent to minimizing the mean absolute error. We will minimize the mean absolute error, since this has better numerical properties.[1]

To compute the mean absolute error, we define a function called maeLoss, which takes the parameters and data as inputs and outputs the associated value of the loss function. The function first computes the error for each observation. It then transforms these values to their absolute values using tf.abs() and then returns the mean across all observations using tf.reduce_mean().

---

[1]Since the mean is the sum divided by the number of observations (i.e., scaled by a constant), minimizing the mean will be equivalent to minimizing the sum. In practice, we will typically minimize means, since computing large sums can result in overflow, which occurs when a number exceeds the allowable range for its data type.

Listing 3-3. Initialize variables and define the loss

```
# Draw initial values randomly.
alphaHat0 = tf.random.normal([1], stddev=5.0)
betaHat0 = tf.random.normal([1], stddev=5.0)

# Define variables.
alphaHat = tf.Variable(alphaHat0, tf.float32)
betaHat = tf.Variable(betaHat0, tf.float32)

# Define function to compute MAE loss.
def maeLoss(alphaHat, betaHat, xSample, ySample):
        prediction = alphaHat + betaHat*xSample
        error = ySample - prediction
        absError = tf.abs(error)
        return tf.reduce_mean(absError)
```

The final step is to perform optimization, which we do in Listing 3-4. To do this, we'll first create an instance of the stochastic gradient descent optimizer named opt using `tf.optimizers.SGD()`. We'll then use that instance to perform minimization. This involves applying the `minimize()` method to opt. To perform a single step of optimization over the entire sample, we pass the function that returns the loss to the `minimize` operation as a `lambda` function. Additionally, we pass the parameters, alphaHat and betaHat, and the first sample of input data, X[:,0] and Y[0:], to `maeLoss()`. Finally, we also need to pass a list of trainable variables, var_list, to `minimize()`. Each increment of the loop performs a minimization step, which updates the parameters and the state of the optimizer. In this example, we have repeated the minimization step 1000 times.

Listing 3-4. Define an optimizer and minimize the loss function

```
# Define optimizer.
opt = tf.optimizers.SGD()

# Define empty lists to hold parameter values.
alphaHist, betaHist = [], []

# Perform minimization and retain parameter updates.
for j in range(1000):

        # Perform minimization step.
        opt.minimize(lambda: maeLoss(alphaHat, betaHat,
        X[:,0], Y[:,0]), var_list = [alphaHat,
        betaHat])

        # Update list of parameters.
        alphaHist.append(alphaHat.numpy()[0])
        betaHist.append(betaHat.numpy()[0])
```

Before we repeat the process for the remaining 99 samples, let's see how successful we were in identifying the true parameter values in the first. Figure 3-2 shows a plot of the values of alphaHat and betaHat at each step in the minimization process. The code for generating this plot is shown in Listing 3-5. Notice that we did not divide the sample into mini-batches, so each step is labeled as an epoch, where an epoch is a complete pass over the sample. The initial values, as we saw earlier, were randomly generated by drawing from a normal distribution with a high variance. Nevertheless, both alphaHat and betaHat appear to converge to their true parameter values after approximately 600 epochs.

Listing 3-5. Plot the parameter training histories

```
# Define DataFrame of parameter histories.
params = pd.DataFrame(np.hstack([alphaHist,
```

```
        betaHist]), columns = ['alphaHat', 'betaHat'])
# Generate plot.
params.plot(figsize=(10,7))

# Set x axis label.
plt.xlabel('Epoch')

# Set y axis label.
plt.ylabel('Parameter Value')
```

Furthermore, alphaHat and betaHat do not appear to adjust any further after they converge on their true parameter values. This suggests that the training process was stable and the stochastic gradient descent algorithm, which we will discuss in detail later in the chapter, was able to identify a clear local minimum, which turned out to be the global minimum in this case.[2]

Now that we've tested the solution method for one sample, we'll repeat the process 100 times with different initial parameter values and different samples. We'll then evaluate the performance of our solution method to determine whether it is sensitive to the choice of initial values or the data sample drawn. Figure 3-3 shows a histogram of the parameter value estimates at the 1000th epoch for each sample. Most estimates appear to be tightly clustered around the true parameter values; however, there are some deviations, due to either the initial values or the sample drawn. If we were planning to use LAD on a dataset with attributes similar to what we've generated in the Monte Carlo experiment, we might want to consider using a higher number of epochs to increase the probability that we converge to the true parameter values.

---

[2]A local minimum is the lowest value of a function in given region, whereas the global minimum is the lowest overall value of the function. In practice, loss functions often have many local minima, making it challenging to identify the global minimum.

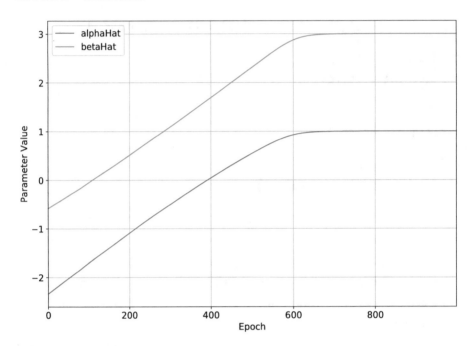

Figure 3-2. *History of parameter values over 1000 epochs of training*

Beyond changing the number of epochs, we may also want to consider adjusting the optimization algorithm's hyperparameters, rather than using the default options. Alternatively, we might consider using a different optimization algorithm altogether. As we will discuss later in the chapter, this is relatively simple to do in TensorFlow.

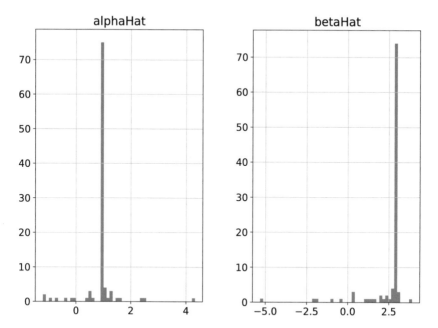

Figure 3-3. *Parameter estimate counts from Monte Carlo experiment*

Other Loss Functions

As we discussed, OLS has an analytical solution, but LAD does not. Since most machine learning models do not permit an analytical solution, LAD can provide an instructive example. The same process we used to construct a model, define a loss function, and perform minimization for LAD will be repeated throughout the chapter and book. Indeed, the steps used to perform LAD can be applied to any form of linear regression by simply modifying the loss function.

There are, of course, reasons to favor OLS beyond the fact that it has a closed-form solution. For instance, if the conditions for the Gauss-Markov Theorem are satisfied, then the OLS estimator has the lowest variance among all linear and unbiased estimators.[3] There is also a large econometric literature which builds on OLS and its variants, making it a natural choice for related work.

In many machine learning applications within economics and finance, however, the objective will often be to perform prediction, rather than hypothesis testing. In those cases, it may make sense to use a different form of linear regression; and using TensorFlow will make this task easier.

Partially Linear Models

In many machine learning applications, we will want to model non-linearities in a way that cannot be satisfactorily achieved using a linear regression model, even with the strategies we outlined earlier. This will require us to use a different modeling technique. In this section, we'll expand the linear model to allow for the inclusion of a non-linear function.

Rather than constructing a purely non-linear model, we'll start with what's called a "partially linear model." Such a model allows for certain independent variables to enter linearly, while others are permitted to enter the model through a non-linear function.

In the context of standard econometric applications, where the objective is typically statistical inference, a partially linear model would usually consist of a single variable of interest, which enters linearly, and a set of controls, which is permitted to enter non-linearly. The objective of such an exercise would be to perform inference on the parameter that enters linearly.

---

[3]The Gauss-Markov Theorem makes five assumptions: (1) the true model is linear in the parameters; (2) the data is sampled randomly; (3) none of the independent variables are perfectly correlated with each other (no perfect collinearity); (4) the error term is exogenous (not correlated with the independent variables); and (5) the variance of the error term is constant and finite.

There are, however, econometric challenges to performing valid statistical inference with partially linear models. First, there is an issue with parameter consistency when the variable of interest and the controls are collinear.[4] This is addressed in Robinson (1988), which constructs a consistent estimator for such cases.[5] Another issue arises when we apply regularization to the non-linear function of controls. If we simply apply the estimator from Robinson (1988), the parameter of interest will be biased. Chernozhukov et al. (2017) demonstrate how to eliminate bias through the use of orthogonalization and sample splitting.

For the purposes of this chapter, we will focus exclusively on the construction and training of a partially linear model for predictive purposes, rather than for statistical inference. In doing so, we will sidestep questions related to consistency and bias and focus on the practical implementation of a training routine in TensorFlow.

We'll start by defining the model we wish to train in Equation 3-12. Here, β is the vector of coefficients that enter the model linearly, and $g(Z)$ is a non-linear function of the controls.

Equation 3-12. A partially linear model.

$$Y = \alpha + \beta X + g(Z) + \epsilon$$

Similar to the example for LAD, we'll use a Monte Carlo experiment to evaluate whether we've correctly constructed and trained the model in TensorFlow and also to determine whether we are likely to encounter numerical issues, given our sample size and model specification.

---

[4]Two regressors, X and Z, are said to be "collinear" if they are not statistically independent.

[5]A consistent estimator converges in probability to the true parameter value as the number of observations goes to infinity.

In order to perform the Monte Carlo experiment, we'll need to make specific assumptions about the values of the linear parameters, as well as the functional form of g(). For the sake of simplicity, we'll assume that there is only one variable of interest, X, and one control, Z, which enters with the functional form $\exp(\theta Z)$. Additionally, the true parameter values are assumed to be $\alpha = 1$, $\beta = 3$, and $\theta = 0.05$.

We'll start the Monte Carlo experiment in Listing 3-6 by generating data. As in the previous example, we'll use 100 samples and 10,000 observations and define the true parameter values using tf.constant(). Next, we'll draw realizations of the regressors, X and Z, and the error term, epsilon. Finally, we use the randomly generated data to construct the dependent variable, Y.

Listing 3-6. Generate data for partially linear regression experiment

```
import tensorflow as tf

# Set number of observations and samples
S = 100
N = 10000

# Set true values of parameters.
alpha = tf.constant([1.], tf.float32)
beta = tf.constant([3.], tf.float32)
theta = tf.constant([0.05], tf.float32)

# Draw independent variable and error.
X = tf.random.normal([N, S])
Z = tf.random.normal([N, S])
epsilon = tf.random.normal([N, S], stddev=0.25)

# Compute dependent variable.
Y = alpha + beta*X + tf.exp(theta*Z) + epsilon
```

The next step, shown in Listing 3-7, is to define and initialize the model parameters: alphaHat0, betaHat0, and thetaHat0. We then deviate slightly from the previous example: rather than computing the loss function immediately, we'll first define a function for the partially linear model, which takes the parameters and a sample of the data as inputs and then outputs a prediction for each observation.

Listing 3-7. Initialize variables and compute the loss

```
# Draw initial values randomly.
alphaHat0 = tf.random.normal([1], stddev=5.0)
betaHat0 = tf.random.normal([1], stddev=5.0)
thetaHat0 = tf.random.normal([1], mean=0.05,
           stddev=0.10)

# Define variables.
alphaHat = tf.Variable(alphaHat0, tf.float32)
betaHat = tf.Variable(betaHat0, tf.float32)
thetaHat = tf.Variable(thetaHat0, tf.float32)

# Compute prediction.
def plm(alphaHat, betaHat, thetaHat, xS, zS):
        prediction = alphaHat + betaHat*xS + \
                        tf.exp(thetaHat*zS)
        return prediction
```

We've now generated the data, initialized the parameters, and defined the partially linear model. The next step is to define a loss function, which we do in Listing 3-8. As with the previous examples, we can use whichever loss function is best suited to our problem. In this case, we'll use the mean absolute error (MAE). Additionally, rather than computing the MAE ourselves, as we did previously, we'll instead use a TensorFlow operation. The first argument to the tf.losses.mae() operation is an array of true values and the second is an array of predicted values.

Listing 3-8. Define a loss function for a partially linear regression

```
# Define function to compute MAE loss.
def maeLoss(alphaHat, betaHat, thetaHat, xS, zS, yS):
        yHat = plm(alphaHat, betaHat, thetaHat, xS, zS)
        return tf.losses.mae(yS, yHat)
```

The final step is to perform minimization, which we do in Listing 3-9. As in the LAD example, we'll do this by instantiating an optimizer and then applying the minimize method. Each time we execute the minimize method, we'll complete an entire epoch of training.

Listing 3-9. Train a partially linear regression model

```
# Instantiate optimizer.
opt = tf.optimizers.SGD()

# Perform optimization.
for i in range(1000):
        opt.minimize(lambda: maeLoss(alphaHat, betaHat,
        thetaHat, X[:,0], Z[:,0], Y[:,0]),
        var_list = [alphaHat, betaHat, thetaHat])
```

After the optimization process terminates, we can evaluate the results, as we did for the LAD example. Figure 3-4 shows the history of parameter value estimates over 1000 epochs of training. Notice that alphaHat, betaHat, and thetaHat all converge to their true values after approximately 800 epochs of training. Additionally, they do not appear to diverge from their true values as the training process continues.

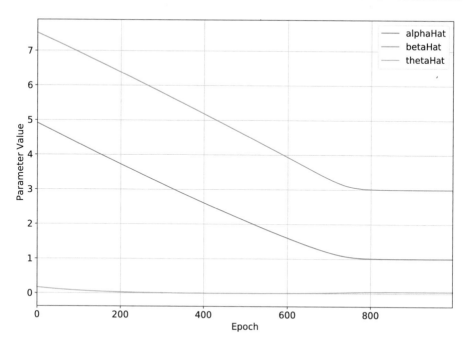

Figure 3-4. *History of parameter values over 1000 epochs of training*

In addition to this, we'll also examine the estimates for all 100 samples to see how sensitive the results are to the initialization and data. The final epoch parameter values for each sample are visualized in histograms in Figure 3-5. From the figure, it is clear that estimates of both alphaHat and betaHat are tightly clustered around their respective true values. While thetaHat appears unbiased, since the histogram is centered around the true value of theta, there appears to be more variation in the estimates. This suggests that we may want to make adjustments to the training process, possibly by using a higher number of epochs.

Performing a LAD regression and a partially linear regression demonstrated that TensorFlow is capable of handling the construction and training of an arbitrary model, including those that contain non-linearities. In the following section, we'll see that TensorFlow can also handle discrete dependent variables. We'll then complete the chapter by discussing the various ways in which we can adjust the training process to improve results.

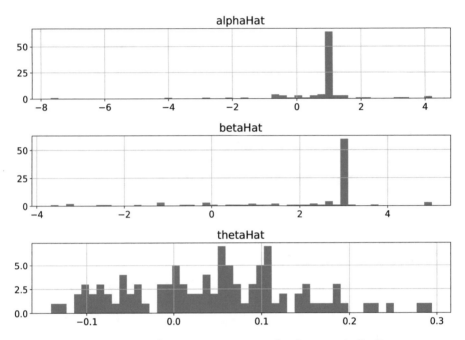

Figure 3-5. *Monte Carlo experiment results for partially linear regression*

Non-linear Regression

In the previous section, we discussed partially linear models, which had both a linear and non-linear component. Solving a fully non-linear model can be accomplished using the same workflow as the partially linear model. We first generate or load the data. Next, we define the model and loss function. And finally, we instantiate an optimizer and perform minimization of the loss function.

Rather than using generated data, as we did in earlier examples, we'll make use of the natural logarithm of the daily exchange rate for US dollar (USD) and British pound (GBP), which is shown in Figure 3-6.[6]

---

[6]The raw series is available for download at https://fred.stlouisfed.org/series/DEXUSUK.

Figure 3-6. *Natural logarithm of the USD-GBP exchange rate at a daily frequency (1970–2020). Source: Federal Reserve Board of Governors*

Since exchange rates are challenging to predict, a random walk is often used as the benchmark model in forecasting exercises. As shown in Equation 3-13, a random walk models the next period's exchange rate as the current period's exchange rate plus some random noise.

Equation 3-13. A random walk model of the nominal exchange rate.

$$e_t = \alpha + e_{t-1} + \epsilon_t$$

A line of literature that emerged in the 1990s argued that threshold autoregressive (TAR) models could generate improvements over the random walk model. Several variants of such models were proposed, including Smooth Transition Autoregressive Models (STAR) and Exponential Smoothed Autoregressive Models (ESTAR).[7]

---

[7]See Taylor et al. (2001) for an overview of the STAR and ESTAR models.

Our exercise will focus on implementing a TAR model in TensorFlow and will deviate from the literature by, among other things, using the nominal, rather than real, exchange rate. Additionally, we will again abstract away from questions related to statistical inference by focusing on prediction.

An autoregressive model assumes that movements in a series are explained by past values of the series and noise. A random walk, for instance, is an autoregressive model of order one – since it contains a single lag – that has an autoregressive parameter of one. The autoregressive parameter is the coefficient on the lagged value of the dependent variable.

A TAR model modifies an autoregression by allowing parameter values to vary according to pre-defined thresholds. That is, parameters are assumed to be fixed within a particular regime, but may vary across regimes. We'll use the regimes given in Equation 3-14. If there's a sharp depreciation of more than 2%, then we're in one regime, associated with one autoregressive parameter value. Otherwise, we're in another.

Equation 3-14. A threshold autoregressive (TAR) model with two regimes.

$$e_t = \begin{cases} \rho_0 e_{t-1} + \epsilon_t, & \epsilon_{t-1} - \epsilon_{t-2} < -0.02 \\ \rho_1 e_{t-1} + \epsilon_t, & \epsilon_{t-1} - \epsilon_{t-2} \geq -0.02 \end{cases}$$

Our first step in the TensorFlow implementation will be to prepare the data. In order to do this, we'll need to load the log of the nominal exchange rate, compute a lag, and compute a lagged first difference. We'll load and transform the data in pandas and numpy. We'll then convert them into tf. constant() objects. For the threshold variable, we'll also need to change its type from a Boolean to 32-bit floating-point number. All steps are shown in Listing 3-10.

Listing 3-10. Prepare the data for a TAR model of the USD-GBP exchange rate

```
import pandas as pd
import numpy as np
import tensorflow as tf

# Define data path.
data_path = '../data/chapter3/'

# Load data.
data = pd.read_csv(data_path+'exchange_rate.csv')

# Convert log exchange rate to numpy array.
e = np.array(data["log_USD_GBP"])

# Identify exchange decreases greater than 2%.
de = tf.cast(np.diff(e[:-1]) < -0.02, tf.float32)

# Define the lagged exchange rate as a constant.
le = tf.constant(e[1:-1], tf.float32)

# Define the exchange rate as a constant.
e = tf.constant(e[2:], tf.float32)
```

Now that the data has been prepared, we'll define the trainable model parameters, rho0Hat and rho1Hat, in Listing 3-11.

Listing 3-11. Define parameters for a TAR model of the USD-GBP exchange rate

```
# Define variables.
rho0Hat = tf.Variable(0.80, tf.float32)
rho1Hat = tf.Variable(0.80, tf.float32)
```

We next define both the model and the loss function in Listing 3-12. We then multiply the autoregressive coefficient by a dummy variable for the regime, de. Finally, this is multiplied by a lag of the exchange rate, le. For the sake of simplicity, we'll use the mean absolute loss function, along with the TensorFlow operation for it.

Listing 3-12. Define model and loss function for TAR model of USD-GBP exchange rate

```
# Define model.
def tar(rho0Hat, rho1Hat, le, de):
        # Compute regime-specific prediction.
        regime0 = rho0Hat*le
        regime1 = rho1Hat*le
        # Compute prediction for regime.
        prediction = regime0*de + regime1*(1-de)
        return prediction

# Define loss.
def maeLoss(rho0Hat, rho1Hat, e, le, de):
        ehat = tar(rho0Hat, rho1Hat, le, de)
        return tf.losses.mae(e, ehat)
```

The final step is to define an optimizer and perform optimization, which we do in Listing 3-13.

Figure 3-7 shows the training history. The autoregressive parameter for the "normal" regime – where no sharp depreciation occurs the previous day – rapidly converges to approximately 1.0. This suggests that the exchange rate is best modeled as a random walk in normal times. However, when we look at cases where a sharp depreciation occurred the previous day, we instead find an autoregressive coefficient of 0.993, suggesting that the rate will be highly persistent, but will tend to drift back toward its mean, rather than remaining permanently lower.

Listing 3-13. Train TAR model of the USD-GBP exchange rate

```
# Define optimizer.
opt = tf.optimizers.SGD()

# Perform minimization.
for i in range(20000):
        opt.minimize(lambda: maeLoss(
        rho0Hat, rho1Hat, e, le, de),
        var_list = [rho0Hat, rho1Hat]
        )
```

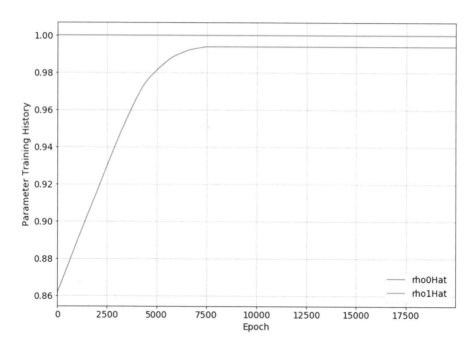

Figure 3-7. *Training history of the TAR model of the USD-GBP exchange rate*

We've now seen how to perform linear regression with different loss functions, partially linear regression, and non-linear regression in TensorFlow. In the next section, we'll examine another type of regression, which has a discrete dependent variable.

Logistic Regression

In machine learning, supervised learning models are typically divided into "regression" and "classification" categories based on whether they have a discrete or continuous dependent variable. As discussed earlier, we will use the definition of regression from econometrics, which also applies to classification models, such as a logistic regression.

A logistic regression or "logit" predicts the class of the dependent variable. In a microeconometric setting, a logit might be used to model the choice of transportation over two options. In a financial setting, it might be used to model whether we are in a crisis or not.

Since the process of constructing and training a logistic regression involves many of the same steps as linear, partially linear, and non-linear regression, we will focus exclusively on what differs.

First, the model takes a specific functional form – namely, that of the logistic curve – which is given in Equation 3-15.

Equation 3-15. The logistic curve.

$$p(X) = \frac{1}{1 + e^{-(\alpha + \beta_0 X_0 + \ldots + \beta_k X_k)}}$$

Notice that the model's output is a continuous probability, rather than a discrete outcome. Since probabilities range from 0 to 1, probabilities greater than 0.5 will often be treated as predictions of outcome 1. While this functional form differs from anything we've dealt with previously in this chapter, it can be handled using all of the same tools and operations in TensorFlow.

Finally, the other difference between a logistic model and those we've defined earlier in this chapter is that it will require a different loss function. Specifically, we will use the binary cross-entropy loss function, which is defined in Equation 3-16.

Equation 3-16. Binary cross-entropy loss function.

$$\Sigma_i - \left(Y_i * \log\left(p\left(X_i\right)\right)\right) + \left(1 - Y_i\right) * \log\left(1 - p\left(X_i\right)\right)$$

We use this particular functional form because the outcomes are discrete and the predictions are continuous. Note that the binary cross-entropy loss sums over the product of the outcome variable and the natural log of the predicted probability for each observation. If, for instance, the true class of Y_i is 1 and the model predicts a 0.98 probability of class 1, then that observation will add 0.02 to the loss. If, instead, the prediction is 0.10, which is far from the true classification, then the addition to the loss will instead be 2.3.

While computing the binary cross-entropy loss function is relatively simple, TensorFlow simplifies it further by providing the operation `tf.losses.binary_crossentropy()`, which takes the true label as its first argument and the predicted probability as its second.

Loss Functions

Whenever we solve a model in TensorFlow, we will need to define a loss function. The minimization operation will make use of this function to determine how to adjust parameter values. Fortunately, it will not always be necessary to define a custom loss function. Rather, we will often be able to use one of the pre-defined loss functions provided by TensorFlow.

There are currently two submodules of TensorFlow that contain loss functions: `tf.losses` and `tf.keras.losses`. The first submodule contains native TensorFlow implementations of loss functions. The second submodule contains the Keras implementations of the loss functions. Keras is a library for performing deep learning that is available as both a stand-alone module in Python and a high-level API in TensorFlow.

TensorFlow 2.3 offers 15 standard loss functions in the `tf.losses` submodule. Each of those loss functions takes the form `tf.loss_function(y_true, y_pred)`. That is, we pass the dependent variable, `y_true`, as the first argument and the model's predictions, `y_pred`, as the second argument. It then returns the value of the loss function.

When we work with high-level APIs in TensorFlow in later chapters, we will make use of the loss functions directly. However, for the purpose of this chapter, which is centered around optimization using low-level TensorFlow operations, we will need to wrap those loss functions within a function of the model's trainable parameters and data. The optimizer will need to make use of the outer function to perform minimization.

Discrete Dependent Variables

The submodule `tf.losses` offers two loss functions for discrete dependent variables in regression settings: `tf.binary_crossentropy()`, `tf.categorical_crossentropy()`, and `tf.sparse_categorical_crossentropy()`. We have previously covered the binary cross-entropy function, which is used in logistic regression. This provides us with a measure of loss when we have a binary dependent variable, such as an indicator for whether the economy is a recession, and a continuous prediction, such as a probability of being in a recession. For convenience, we repeat the formula for binary cross-entropy in Equation 3-17.

Equation 3-17. Binary cross-entropy loss function.

$$L(Y, p(X)) = \Sigma_i -(Y_i * \log(p(X_i)) + (1 - Y_i) * \log(1 - p(X_i))$$

The categorical cross-entropy loss is simply the extension of the binary cross-entropy loss to cases where the dependent variable has more than two categories. Such models are commonly used in discrete choice problems, such as a model of the decision to commute by subway, bicycle, car, or foot. Within machine learning, categorical cross-entropy is the standard loss function for classification problems with more than two classes and is commonly used in neural networks that perform image and text classification. The equation for categorical cross-entropy is given in Equation 3-18. Note that (Y_i==k) is a binary variable equal to 1 if Y_i is class k and 0 otherwise. Additionally, $p_k(X_i)$ is the probability that the model assigns to X_i being class k.

Equation 3-18. Categorical cross-entropy loss function.

$$L\left(Y, p\left(X\right)\right) = -\Sigma_i \Sigma_k \left(Y_i == k\right) * \log\left(p_k\left(X_i\right)\right)$$

Finally, if we have a problem with a dependent variable that may belong to multiple categories – that is, a "multi-label" problem – we'll use the sparse categorical cross-entropy loss function, rather than categorical cross-entropy. Notice that the normal cross-entropy loss function assumes that the dependent variable can have only one class.

Continuous Dependent Variables

For continuous dependent variables, the most common loss functions are the mean absolute error (MAE) and mean squared error (MSE). MAE is used in LAD and MSE in OLS. Equation 3-19 defines the MAE loss function, and Equation 3-20 defines the MSE loss. Recall that $\hat{Y}_i$ is the model's predicted value for observation *i*.

Equation 3-19. Mean absolute error loss.

$$L\left(Y, \hat{Y}\right) = \frac{1}{n} \sum_i \left|Y_i - \hat{Y}_i\right|$$

Equation 3-20. Mean squared error loss.

$$L\left(Y, \hat{Y}\right) = \frac{1}{n} \sum_i \left(Y_i - \hat{Y}_i\right)^2$$

Note that we can compute the losses using `tf.losses.mae()` and `tf.losses.mse()`.

Other common loss functions for linear regression include the mean absolute percentage error (MAPE), the mean squared logarithmic error (MSLE), and the Huber error, which are defined in Equations 3-21, 3-22, and 3-23. Respectively, these are available as `tf.losses.MAPE()`, `tf.losses.MSLE()`, and `tf.losses.Huber()`.

Equation 3-21. Mean absolute percentage error.

$$L(Y,\hat{Y}) = 100 * \frac{1}{n}\sum_i \left| \left(Y_i - \hat{Y}_i\right)\middle/\hat{Y}_i \right|$$

Equation 3-22. Mean squared logarithmic error.

$$L(Y,\hat{Y}) = \frac{1}{n}\sum_i \left(\log(Y_i+1) - \log(\hat{Y}_i+1)\right)^2$$

Equation 3-23. Huber error.

$$L(Y,\hat{Y}) = \begin{cases} \frac{1}{2}\left(Y_i - \hat{Y}_i\right)^2 & \text{for } \left|Y_i - \hat{Y}_i\right| \le \delta \\ \delta\left(\left|Y_i - \hat{Y}_i\right| - \frac{1}{2}\delta\right)^2 & \text{otherwise} \end{cases}$$

Figure 3-8 provides a comparison of selected loss functions. For each loss function, the loss value is plotted against the error value. Notice that the MAE loss scales linearly in the error. To the contrary, the MSE loss increases slowly near zero, but grows much faster far away from zero, leading to the application of a substantial penalty on outliers. Finally, the Huber loss is similar to the MSE loss near zero, but similar to the MAE loss as the error increases in size.

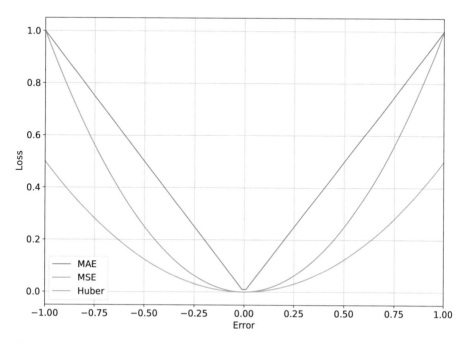

Figure 3-8. *Comparison of common loss functions*

Optimizers

The last topic we'll consider in this chapter is the use of optimizers in TensorFlow. We have already seen how optimizers work when we applied them in the context of linear regressions. In each case, we used the stochastic gradient descent (SGD) optimizer, which is simple and interpretable, but is less commonly used in more recent work on machine learning. In this section, we'll expand the set of optimizers we discuss.

Stochastic Gradient Descent (SGD)

Stochastic gradient descent (SGD) is a minimization algorithm that updates parameter values through the use of the gradient. In this case, the gradient is a tensor of partial derivatives of the loss function with respect to each of the parameters.

The parameter update process is given in Equation 3-24. To ensure compatibility with the equivalent TensorFlow operation, we use the definition provided in the documentation. Note that θ_t is a vector of parameter values at iteration t, lr is the learning rate, and g_t is the gradient computed in iteration i.

Equation 3-24. Stochastic gradient descent in TensorFlow.

$$\theta_t = \theta_{t-1} - lr * g_t$$

You might wonder in what sense SGD is "stochastic." The stochasticity arises from the sampling process used to update the parameters. This differs from gradient descent, where the entire sample is used at each iteration. The benefits of the stochastic version of gradient descent are that it increases iteration speed and alleviates memory constraints.

Let's take a look at a single SGD step for a linear regression with an intercept term and a single variable, where $\theta_t = [\alpha_t, \beta_t]$. We'll start at iteration 0 and assume we've computed the gradient, g_0, for the batch of data as [−0.25, 0.33]. Additionally, we'll set the learning rate, lr, to 0.01. What does this imply for θ_1? Using Equation 3-24, we can see that $\theta_1 = [\alpha_0 + 0.025, \beta_0 − 0.033]$. That is, we decrease α_0 by 0.025 and increase β_0 by 0.033.

Why do we increase a parameter value when the partial derivative is negative and decrease it when it is positive? Because the partial derivatives tell us how the loss function changes in response to a change in a given parameter. If the loss function is increasing, we're moving further away from the minimum, so we want to change direction; however, if the loss function is decreasing, we're moving toward a minimum, so we want to continue on the same direction. Furthermore, if the loss function is neither increasing nor decreasing, this means we're at a minimum and the algorithm will naturally terminate.

Figure 3-9 illustrates this for the partial derivative of the loss function with respect to the intercept term. We focus on a narrow window around the true value of the intercept and plot both the loss function and its derivative. We can see that the derivative is initially negative, but increases to 0 at the true value of the intercept. It then becomes positive and increasing thereafter.

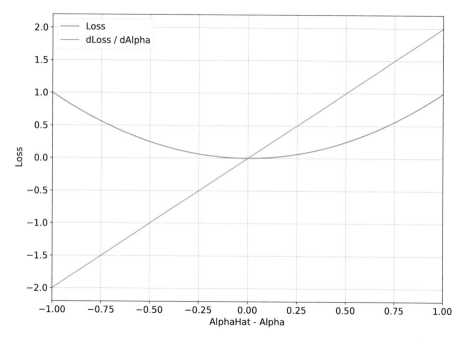

Figure 3-9. *Loss function and its derivative with respect to the intercept*

Returning to Equation 3-24, notice that the selection of the learning rate can also be quite consequential. If we select a high learning rate, we'll take larger steps with each iteration, which could bring us closer to a minimum faster. However, taking larger steps could also lead us to skip over the minimum, missing it entirely. The selection of the learning rate should take this trade-off into consideration.

Finally, it is worth mentioning that the "minima" we're identifying are local and, thus, may be higher than the global minimum. That is, SGD makes no distinction between the lowest point in an area and the lowest value of the loss function. Consequently, it may be worthwhile to re-run the algorithm for several different sets of initial parameter values to see if we always converge to the same minimum.

Modern Optimizers

While SGD is easy to understand, it is rarely used in machine learning applications in its original form. This is because modern extensions typically offer more flexibility and robustness and perform better on benchmark tasks. The most common extensions of SGD are root mean square propagation (RMSProp), adaptive moment estimation (Adam), and adaptive gradient methods (Adagrad and Adadelta).

There are several advantages to using modern extensions of SGD. First, starting with RMSProp, which is the oldest, they allow for the application of separate learning rates to each parameter. In many optimization problems, there will be orders of magnitude differences between partial derivatives in the gradient. Consequently, applying a learning rate of 0.001, for instance, may be sensible for one parameter, but not for another. RMSProp allows us to overcome this problem. It also allows for the use of "momentum," where the gradients accumulate over mini-batches, making it possible for the algorithm to break out of local minima.

Adagrad, Adadelta, and Adam all offer variants on the use of momentum and adaptive updates for each individual parameter. Adam tends to work well for many optimization problems with its default parameters. Adagrad is centered around the accumulation of gradients and the adaptation of learning rates for individual parameters. And Adadelta modifies Adagrad by introducing a window over which accumulated gradients are retained.[8]

---

[8]For an extended discussion of the theoretical properties of optimizers, see Goodfellow et al. (2017).

In all cases, the use of optimizers will follow a familiar two-step process. We'll first instantiate an optimizer and will set its parameter values in the process using the tf.optimizer submodule. And second, we'll iteratively apply the minimize function and pass the loss function to it as a lambda function.

Since we have performed the second step multiple times, we'll focus exclusively on the first step in Listing 3-14. There, we've instantiated SGD, RMSProp, Adagrad, and Adadelta optimizers and have emphasized how to set their respective parameter values.

Listing 3-14. Instantiate optimizers

```
# Instantiate optimizers.
sgd = tf.optimizers.SGD(learning_rate = 0.001,
        momentum = 0.5)
rms = tf.optimizers.RMSprop(learning_rate = 0.001,
        rho = 0.8, momentum = 0.9)
agrad = tf.optimizers.Adagrad(learning_rate = 0.001,
        initial_accumulator_value = 0.1)
adelt = tf.optimizers.Adadelta(learning_rate = 0.001,
        rho = 0.95)
adam = tf.optimizers.Adam(learning_rate = 0.001,
        beta_1 = 0.9, beta_2 = 0.999)
```

For SGD, we set the learning rate and the momentum. If we're concerned that there are many local minima, we can increase momentum to a higher value. For RMSProp, we not only set a momentum parameter but also set rho, which is the rate at which information about the gradient decays. The Adadelta parameter, which retains gradients for a period of time, also has the same decay parameter, rho. For Adagrad, we set an initial accumulator value, related to the intensity with which gradients are accumulated over time. Finally, for the Adam optimizer, we set decay rates for the accumulation of information about the mean and variance of the gradients. In this case, we have used the default values for the Adam optimizer, which generally perform well in large optimization problems.

We've now introduced the main optimizers we will use throughout the book. We will return to them again in detail when we apply them to train models. The modern variants of SGD will be particularly useful when we train large models with thousands of parameters.

Summary

The most commonly used empirical method in economics is the regression. In machine learning, the term regression refers to a supervised learning model with a continuous target. In economics, the term "regression" is more broadly defined and may refer to cases with binary or categorical dependent variables, such as logistic regression. For the purposes of this book, we adopt the economics terminology.

In this chapter, we introduced the concept of a regression, including the linear, partially linear, and non-linear varieties. We saw how to define and train such models in TensorFlow, which will ultimately form the basis for solving any arbitrary model in TensorFlow, as we will see in later chapters.

Finally, we discussed the finer details of the training process. We saw how to construct a loss function and what pre-defined loss functions were available in TensorFlow. We also saw how to perform minimization with a variety of different optimization routines.

Bibliography

Chernozhukov, V., D. Chetverikov, M. Demirer, E. Duflo, C. Hansen, W. Newey, and J. Robins. 2017. "Double/debiased machine learning for treatment and structural parameters." *The Econometrics Journal* 21 (1).

Goodfellow, I., Y. Bengio, and A. Courville. 2017. *Deep Learning.* Cambridge, MA: MIT Press.

Robinson, P.M. 1988. "Root-N-Consistent Semiparametric Regression." *Econometrica* 56 (4): 931–954.

Taylor, M.P., D.A. Peel, and L. Sarno. 2001. "Nonlinear Mean-Reversion in Real Exchange Rates: Toward a Solution to the Purchasing Power Parity Puzzles." *International Economic Review* 42 (4): 1015–1042.

CHAPTER 4

Trees

Tree-based models have proven to be remarkably useful for prediction tasks in machine learning and have recently been applied to and modified for problems in economics and finance. The fundamental unit of any tree-based model is a decision tree, which explains an outcome using a sequence of data partitions. Such a model can be naturally visualized as a flowchart.

While TensorFlow was developed for the purpose of solving deep learning problems, it has recently added libraries for tree-based models in its high-level `Estimators` API. In this chapter, we'll examine those libraries and will apply them to train tree-based models on Home Mortgage Disclosure Act (HMDA) application data for the state of Alaska.[1]

Decision Trees

A decision tree is analogous to a flowchart with specific numerical and categorical thresholds, typically constructed using the family of algorithms introduced in Breiman et al. (1984). In this section, we'll introduce decision trees on a conceptual level, focusing on basic definitions and

---

[1]The HMDA dataset is available for download from the Consumer Financial Protection Bureau (CFPB): `www.consumerfinance.gov/data-research/hmda/`. It is publicly available and provides data from many mortgage lenders on application features and decisions. We use all application data from Alaska for 2017.

© Isaiah Hull 2021
I. Hull, *Machine Learning for Economics and Finance in TensorFlow 2*,
https://doi.org/10.1007/978-1-4842-6373-0_4

the training process. Later in the chapter, we'll focus on implementing decision trees in TensorFlow. See Athey and Imbens (2016, 2019) for an overview of decision tree use in economics and Moscatelli et al. (2020) for an application to corporate default forecasting.

Overview

A decision tree consists of branches and three types of nodes: the root, internal nodes, and leaves. The root is where the first sample split occurs. That is, we enter the tree with the full sample of data and then pass through the root, which splits the sample. Each split is associated with a branch, which connects the root to internal nodes and potentially to leave nodes. Much like the root, internal nodes impose a condition that splits the sample. Internal nodes are connected to additional internal nodes or leaves by branches, which again are each associated with a sample split. Finally, the tree terminates at the leave nodes, which yield either a prediction or a probability distribution over categories.

To fix an example, let's consider the HMDA mortgage application data. We'll build a simple classifier that takes features from a mortgage application and then predicts whether it will be accepted or rejected. We'll start off with a tree model that has only one feature: applicant income in thousands of dollars. Our objective is only to train the model and see how it splits the sample. That is, we want to know what income level is associated with a split between acceptance and rejection, given that we don't condition on anything else, such as the size of the mortgage or the borrower's credit rating. Figure 4-1 shows this chart.

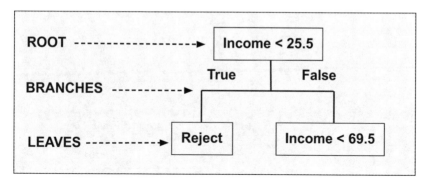

Figure 4-1. *A simple decision tree (DT) model using the HMDA data*

As we will discuss later in the chapter, one parameter of a decision tree is its maximum depth. We can measure the depth of a tree by counting the number of branches between the root and the most distant leaf. In this case, we've selected a maximum depth of one. Such trees are sometimes referred to as "decision stumps." Our simple model predicts that applicants with incomes below $25,500 are rejected, whereas applicants with incomes greater than or equal to $25,500 are accepted. The model is, of course, too simple to be useful for most applications; however, it provides us with a starting point.

In Figure 4-2, we extend this exercise further by increasing the maximum depth of the tree to three and adding a second feature: the ratio of census tract income to metropolitan statistical income, multiplied by 100. Note that we've used "Area Income" to describe this feature in the figure.

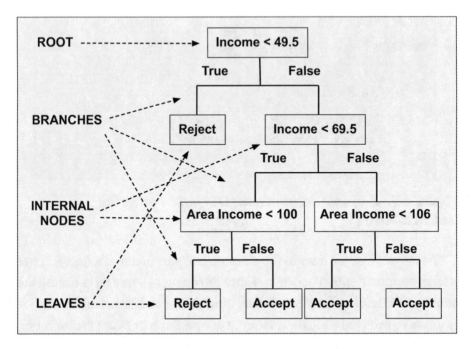

Figure 4-2. *A decision tree model trained on the HMDA data with two features and a max depth of three*

Starting again at the root, we can see that the decision tree first partitions the sample by applicant income. Low-income applicants are rejected. It then performs another partition among the remaining applicants. For lower-income households, the next internal node checks whether the income of the area in which they live is below average. If it is, they're rejected, but if isn't, they're accepted. Similarly, for high-income households, the tree checks the level of income in the house's area. However, irrespective of whether it is high or low, the application is accepted.

There are a few other things worthy of observation in the diagram. First, now that we have sufficient depth, the diagram has "internal nodes" – that is, nodes that are not the root or the leaves. And second, not all pairs of leaves must contain both an "accept" and "reject" class. In fact, the class of the leaf will depend on the empirical distribution of classes that are associated with the leaf. By convention, we might treat a leaf with more than 50% accept observations as an "accept" leaf. Alternatively, we might instead state the distribution over outcomes for the leaf, rather than associating it with a particular class.

Feature Engineering

The term "feature engineering" isn't used often in this book, since TensorFlow was designed primarily for deep learning, which typically performs feature extraction automatically. It's worthwhile, however, to point out that feature engineering is necessary for decision tree models, since they have a restrictive functional form.

In particular, decision trees are constructed by performing increasingly granular sample splits. If the functional form of the relationship isn't captured by a threshold for an individual feature, then a tree-based model will struggle to discover it. A linear relationship between one feature and the dependent variable, for instance, couldn't be captured by an intercept and slope. It would require a complicated step function, constructed from potentially hundreds of thresholds.

A clear example of this is the use of applicant income in the HMDA example we gave in Figures 4-1 and 4-2. While some minimum level of income may be needed to obtain a mortgage of any kind, it is clear that lower incomes should be permissible for smaller mortgages. Thus, what we might actually want is the debt-to-income ratio, which is commonly used to assess lending decisions.

However, if we don't compute the debt-to-income ratio and include it as a feature, the decision tree will require many internal nodes to achieve what we were able to do by taking a ratio. For this reason, decision trees still rely on expert judgment to inform the feature engineering process.

Training

We now know that decision trees make use of recursive sample splitting, but we haven't yet said how the sample splits themselves are selected. In practice, decision tree algorithms will perform sample splits by sequentially selecting the variable and threshold that generates the lowest Gini impurity or the greatest "information gain." The Gini impurity is given in Equation 4-1.

Equation 4-1. Gini impurity for dependent variable with K classes.

$$G(p) = 1 - \sum_{k \in K} p_k^2$$

The Gini impurity is computed over the empirical distribution of classes in a node. It tells us the extent to which the distribution is dominated by a single class. As an example, let's consider the model used in Figure 4-1, where we performed a single sample split on applicant income. We did not mention this earlier, but among the applicants with an income below the $25,500 threshold, the probability of acceptance was 0.656 and the probability of rejection was 0.344. This gives us a Gini impurity measure of 0.451. For those with incomes higher than $25,500, it was 0.075 for rejection and 0.925 for acceptance, yielding a Gini impurity of 0.139.[2]

Note that if the split had perfectly divided applicants into rejections and acceptances, then the Gini impurity for each group would have been zero. That is, we want a low Gini impurity and the algorithm achieves it by performing splits that tend to reduce heterogeneity within each node after a split.

---

[2]We arrive at a Gini impurity of 0.451 by computing 1-(0.656**2 + 0.344**2). Additionally, we arrive at a Gini impurity of 0.139 by computing 1-(0.075**2 + 0.925**2).

Next, we'll consider the information gain, which is the other common measure of the quality of a split. Similar to Gini impurity, it measures the change in the level of disorder that arises as a result of splitting a sample into nodes. In order to understand information gain, it will be necessary to first understand the concept of information entropy, which we define in Equation 4-2.

Equation 4-2. Information entropy for K-class case.

$$E(p) = -\sum_{k \in K} p_k \log_2 p_k$$

Let's return to the example we considered for Gini impurity. If we have a leaf with an empirical probability of acceptance of 0.656 and 0.344 for rejection, then the information entropy will be 0.929. Similarly, for the other leaf, with acceptance and rejection probabilities of 0.075 and 0.925, it will be 0.384.[3]

Since our objective is to reduce entropy in the data, we'll use a measure called the "information gain." This will measure how much entropy is removed from the system by performing a sample split. In Equation 4-3, we define the information gain as the difference between the entropy of a parent node and the weighted entropies of its child nodes.

Equation 4-3. Information gain.

$$IG = E(p_p) - \sum_k w_k E(p_{ck})$$

Between any nodes connected by a branch, a "child" node is subsample of the "parent" node that arises from a split. In Equation 4-3, we have already computed the entropies of the two child nodes as 0.929 and 0.384. The weights for the nodes, w_k, are their respective shares of the

---

[3]We compute the information entropy value as $-(0.656 * \log_2 0.656 + 0.344 * \log_2 0.344)$ for the first leaf and $-(0.075 * \log_2 0.075 + 0.925 * \log_2 0.925)$ for the second.

total sample. Let's assume the first leaf contains 10% of observations and the second contains the remaining 90%. This yields a value of 0.4385 for the weighted sum of child node entropies.

Before we can compute the information gain, we must first compute the parent node's entropy. For the sake of illustration, let's assume that an observation in the root node has a 0.25 probability of being a rejection and a 0.75 probability of being an acceptance. This yields an entropy of 0.811 for the parent node. Thus, the information gain or reduction in entropy is 0.3725 (i.e., 0.811–0.4385).

TensorFlow will allow for flexibility in the choice of splitting algorithm; however, we will delay discussing the details of implementation in TensorFlow until the "Random Forests" section. This is because TensorFlow currently only supports gradient boosted random forests, which will require the introduction of additional concepts.

Regression Trees

Decision trees, which we discussed in the previous section, use a flowchart-like structure to model a process with a categorical outcome. In most economics and finance applications, however, we have a continuous dependent variable, which means that we cannot use decision trees. For such problems, we can instead use a "regression tree," where "regression" is used in the machine learning context and denotes a continuous dependent variable.

A regression tree is nearly identical in structure to a decision tree. The only difference is in the leaves. Rather than associating a leaf with a class or a probability distribution over classes, it is instead associated with the mean value of the dependent variable for the observations in the leaf.

We'll follow the treatment of regression trees given in Athey and Imbens (2019), but will tie it to the HMDA dataset. To start, we'll assume that we have one feature, X_i, and a continuous dependent variable, Y_i. For the feature, we'll use applicant income in thousands of dollars. For the dependent variable, we'll use the size of the loan in thousands of dollars. If we use the sum of squared errors as the loss function, we may compute the loss at the root, prior to the first split, as in Equation 4-4.

Equation 4-4. Initial sum of squared errors at root.

$$SSE = \sum_i \left(Y_i - \bar{Y}\right)^2$$

That is, we do not split the sample, so all observations are in the same leaf. The predicted value for that leaf is simply the mean over the values of the dependent variable, denoted as $\bar{Y}$.

Using the notation from Athey and Imbens (2019), we'll use l to denote the "left" branch, r to denote the right branch of a split, and c to denote the threshold. Now, let's assume we decide to perform a single split at the root on the applicant income variable. The sum of squared errors can be computed using Equation 4-5.

Equation 4-5. Sum of squared errors after one split.

$$SSE = \sum_{i:X_i \le c} \left(Y_i - \bar{Y}_{l,r}\right)^2 + \sum_{i:X_i > c} \left(Y_i - \bar{Y}_{c,r}\right)^2$$

Notice that we now have two leaves, which means we must compute two sums of squared errors – one for each leaf. Starting with the leaf connected to the left branch, we compute the mean over all observations in the leaf, which is denoted as $\bar{Y}_{l,r}$. We then sum the squared differences between each observation in the leaf and the leaf mean and add to this to the sum of squared differences for the right leaf, computed in the same way.

As with decision trees, we may repeat this process for additional splits, depending on the choice of model parameters, such as the maximum tree depth. In general, however, we will typically not use regression and decision trees in isolation. Rather, we will use them in the context of a random forest, which we will discuss in the following section.

There are, however, some benefits to using single trees in isolation. One clear advantage is the interpretability of trees. In some cases, such as credit modeling, interpretability may be a legal requirement. Another benefit of using a regression tree, which Athey and Imbens (2019) discuss, is that they have good statistical properties. The tree's output is a mean and it is relatively straightforward to compute a confidence interval for it. They do, however, point out that the mean is not necessarily unbiased, but provide a procedure in Athey and Imbens (2016) to correct the bias using sample splitting.

Random Forests

While there are some advantages to using individual decision and regression trees, it is not common practice in most machine learning applications. The reason for this is primarily related to the predictive efficacy of random forests, which were introduced in Breiman (2001). As the name suggests, a random forest consists of many trees, rather than just one.

Athey and Imbens (2019) point out two differences between random forests and regression (or decision) trees. First, unlike regression trees, individual trees in a random forest only make use of part of the sample. That is, for each individual tree, the sample is bootstrapped by drawing a fixed number of observations at random and with replacement. This process sometimes referred to as "bagging." The second is that a random set of features is selected at each stage for the purpose of splitting. This differs from regression trees, which optimize over all features in the model.

The machine learning field has generally found random forests to have a high degree of predictive accuracy. They perform well in the literature, in machine learning contests, and in industry applications. Athey and Imbens (2019) point out that random forests also improve over regression trees by adding smoothness to the computed averages.

While random forests are almost exclusively used as a tool for prediction, recent work has demonstrated how they can be used to perform hypothesis testing and statistical inference. Wager and Athey (2017), for example, demonstrate the conditions under which leaf-level means (i.e., model predictions) are asymptotically normal and unbiased and also show how confidence intervals can be constructed for the model predictions.

Figure 4-3 illustrates the prediction process for a random forest model. In the first step, the set of features is passed to each of the individual decision or regression trees. A sequence of thresholds is then applied, which will depend on the structure of the trees themselves. Since there is randomness in the training process – in both the selection of features and the selection of observations – the trees will not have an identical structure.

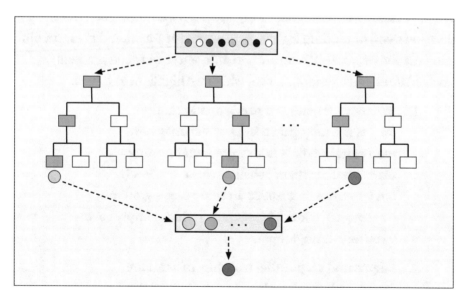

Figure 4-3. *Generating a prediction from a random forest model*

Each tree in the random forest will produce a prediction. The predictions will then be aggregated using some function. In classification trees, it is common to use a majority vote over the trees' predictions to determine the forest's classification. In regression trees, averaging over the trees' predictions is a common choice.

Finally, trees in a random forest are trained simultaneously, and the weights on individual trees, which are used for aggregation purposes, do not update during the training process itself. In the following section, we will take a look at gradient boosted trees, which modify random forests in a couple of ways and, most importantly, have an implementation in TensorFlow.

Gradient Boosted Trees

While TensorFlow doesn't offer a high-level API for regression trees, decision trees, or random forests, it does provide functionality for training gradient boosted trees. There are two differences between gradient boosted trees and a random forest, which we highlight as follows:

1. **Strong vs. weak learners**: Whereas random forests use fully grown trees, which may have many intermediate nodes, gradient boosting uses "weak learners": shallow trees with few (if any) intermediate nodes. In some cases, gradient boosting uses "decision stumps," which simply have a root and a single split.

2. **Sequential vs. parallel training**: In a random forest, each tree is trained in parallel and the weighting scheme over the trees does not depend on the training process. In gradient boosting, each tree is trained in sequence and can account for deficiencies in the model, given the previously trained trees.

The gradient boosting process relies on techniques that are familiar to economists, even if tree-based models are not. To clarify how such models are constructed, we will step through an example, where we use least squares as a loss function. We'll start by defining a function, $G_i(X)$, which yields predictions for the model's target, Y, after i iterations. Relatedly, we'll define a tree-based model, $T_i(X)$, which is introduced in iteration i as an improvement over $G_i(X)$ and a contributor to $G_{i+1}(X)$. The relationship between the functions is summarized in Equation 4-6.

Equation 4-6. Relationship between tree and prediction function in gradient boosting.

$$G_{i+1}(X) = G_i(X) + T_i(X)$$

Since $G_{i+1}(X)$ is a model that yields a prediction from features, it can be written in terms of the target variable, Y, and the prediction error or residual, ϵ, as in Equation 4-7.

Equation 4-7. Define model residual.

$$Y = G_i(X) + T_i(X) + \epsilon$$

$$\rightarrow \epsilon = Y - G_i(X) - T_i(X)$$

Notice that $Y - G_i(X)$ is fixed at iteration i. Thus, adjusting the parameters of tree model $T_i(X)$ will affect the residuals, ϵ. We can train $T_i(X)$ by minimizing the sum of squared errors, $\epsilon'\epsilon$. Alternatively, we could use a different loss function. Once $T_i(X)$ has been trained, we can update the predictive function, $G_{i+1}(X)$, and then repeat the process in another iteration to add another tree.

At each step, we'll use the residuals from the previous iteration as a target. If, for instance, our first tree is positively biased in a problem with a continuous target, then the second tree will likely develop a negative bias that, when combined with the first, reduces the model bias.

Classification Trees

Let's look at an example of implementing gradient boosted decision trees in TensorFlow. We'll make use of the HMDA data. Since we're using decision trees, we'll need a discrete dependent variable and will make use of the application outcome, which can either be acceptance or rejection.

In Listing 4-1, we'll start the process by importing pandas and tensorflow. We'll then load the HMDA data using pandas and assign it to the pandas DataFrame hmda. Next, we'll define containers to hold the data called feature columns using the operation feature_column.numeric_ column(). We'll name them to match the variables they will contain: applicantIncome and areaIncome. We'll then combine the two feature columns into a single list named feature_list.

Listing 4-1. Prepare data for use in gradient boosted classification trees

```python
import pandas as pd
import tensorflow as tf

# Define data path.
data_path = '../chapter4/hmda.csv'

# Load hmda data using pandas.
hmda = pd.read_csv(data_path+"hmda.csv")

# Define applicant income feature column.
applicantIncome = tf.feature_column.numeric_
column("applicantIncome")
```

```
# Define applicant msa relative income.
areaIncome = tf.feature_column.numeric_column("areaIncome")

# Combine features into list.
feature_list = [applicantIncome, areaIncome]
```

The next step, given in Listing 4-2, is to define an input function for the training data. This function will return the features and labels and will later be passed to the train operation. We will typically want to define separate functions for the training and evaluation process, but for the purpose of this example, we will keep things as simple as is possible.

Since we have defined a minimal version of this function, it will take no arguments. It constructs a dictionary called features, which uses variables for personal income and the median income in the area. It then defines the labels using accepted applications from the hmda dataset.

We can now define and train the model, which we do in Listing 4-3. We'll first use the BoostedTreesClassifier from the high-level Estimators API to define the model. At a minimum, we'll need to supply the list of feature columns, feature_columns, and the number of batches the sample is divided into, n_batches_per_layer. Since the dataset is sufficiently small to be processed in a single batch, we set the second parameter to one.

Listing 4-2. Define function to generate input data function

```
# Define input data function.
def input_fn():
        # Define dictionary of features.
        features = {"applicantIncome": hmda['income'],
        "areaIncome": hmda['area_income']}

        # Define labels.
        labels = hmda['accepted'].copy()

        # Return features and labels.
        return features, labels
```

Listing 4-3. Define and train a boosted trees classifier

```
# Define boosted trees classifier.
model = tf.estimator.BoostedTreesClassifier(
        feature_columns = feature_list,
        n_batches_per_layer = 1)

# Train model using 100 epochs.
model.train(input_fn, steps=100)
```

Finally, we use the `train` operation, along with the input function we defined earlier, to train the model. For the sake of simplicity, we only will set the `steps` parameter, which determines the number of training epochs, to 100.

Once the training process is complete, we can apply the `evaluate` operation, along with our input function and a number of steps as arguments. We'll use the same input function defined earlier, which means we'll evaluate in-sample. While this is not recommended practice in general, we will do it here for the sake of providing a minimal example. The code for performing evaluation and printing the results is given in Listing 4-4.

Listing 4-4. Evaluate a boosted trees classifier

```
# Evaluate model in-sample.
result = model.evaluate(input_fn, steps = 1)

# Print results.
print(pd.Series(result))
```

```
accuracy                    0.635245
accuracy_baseline           0.598804
auc                         0.665705
auc_precision_recall        0.750070
average_loss                0.632722
```

label/mean	0.598804
loss	0.632722
precision	0.628028
prediction/mean	0.598917
recall	0.958663
global_step	100.000000

dtype: float64

We can see that the console output contains a number of different measures of performance, including the loss, the share of correct predictions (accuracy), and the area under the curve (AUC). We will not cover these metrics in detail here, but it is worthwhile to point out that they are produced automatically by the evaluate operation.

Regression Trees

If we have a continuous dependent variable, then we'll need to use gradient boosted regression trees, rather than classification trees. Much of the code will be identical, but with a few changes. To fix an example, let's assume that we now want to predict the loan amount in thousands of dollars, rather than the application outcome, but we still want to use the same two features.

To do this, we only need to modify the data input function and define a BoostedTreesRegressor, rather than classifier. Both steps are shown in Listing 4-5.

Listing 4-5. Define and train a boosted trees regressor

```
# Define input data function.
def input_fn():
        features = {"applicantIncome": data['income'],
        "msaIncome": data['area_income']}
        targets = data['loan_amount'].copy()
        return features, targets
```

```
# Define model.
model = tf.estimator.BoostedTreesRegressor(
        feature_columns = feature_list,
        n_batches_per_layer = 1)
```

Since all other steps are identical, we'll skip to printing the results of the evaluation operation, which are given in Listing 4-6.

Listing 4-6. Evaluate a boosted trees regressor

```
# Evaluate model in-sample.
result = model.evaluate(input_fn, steps = 1)

# Print results.
print(pd.Series(result))
```

```
average_loss        8217.281250
label/mean           277.759064
loss                8217.281250
prediction/mean      277.463928
global_step          100.000000
dtype: float64
```

Notice that we now have a different set of metrics in Listing 4-6. This is because we have a continuous target, rather than categorical labels. Measures such as accuracy and the AUC are no longer meaningful in this context.

Model Tuning

Finally, we'll end this chapter by discussing model tuning, which is the process by which we adjust model parameters to improve training results. We'll focus on five model parameters that are common to both gradient boosted classification and regression trees:

1. **Number of trees**: This is specified by the n_trees parameter and determines how many individual trees will be created in the training process. The default value is 100, but can be increased if the model is underfitting the data or decreased if it is overfitting.

2. **Maximum tree depth**: This is set using the max_depth parameter and is 6 by default. The maximum tree depth measures the number of branches between the root and the most distant leaf. Gradient boosted trees typically use lower values than random forests or individual decision trees. If overfitting is an issue, you can reduce the maximum tree depth.

3. **Learning rate**: Since gradient boosted trees can be trained using a least squares loss function, it is possible to perform optimization using stochastic gradient descent or one of its variants. Consequently, we'll need to set a learning rate, which is 0.1 by default. In applications where convergence proves elusive, we may want to lower the learning_rate parameter and increase the number of epochs.

4. **Regularization**: If we're concerned with overfitting, it makes sense to apply regularization to trees, which will penalize them for being deep and having many nodes. Setting the l1_regularization parameter will penalize the absolute values of the weights applied to nodes, whereas l2_regularization will penalize squared weights. We can also penalize the number of leaves using the tree_complexity parameter.

5. **Pruning mode**: By default, trees will not be pruned
by the gradient boosting algorithms in TensorFlow.
To apply pruning, you will have to set a positive
value for the `tree_complexity` parameter and
then set the `pruning_mode` to either `pre` or `post`.
Pre-pruning trees is faster, as the growth of trees
is terminated when a pruning threshold has been
reached. Post-pruning is slower, since it requires
us to grow the tree first – and then prune it – but it
may also allow the algorithm to discover additional
useful relationships that it would otherwise not
identify.

In general, when we apply pruning, our primary concern will be the
mitigation of overfitting. We want to train a model that predicts the data
well out of sample, but not by memorizing it. Adjusting the values of the
five parameters we defined in this section will help us to achieve this
objective.

Summary

In this chapter, we introduced the concept of tree-based models. We saw
that there are decision trees, used for the purpose of classification, and
regression trees, which are used to predict continuous targets. In general,
trees are not typically used in isolation, but are combined in random
forests or using gradient boosting. Random forests use "fully grown" trees,
which are trained in parallel, and generate predictions by averaging or
applying a majority vote to individual tree outputs. Gradient boosted
trees are trained sequentially by minimizing the model residual from the
previous iteration. This process can use a least squares loss function and
can be trained using stochastic gradient descent or some variation thereof.

TensorFlow was structured around deep learning and, thus, was not originally suitable for training other types of machine learning models, including decision and classification trees. With the introduction of the high-level `Estimators` API and TensorFlow 2, that has changed. TensorFlow now offers robust, production-quality operations for training and evaluating gradient boosted trees. In addition to this, it offers a variety of useful parameters through which we can tune models to prevent over- and underfitting. In general, we will do this by iterating over training, evaluation, and tuning steps.

Bibliography

Athey, S., and G.W. and Imbens. 2016. "Recursive partitioning for heterogeneous causal effects." *Proceedings of the National Academy of Sciences* 27 (113): 7353–7360.

Athey, S., and G.W. Imbens. 2019. "Machine Learning Methods Economists Should Know About." *arXiv.*

Breiman, L. 2001. "Random forests." *Machine Learning* 45 (1): 5–32.

Breiman, L., J. Friedman, C.J Stone, and R.A. Olshen. 1984. "Classification and Regression Trees." (CRC Press).

Moscatelli, M., F. Parlapiano, S. Narizzano, and G. Viggiano. 2020. "Corporate Default Forecasting with Machine Learning." *Expert Systems with Applications* 161.

Wager, S., and S. Athey. 2017. "Estimation and inference of heterogeneous treatment effects using random forests." *Journal of the American Statistical Association* 1228–1242.

CHAPTER 5

Image Classification

Image classification was once a task that required domain expertise and the use of problem-specific models. Much of this has changed with the emergence of deep learning as general-purpose modeling technique for predictive tasks in computer vision. Both the machine learning literature and image classification contests are now dominated by deep learning models that often do not require domain expertise, since such models identify and extract features automatically, eliminating the need for feature engineering.

While academic economists have recently begun to import methods from machine learning, widespread use of deep learning for image classification purposes has lagged behind. Much of the existing work in economics that involves image data makes use of pre-processed night-time luminosity values. Such data can be used to proxy for economic variables,[1] measure output growth at different levels of geography,[2] and evaluate the impact of infrastructure investment.[3] For an overview of this literature, see Donaldson and Storeygard (2016) and Gibson et al. (2020).

---

[1]See Chen and Nordhaus (2011), Nordhaus and Chen (2015), and Addison and Stewart (2015).

[2]See Henderson et al. (2012), Bluhm and Krause (2018), Bickenbach et al. (2016), and Goldblatt et al. (2019).

[3]See Mitnik et al. (2018).

Image datasets remain underused in economics and finance research; however, there have been some recent noteworthy applications. Naik et al. (2017) use computer vision techniques to measure changes in the visual appearance of neighborhoods. They then test theories of urban economics by determining which neighborhood characteristics are associated with future appearance improvements. Borgshulte et al. (2019) use deep learning to measure the impact of stress events on the apparent ages of CEOs. They show that stress caused by the Great Recession is associated with an approximately 1-year increase in apparent CEO age.

Beyond academic work, computer vision applications – and particularly those that involve deep learning – have become common in industry settings. Furthermore, they are likely to gain increased use both in academia and private industry as a consequence of the proliferation of image datasets and the quality of off-the-shelf models.

In this chapter, we'll provide a broad overview of image data and its potential uses in economics and finance. We will focus on the development of deep neural networks that are specialized for the purpose of classifying images and their implementation in `TensorFlow` and its high-level APIs, including `Keras` and `Estimators`. We'll also talk about using pretrained models and fine-tuning them to improve performance.

Image Data

Before we discuss methods and models, let's first define what an image is. For our purposes, an image is a k-tensor of pixel intensities. For instance, a grayscale image of dimensions 600x400 is a matrix with 600 rows and 400 columns. Each element of the matrix is an integer value between 0 and 255, where the value corresponds to the intensity of the pixel it represents. A value of 0, for instance, corresponds to the color black, whereas a value of 255 corresponds to white.

Color images have several tensor representations, but the most common one – and the one we'll almost exclusively use in this book – is a 3-tensor. Such images are 3-tensors because they contain a matrix with identical dimensions for three different color channels: red, green, and blue (RGB). Each matrix holds pixel intensity values for its respective color, as shown in Figure 5-1.

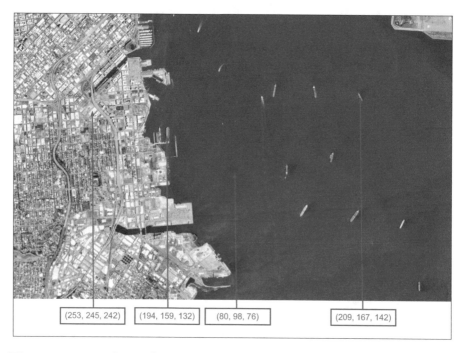

Figure 5-1. *Each pixel in an RGB image corresponds to an element in a 3-tensor. Four such elements are labeled in the figure. Source:* www.kaggle.com/rhammell/ships-in-satellite-imagery/data

Throughout this chapter, we'll use images from the "Ships in Satellite Imagery" dataset, which is available for download on Kaggle.[4] It contains 80x80x3 pixel color images, which are extracted from larger images.

---

[4]The dataset is available for download on Kaggle: www.kaggle.com/rhammell/ships-in-satellite-imagery/data. It contains a JSON file with metadata, including labels, as well as a folder that contains images of ships and non-ships.

The sub-images are labeled 1 if they contain a ship and 0 otherwise. The non-ship images contain a variety of different types of land cover, including buildings, vegetation, and water. Figure 5-2 shows a selection of random images from this dataset.

There are several ways in which we could use satellite images of ships in economics and finance applications. In this chapter, we'll use them to build a classifier. Such a classifier could be used to count ship traffic at locations of interest. With the increased availability of daily satellite data, this could be used to estimate trade flows at a higher frequency than official statistics.

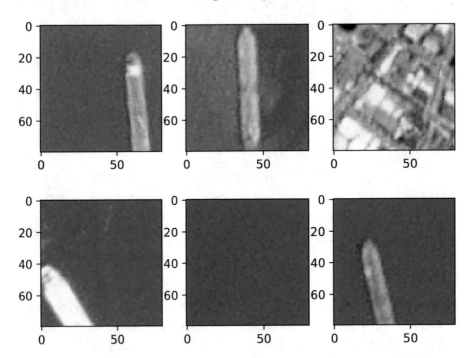

Figure 5-2. *Examples of ships from "Ships in Satellite Imagery" dataset*

We'll start by loading and preparing the data in Listing 5-1. The first step is to import the relevant modules. This includes matplotlib.image as mpimg, which we'll use to load and manipulate images; numpy as np to convert images into tensors; and os, which we'll use to perform various tasks using the operation system. Next, we apply listdir() to the directory where the downloaded images are located, which yields a list of filenames.

Now that we can construct the path to each file, we'll load the images, convert them to numpy arrays, and store them in two lists: one for ship images and one for images that do not contain ships. We'll do this by using a list comprehension to construct the path to each image and using the first character in each filename to identify whether the corresponding image contains a ship. The file 0__20150718_184300_090b__ -122.35324421973536_37.772113980272394.g, does not contain a ship, whereas 1__20180708_180908_0f47__-118.15328750044623_ 33.735783554733885.png does.

Listing 5-1. Prepare image data for use in TensorFlow

```
import matplotlib.image as mpimg
import numpy as np
import os

# Set image directory.
data_path = '../data/chapter5/shipsnet/'

# Generate file list.
images = os.listdir(image_path)

# Create list of ship images.
ships = [np.array(mpimg.imread(image_path+image))
for image in images if image[0] == '1']

# Create list of no-ship images.
noShips = [np.array(mpimg.imread(image_path+image))
for image in images if image[0] == '0']
```

Now that we've loaded our data into lists, we'll explore it in Listing 5-2. We'll first import matplotlib.pyplot as plt, which we can use to plot images. We'll then print the shape of one of the items in ships. This returns the tuple (80, 80, 3), which means that the image is a 3-tensor of pixels. We may also print an arbitrary pixel by selecting a coordinate in the tensor. Finally, we use the imshow() function to render the image, which is shown in Figure 5-3.

Listing 5-2. Exploring image data

```
import matplotlib.pyplot as plt
```

```
# Print item in list of ships.
print(np.shape(ships[0]))
```

```
(80, 80, 3)
```

```
# Print pixel intensies in [0,0] position.
print(ships[0][0,0])
```

```
[0.47058824 0.47058824 0.43137255]
```

```
# Show image of ship.
plt.imshow(ships[0])
```

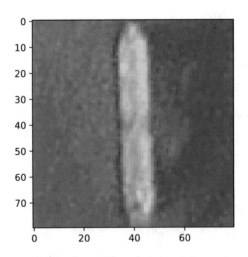

Figure 5-3. *Image of ship from dataset*

When we printed the color channels for a particular pixel, notice that the values were not integers between 0 and 255. Rather, they were real numbers between 0 and 1. This is because the tensor has been normalized by dividing all elements by 255. We will typically need to do this before using images as an input to neural network models designed for image processing tasks, since they typically require inputs in the [0, 1] or [–1, 1] range.

Neural Networks

Before we introduce the high-level APIs in TensorFlow that were designed for the purpose of constructing and training image classification models, we'll first discuss neural networks, since all models we consider in this chapter will be some variant of a neural network.

Figure 5-4 shows a neural network with an input layer, a hidden layer, and an output layer.[5] The input layer contains eight "nodes" or input features. These nodes are multiplied by weights, which are represented by the lines in the diagram. After the multiplication step is applied, the resulting output is transformed using a non-linear "activation function." This yields the next layer of "nodes," which is called a hidden layer because it is not observed like the input and output layers. Just as with the input layer, we multiply the hidden layer by weights and then apply an activation function, yielding the output layer.

---

[5]The diagram was generated by LeNail (2019) and modified by this author. To access the tool, see https://doi.org/10.21105/joss.00747.

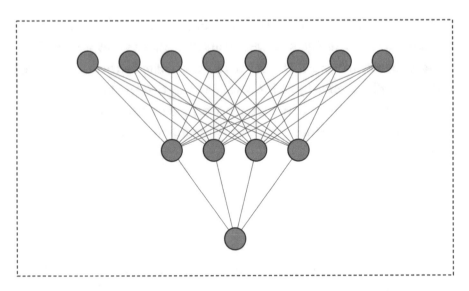

Figure 5-4. *A neural network with an input layer, hidden layer, and output layer*

Note that the output layer is a prediction. In a binary classification problem (i.e., ship or no-ship), the output could be interpreted as the probability that the image contained a ship and, thus, would be a real number between 0 and 1. In a problem with a continuous target, the output layer would yield a prediction in the real numbers.

In contrast to a neural network, a linear regression model does not apply activation functions and does not have hidden layers. The diagram of the familiar linear regression model is shown in Figure 5-5 for comparison. Notice that the input and output layers of the linear regression do not differ from a neural network.

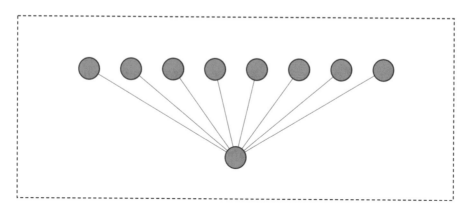

Figure 5-5. *A linear regression model*

Another similarity between the diagrams for neural networks and linear regressions is that edges connect all nodes between two consecutive layers. In a linear regression, we know that there are only two layers and that multiplying the input layer by weights (coefficients) yields the output layer (fitted values). In a neural network, we perform a similar operation whenever we use something called a "dense" or "fully connected" layer: that is, we multiply a matrix of weights by the values associated with nodes.

To fix an example, let's consider the case shown in Figure 5-4. We'll start by performing a step called "forward propagation," which is the process by which we compute a prediction for a given set of features. Starting in the input layer, the first operation multiplies the features, X_0, by weights, w_0. We then apply an activation function, $f()$, which yields the next layer of nodes, X_1. Once again, we multiply by the next set of weights, w_1, and apply another activation function, yielding the output, Y. This is shown in Equation 5-1.

Equation 5-1. Forward propagation in a neural network with dense layers.

$$X_1 = f\left(X_0 w_0\right)$$

$$Y = f\left(X_1 w_1\right)$$

We may also write this in a single line by nesting the functions, as is done in Equation 5-2.

Equation 5-2. Compact expression for forward propagation.

$$Y = f\left(f\left(X_0 w_0\right)w_1\right)$$

What must be true about the shapes of X_0, w_0, and X_1? If we have N observations, then the shape of X_0 will be Nx8, since we have eight features. This means that w_0 must have eight rows, since the number of rows in w_0 must equal the number of columns in X_0 to perform matrix multiplication. Furthermore, the shape of the product of X_0 and w_0 will be equal to the number of rows in X_0, which is N, and the number of columns in w_0. Since we know that the next layer has four nodes, w_0 must be 8x4. Similarly, since X_1 is Nx4 and Y is Nx1, w_1 must be 4x1.

Note that dense layers are just one type of layer used in neural networks. When working with image classification models, for instance, we will often make use of specialized layers, such as convolutional layers. We will delay this discussion until we implement such networks in TensorFlow later in the chapter.

Keras

TensorFlow 2 provides tighter integration of high-level APIs. Keras, for instance, is now a submodule of TensorFlow, whereas it was previously a stand-alone module that allowed for optional use of TensorFlow as a back end. In this section, we will discuss how to use the Keras submodule in TensorFlow to define and train neural networks.

Whenever we define a model in Keras, we'll have the choice to do it using one of two APIs: the "sequential" API or the "functional" API. The sequential API has a simple syntax, but limited flexibility. The functional API is highly flexible, but comes at the cost of a more complicated syntax. We will start by defining the neural network in Figure 5-4 using the sequential API.

The Sequential API

The neural network in Figure 5-4 consisted of an input layer, a hidden layer, and an output layer. Additionally, it was constructed using dense layers, as indicated by the edges connecting each node in layer *i* to each node in layer *i+1*. We will construct this simple neural network in Listing 5-3 as a first demonstration of the Keras API.

We start by importing `tensorflow` as `tf`. Next, we define a sequential model in Keras using `tf.keras.Sequential()`. Once we have defined a sequential model, we can add layers through the use of the `add()` method. We first add an input layer with eight feature columns using `tf.keras.Input()`. We next define the hidden layer, specifying that it has four output nodes, as is indicated in Figure 5-4. We also indicate that it is dense by using `tf.keras.layers.Dense()` to construct the layer. We must also specify an activation function, which applies a non-linear transformation to the product of the inputs and weights. In this case, we've used a `sigmoid` transformation.

Finally, we again use the `add()` method to append another dense layer to the model, which has a single output node and uses a `sigmoid` activation function. As a consequence of this choice of activation function, the output of the model will be a predicted probability between 0 and 1. If we had a continuous target, rather than a discrete one, we could have used a `linear` activation function instead, which would have allowed for a linear prediction.

Listing 5-3. Implement a simple neural network in Keras

```
import tensorflow as tf

# Define sequential model.
model = tf.keras.Sequential()

# Add input layer.
model.add(tf.keras.Input(shape=(8,)))
```

```
# Define hidden layer.
model.add(tf.keras.layers.Dense(4,
activation="sigmoid"))
```

```
# Define output layer.
model.add(tf.keras.layers.Dense(1,
activation="sigmoid"))
```

Let's say we want to consider a more meaningful problem, such as the classification of ships. What would we need to modify? At a minimum, we'd have to change the input layer, which has the wrong shape. The images in our dataset are 80x80x3 pixels. If we want to use them as an input to a network with only dense layers, we would have to reshape the images. Since there are 19,200 pixels (i.e., 80*80*3), we would need to have 19,200 nodes in the input layer.

In Listing 5-1, we loaded the images, converted them into numpy arrays, and stored them as two lists, ships and noShips. In Listing 5-4, we'll reshape the 80x80x3 tensors into 19,200-element vectors using list comprehensions. We'll also create a corresponding dependent variable called labels and stack the flattened features into a numpy array.

Two steps remain before we can train our network. The first is to randomly shuffle the data and then split it into train and test samples. The shuffling ensures that we do not have long clusters of ship or no-ship images in a sequence, which can make it difficult to learn using stochastic gradient descent (SGD). Additionally, splitting off a test sample is a standard practice in machine learning that is used to ensure that we do not evaluate model fit with the same observations that were used to train the model. This allows us to identify when overfitting occurs.

Listing 5-4. Reshape images for use in a neural network with dense layers

```python
import numpy as np

# Reshape list of ship images.
ships = [ship.reshape(19200,) for ship in ships]

# Reshape list of non-ship images.
noShips = [noShip.reshape(19200,) for noShip in
noShips]

# Define class labels.
labels = np.vstack([np.ones((len(ships), 1)),
                np.zeros((len(noShips), 1))])

# Stack flattened images into numpy array.
features = np.vstack([ships, noShips])
```

In Listing 5-5, we'll handle the first step using the model_selection submodule of sklearn. From that module, we'll use train_test_split, which will allow us to specify labels, features, the share of observations that should be in the test sample, and a random seed to ensure reproducibility. By default, the parameter shuffle is set to True, so we will not need to adjust it.

Once our sample has been shuffled and split, the final step is to modify the network to allow for 19,200 nodes in the input layer. Listing 5-6 shows the revised architecture for the network. Note that this is not ideal for the problem under consideration, but will be helpful for understanding how to construct, train, and evaluate neural networks.

Listing 5-5. Shuffle and split data into train and test samples

```
from sklearn.model_selection import train_test_split

# Shuffle and split sample.
X_train, X_test, y_train, y_test = \
        train_test_split(features, labels,
        test_size = 0.20, random_state=0
)
```

Before we start the training process, we might want to get a high-level overview of our model. We can do this using summary() method, as is shown in Listing 5-7. As the output indicates, our model has 76,809 parameters. This might already give us cause for concern that the model will overfit, but we will see that machine learning offers many strategies for managing this problem.

We can also see that most of the parameters seem to be located in the hidden layer. This is where we multiplied the 19,200 input nodes by the weights. This means we'll need a weight matrix that can transform an Nx19200 matrix input into Nx4 matrix. Consequently, it will have to have the shape 19200x4, which is 76,800 parameters. The remaining four parameters are called "biases," which are equivalent to the constant term in a regression. We will have one for each node in the hidden layer. Similarly, for the output layer, we need to transform an Nx4 matrix into an Nx1 matrix, which will require a 4x1 matrix of weights, as well as one bias term, giving us five additional parameters.

Another thing we may notice from the summary output is that parameters are divided into two categories: "trainable params" and "non-trainable params." This is because Keras gives us the option to freeze parameters, making them untrainable. We will not make use of this feature here, but we will return to it later.

Listing 5-6. Modify a neural network to fit the input shape

```python
import tensorflow as tf

# Define sequential model.
model = tf.keras.Sequential()

# Add input layer.
model.add(tf.keras.Input(shape=(19200,)))

# Define hidden layer.
model.add(tf.keras.layers.Dense(4,
activation="sigmoid"))

# Define output layer.
model.add(tf.keras.layers.Dense(1,
activation="sigmoid"))
```

Listing 5-7. Print a model summary in Keras

```python
print(model.summary())
```

Layer (type)	Output Shape	Param #
dense (Dense)	(None, 4)	76804
dense_1 (Dense)	(None, 1)	5

```
Total params: 76,809
Trainable params: 76,809
Non-trainable params: 0
```

We have now seen how to define a model in Keras and interpret its architecture. The next step is to "compile" the model by specifying a loss function, an optimizer, and metrics to compute during the training process. We do this in Listing 5-8, selecting the `binary_crossentropy` loss, the adam optimizer, and the `accuracy` metric (i.e., share of correct predictions).

We can now apply the `fit()` method to the model, which will initiate the training process. We must specify the number of epochs and the `batch_size`. The number of epochs corresponds to the number of times the training process should loop over the full sample, whereas the `batch_size` parameter determines the number of observations used in each increment of the loop.

Listing 5-8. Compile and train the model in Keras

```
# Compile the model.
model.compile(loss='binary_crossentropy',
        optimizer='adam', metrics=['accuracy'])

# Train the model.
model.fit(X_train, y_train, epochs=100,
        batch_size=32, validation_split = 0.20)
```

Notice that we also set an optional parameter, `validation_split`, to 0.20. This will split off an additional 20% of our sample, which will not be used to train the model. During the training process, we will compare metric performance for the model both in the training and validation samples. If the two start to diverge, this tells us that the model is overfitting and that we may want to terminate the training process or tune the model's parameters.

At each epoch, the model outputs the value of the loss and the accuracy of the predictions, both in the training and validation samples. According to the accuracy measure, the model appears to perform quite well, correctly predicting 75% of observations in both the training and validation samples. Since we did not tune the model at all, we do not have to worry that the validation sample's accuracy is inflated by our choice of training and model parameters. As such, evaluating the test sample is not strictly necessary, but we will do it, anyway, in Listing 5-9 for the sake of illustration.

Listing 5-9. Evaluate the model on the test sample

```
# Evaluate the model.
model.evaluate(X_test, y_test)

loss: 0.5890 - accuracy: 0.7262
```

We can see that accuracy is slightly lower, but not enough to concern us that overfitting might be an issue. There's one last measure of performance we'll check, which is the confusion matrix. This provides an improvement over accuracy by indicating whether we're misclassifying 0s as 1s or 1s as 0s. Listing 5-10 provides code for computing the confusion matrix.

We'll first import `confusion_matrix` from `sklearn.metrics`. Next, we'll use the model to make predictions for the test sample labels. The predictions are probabilities, but we'll use a threshold of 0.5 to indicate that the model has predicted that an image contains a ship. We'll then pass the true labels, `y_test`, and predictions, `y_pred`, to `confusion_matrix()`. The resulting matrix contains the true values in the rows and the predictions in the columns. The row 0, column 1 element, for instance, indicates what number of observations were truly 0s, but classified as 1s.

The confusion matrix indicates that all predictions are 0s – that is, non-ships. Thus, even though performance was good in the train, validation, and test samples, our model simply noticed that 75% of the observations were 0s and then predicted 0s for all, rather than trying to learn patterns in the data.

Listing 5-10. Evaluate the confusion matrix

```
from sklearn.metrics import confusion_matrix

# Generate predictions.
y_pred = model.predict(X_test)>0.5

# Print confusion matrix.
print(confusion_matrix(y_test, y_pred))

array([[581,   0],
       [219,   0]])
```

This, unfortunately, is a common problem we'll encounter when training neural networks: samples will often be unbalanced. Since getting a 75% classification accuracy is challenging, the model will quickly converge on predicting the most common class, rather than learning meaningful abstractions. There are two ways to avoid this problem. The first is to balance the sample by randomly removing observations from noShips. The second is to apply weights in the loss function that scale up the contribution of instances of the ships class. We'll adopt the second approach, which is implemented in Listing 5-11.

We'll start by computing weights for the ships and noShips classes. This requires us to set a multiplicative constant for each class, such that the product of the weight and the number of observations for a class is the same for all classes. In our case, we have 1000 ships and 3000 non-ship images. The ship images are coded as 1s and the non-ship images as 0s. If we compute the mean of y_train, that'll give us the share of 1s in the sample, which is 0.25.

We'll set 0.25 as the weight for noShips, cw_0, which will scale down its contribution to the loss. We can then set the weight for ships, cw_1, as $1.0 - cw_0$ or 0.75. Since $0.25 * 3000 = 0.75 * 1000 = 750$, the scheme we've selected is valid. Finally, we define a dictionary, class_weights, which uses the classes (0 or 1) as keys and the weights as values. We then pass it to the class_weight parameter of fit().

Listing 5-11. Train the model with class weights

```
# Compute class weights.
cw0 = np.mean(y_train)
cw1 = 1.0 - cw0
class_weights = {0: cw0, 1: cw1}

# Train the model using class weights.
model.fit(X_train, y_train, epochs=100,
        class_weight = class_weights,
        batch_size=32,
        validation_split = 0.20)
```

This time, model prediction accuracy improves to over 0.87 in the training, validation, and test samples. This is sufficiently high to rule out the possibility that the model is simply predicting the most common class; however, we'll check the confusion matrix again to see how well the weighting scheme worked to resolve this issue.

The confusion matrix is shown in Listing 5-12. The elements on the diagonal show correct predictions. The elements off of the diagonal show incorrect predictions. We can see that the model no longer seems to overpredict 0s (non-ships). Rather, most of the classification errors are now for ships that are misclassified as non-ships.

We've now seen how to perform image classification using a neural network with dense layers and have addressed many of the common problems we'll encounter in the training and evaluation process. In the following sections, we'll see how we can apply different layers and make other modifications to the training process to improve model performance further.

Listing 5-12. Evaluate the impact of class weights on the confusion matrix

```
# Generate predictions.
y_pred = model.predict(X_test)>0.5
```

```
# Print confusion matrix.
print(confusion_matrix(y_test, y_pred))
```

```
[[487  94]
 [  5 214]]
```

The Functional API

While the sequential API in Keras simplifies model building, the functional API allows for flexibility, but at the cost of a slight increase in complexity. To see how the functional API works, let's start by re-defining the model from Listing 5-6, but using the functional API. This is given in Listing 5-13.

We'll first define the input layer by using the `tf.keras.Input()` method and supplying a shape. Next, we define a dense layer, using `tf.keras.layers.Dense()`. Notice that we've passed the input layer as an argument to the dense layer that followed it. Similarly, we define an output layer, again using a dense layer and again passing the preceding layer as an argument to it. The final step is to define the model by specifying the input and output layer.

We now have a model that is no different from the one we specified using the sequential API. We can compile it, summarize it, and train it using the exact same methods.

It might not be immediately obvious that there are advantages to using the functional API, since we have simply reproduced what the sequential API did, but using more lines of code. To see where the functional API might be useful, consider a case where we have an additional set of inputs that we'd like to include in the model, but want to isolate them from the image network itself.

Listing 5-13. Define a model in Keras with the functional API

```
import tensorflow as tf

# Define input layer.
inputs = tf.keras.Input(shape=(19200,))

# Define dense layer.
dense = tf.keras.layers.Dense(4,
        activation="sigmoid")(inputs)

# Define output layer.
outputs = tf.keras.layers.Dense(1,
        activation="sigmoid")(dense)

# Define model using inputs and outputs.
model = tf.keras.Model(inputs=inputs,
        outputs=outputs)
```

In the ship detection example, we might have metadata about the location of the ship, such as its longitude and latitude. If the model were able to learn something about the likelihood of observing ships in different locations, it could combine that with the features extracted from the image to assign a class probability.

It isn't possible to do this with the sequential API, since we can only stack layers on top of each other, whereas our objective is to create two parallel networks, which are joined somewhere at or above the output node. Listing 5-14 demonstrates how we can do this with the functional API. We'll assume that we have the image input and 20 features of metadata inputs, and we'll define two separate input layers, img_inputs and meta_inputs. We'll then isolate those inputs into separate networks, since it will otherwise be difficult for the model to determine how best to

use the 20 features when they are mixed in with 19,200 pixel values. We'll
do this by passing them to separate dense layers, img_dense and meta_
dense. Notice, again, that this would not be possible with the sequential
API, since we must define the connections between layers explicitly.

Listing 5-14. Define a multi-input model in Keras with the
functional API

```python
import tensorflow as tf

# Define input layer.
img_inputs = tf.keras.Input(shape=(19200,))
meta_inputs = tf.keras.Input(shape=(20,))

# Define dense layers.
img_dense = tf.keras.layers.Dense(4,
          activation="sigmoid")(img_inputs)
meta_dense = tf.keras.layers.Dense(4,
          activation="sigmoid")(meta_inputs)

# Concatenate layers.
merged = tf.keras.layers.Concatenate(axis=1)([
          img_dense, meta_dense])

# Define output layer.
outputs = tf.keras.layers.Dense(1,
          activation="sigmoid")(merged)

# Define model using inputs and outputs.
model = tf.keras.Model(inputs=
          [img_inputs, meta_inputs],
          outputs=outputs)
```

Next, we use the `tf.keras.layers.Concatenate()` operation to merge the outputs of the two dense layers. This recombines the initially separated networks into a single network, which takes four features from the image and four features from the metadata. This is then passed to an output layer, which allows us to define the complete model, which now requires a list of the two input layers.

In addition to defining multi-input models, we can also define multi-output models using the functional API. For instance, rather than using metadata as an input, we might want to train a model to predict it as an output. We might use the model with image inputs to predict both a class label (ship or non-ship) and GPS coordinates. For an example of the use of multi-input models in economics, see Grodecka and Hull (2019).

Estimators

We previously mentioned the Estimators API in the Chapter 4. TensorFlow also offers the possibility of using the Estimators API to train and make predictions with neural networks. In general, you will want to consider using the Estimators API over Keras if you are working in a production setting and do not require a high degree of flexibility, but do require reliability and want to minimize the likelihood of errors.

The Estimators API will allow you to fully specify a neural network's architecture using a small number of parameters. Let's consider an example for a deep neural network classifier. We'll first define feature columns to contain our images and will store this as `features_list` in Listing 5-15. After this, we'll define our input function, which returns the features and labels that will be used in the training process. We'll then define an instance of `tf.estimator.DNNClassifier()`, specifying feature columns and a list of the number of hidden units as inputs. For the sake of illustration, we'll select an architecture that uses four hidden layers with 256, 128, 64, and 32 nodes.

Note that we have intentionally set only the required parameter values for the DNNClassifier. For everything else, we have used the defaults. This was only to demonstrate the simplicity of defining and training a DNNClassifier with four hidden layers. We can also use the syntax in Listing 5-16 to evaluate the model.

Listing 5-15. Define a deep neural network classifier using Estimators

```
# Define numeric feature columns for image.
features_list =
        [tf.feature_column.numeric_column("image",
        shape=(19200,))]

# Define input function.
def input_fn():
        features = {"image": X_train}
        return features, y_train

# Define a deep neural network classifier.
model = tf.estimator.DNNClassifier(
        feature_columns=features_list,
        hidden_units=[256, 128, 64, 32])

# Train the model.
model.train(input_fn, steps=20)
```

Listing 5-16. Evaluate deep neural network classifiers using Estimators

```
# Evaluate model in-sample.
result = model.evaluate(input_fn, steps = 1)
```

Finally, beyond what we have listed here, DNNClassifier has other parameters that can be adjusted to modify the model's architecture or training process. We describe six of them below.

1. **Number of classes**: By default, the number of classes is set to two; however, for multi-class problems, we can set the n_classes parameter to a different value.

2. **Weight column**: In cases with unbalanced samples, such as the one we considered earlier, it is necessary to specify a weight column, so that classes are properly weighted in the loss function. DNNClassifier takes this through the weight_column parameter.

3. **Optimizer**: By default, DNNClassifier uses the Adagrad optimizer. If you would prefer to use a different optimizer, you can specify it using the optimizer parameter.

4. **Activation function**: DNNClassifier applies the same activation function to all layers. By default, it will use a rectified linear unit (ReLU) activation; however, you can supply an alternative, such as tf.nn.sigmoid, through the activation_fn parameter.

5. **Dropout**: In models with a large number of parameters, dropout can be used to prevent overfitting. Set a number between 0 and 1 through the dropout parameter. This is the probability with which a given node in the model will be ignored during the training process. Common choices range between 0.10 and 0.50. By default, no dropout is applied.

6. **Batch normalization**: For many applications, batch normalization reduces training time. It functions by normalizing the mean and variance of observations within each mini-batch. You can use batch normalization by setting `batch_norm` to `True`.

In addition to `tf.estimator.DNNClassifier()`, the Estimators API also has a deep neural network model for continuous targets, `tf.estimator.DNNRegressor()`. It also has specialized models, such as deep-wide networks – introduced in Cheng et al. (2016) and applied within economics in Grodecka and Hull (2019) – which combine a linear model that can be used to incorporate one-hot encoded variables, such as fixed effects, and deep neural network for continuous features. These are available as `tf.estimator.DNNLinearCombinedClassifier()` and `tf.estimator.DNNLinearCombinedRegressor()`.

Convolutional Neural Networks

We started the chapter by training a neural network with dense layers to perform image classification. While there is nothing wrong with this approach, it will typically be dominated by alternative neural network architectures. Networks with convolutional layers, for instance, will typically yield both an increase in accuracy and a reduction in model size. In this section, we will introduce convolutional neural networks (CNNs) and use one to train an image classifier.

The Convolutional Layer

A convolutional neural network (CNN) makes use of convolutional layers, which are designed to handle image data. Figure 5-6 demonstrates how such layers work. For simplicity, we'll assume that we're working with a 4x4 pixel grayscale image, which is shown in pink in the figure. The convolutional layer will apply filters, such as the one shown in blue, by performing elementwise multiplication of the filter and image segment and then summing the elements of the resulting matrix. In this case, the filter is 2x2 and is first applied to the red segment of the image, yielding the scalar value 0.7. The filter is then moved to the right and applied to the next 2x2 segment of the image, yielding a 0 value. The process is repeated for all 2x2 segments of the image, yielding a 3x3 matrix, which is shown in yellow.

Figure 5-7 demonstrates how convolutional layers fit into a CNN.[6] The first layer is an input layer, which accepts color image tensors of shape (64, 64, 3). Next, a convolutional layer with 16 filters is applied. Notice that each filter is applied across the color channel, yielding an output of 64x64x16. In addition to performing the multiplication step illustrated in Figure 5-7, the layer also applies an activation function to each element of the output, which leaves the shape unchanged. Note that the 16 64x64 matrices that resulted from the operations in this layer each are referred to as "feature maps."

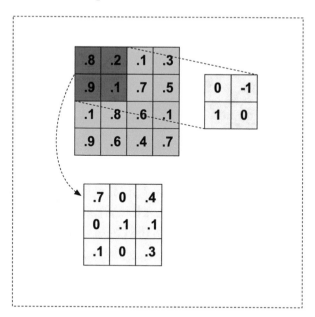

Figure 5-6. *A 2x2 convolutional filter applied to a 4x4 image*

---

[6]The diagram was generated by LeNail (2019) and modified by this author. To access the tool, see https://doi.org/10.21105/joss.00747.

The output of the convolutional layer is then passed to a "max pooling" layer. This is a type of filter that outputs the maximum value of a group of elements. In this case, it'll take the maximum element from each 2x2 block of each feature map. We'll use a "stride" of 2, which means that we'll move the max pooling filter two elements to the right (or down) after each application. This layer will take an input of dimension 64x64x16 and reduce it to 32x32x16.

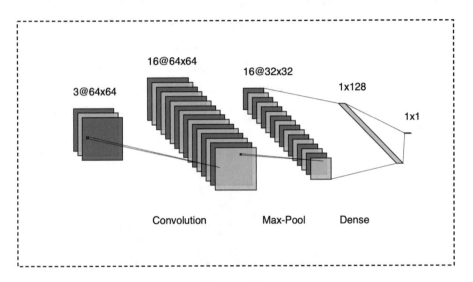

Figure 5-7. *A minimal example of a convolutional neural network*

We next flatten the 32x32x16 max pooling layer output into a 32*32*16x1 (16384,1) vector and pass it to a 128x1 dense layer, which functions as we described earlier in the chapter. Finally, we pass the dense layer output to an output node, which will yield a predicted class probability.

Training a Convolutional Neural Network

Earlier in the chapter, we introduced a dataset of ship and non-ship images. We then constructed a neural network out of dense layers and used the dataset to train a ship classifier. As we have noted, using a dense neural network to train an image classifier is inefficient, since it does not take advantage of the structure of images, including the spatial correlation in pixel values and in the location of features.

In this subsection, we'll use the high-level Keras API in TensorFlow to define a CNN for the same classification problem. As we'll see, this substantially improves efficiency. Not only will the number of model parameters decline, but the accuracy of the model will actually improve.

Listing 5-17 defines a convolutional neural network with an architecture that is designed to match our problem. As usual, we start by defining a sequential model using `tf.keras.Sequential()`. Next, we add the input layer, which accepts images of shape (80, 80, 3) and applies a convolutional layer, which has 8 filters that have a `kernel_size` of 3 (i.e., are 3x3). We also specify that the layer should apply a `relu` activation function to each element of its output. A `relu` activation simply applies the function `max(0,x)`, which thresholds the values of the feature map.

The second layer is also convolutional. It has 4 filters, a `kernel_size` of 3, and a `relu` activation function. The final hidden layer transforms the feature map outputs of the convolutional layer by flattening them into a vector. Flattening allows us to pass the feature maps to the output layer, which is dense and requires a vector input. Notice that, as usual, we use a `sigmoid` activation function in the output layer, since we are performing classification with two classes.

Listing 5-17. Define a convolutional neural network

```
import tensorflow as tf

# Define sequential model.
model = tf.keras.Sequential()

# Add first convolutional layer.
model.add(tf.keras.layers.Conv2D(8,
        kernel_size=3, activation="relu",
        input_shape=(80,80,3)))

# Add second convolutional layer.
model.add(tf.keras.layers.Conv2D(4,
        kernel_size=3, activation="relu"))

# Flatten feature maps.
model.add(tf.keras.layers.Flatten())

# Define output layer.
model.add(tf.keras.layers.Dense(1,
        activation='sigmoid'))
```

Next, we'll use the summary() method to view the model's architecture. This will help us to determine the extent to which we were able to reduce the model size by exploiting the fact that the inputs are images. This is shown in Listing 5-18. Notice that the number of parameters falls from over 75,000 to 23,621. Additionally, of those 23,621 parameters, 23,105 are located in the dense layer. The convolution layers only have 516 parameters in total. This suggests that we can achieve sizable improvements in efficiency by moving from dense layers to convolutional layers.

Before we can train the model, we have to prepare the data. This time, rather than flattening the images, as we did for the dense neural network, we'll instead make use of the images themselves as inputs. Listing 5-19 loads, prepares, and splits the data into train and test samples. It also computes class weights. Note that Listing 5-18 starts from the end of Listing 5-1.

Listing 5-18. Summarize the model architecture

```
# Print summary of model architecture.
print(model.summary())
```

Layer (type)	Output Shape	Param #
conv2d_9 (Conv2D)	(None, 78, 78, 8)	224
conv2d_10 (Conv2D)	(None, 76, 76, 4)	292
flatten_3 (Flatten)	(None, 23104)	0
dense_3 (Dense)	(None, 1)	23105

Total params: 23,621
Trainable params: 23,621
Non-trainable params: 0

Now that the data has been loaded and prepared and the model has been defined, the next steps are to compile and train it. Listing 5-20 shows this process, along with the evaluation step, where we compile the accuracy of model predictions on the test dataset.

In a mere 25 epochs, the CNN model achieves a 0.96 training accuracy and 0.95 validation accuracy. Additionally, when we evaluate the model using the test dataset, we again find an accuracy of 0.95. Even though this network had fewer parameters than the network constructed entirely out of dense layers, we were able to achieve a higher accuracy in fewer training epochs because we exploited the structure of images.

Listing 5-19. Prepare image data for training in a CNN

```
# Define class labels.
labels = np.vstack([np.ones((len(ships), 1)),
                np.zeros((len(noShips), 1))])

# Stack flattened images into numpy array.
features = np.vstack([ships, noShips])

# Shuffle and split sample.
X_train, X_test, y_train, y_test = \
        train_test_split(features, labels,
        test_size = 0.20, random_state=0
)

# Compute class weights.
w0 = np.mean(y_train)
w1 = 1.0 - w0
class_weights = {0: w0, 1: w1}
```

Listing 5-20. Train and evaluate the model

```
# Compile the model.
model.compile(loss='binary_crossentropy',
        optimizer='adam', metrics=['accuracy'])

# Train the model using class weights.
model.fit(X_train, y_train, epochs = 10,
        class_weight = class_weights,
        batch_size = 32,
        validation_split = 0.20)

# Evaluate model.
model.evaluate(X_test, y_test)
```

Pretrained Models

In many cases, there will not be sufficient image data to train a CNN using a state-of-the-art architecture. Fortunately, this is rarely necessary, since the "convolutional base" of the CNN – that is, the convolutional and pooling layers – extracts general features from images and can often be repurposed for use in a variety of models, including those which use different classes.

In general, we will use pretrained models to perform two tasks: feature extraction and fine-tuning. Feature extraction entails using the model's convolutional layers to identify general features of an image, which will then be fed into a dense layer and trained on your image dataset. You will typically use this when you want to train a model with a different set of classes than the original model was trained on. After you have trained a classifier, you can then optionally perform "fine-tuning," which involves training the entire model, including the convolutional base at a low learning rate. This will slightly modify the model's vision filters to align better with your classification task.

One benefit of not needing to fully train the model on your dataset is that you can use more sophisticated architectures, including state-of-the-art models like ResNet, Xception, DenseNet, and EfficientNet. In addition to this, rather than using convolutional layers trained on a small number of images, you will be able to make use of state-of-the-art general vision filters, trained on large datasets, such as ImageNet.

Feature Extraction

We'll start by examining the use of pretrained models as feature extractors. The first step will be to load a pretrained model, which we can do using either the `applications` submodule of Keras or TensorFlow Hub. For the purpose of this example, we'll use Keras.

In Listing 5-21, we'll use TensorFlow to define a ResNet50 model, setting the weights parameter to imagenet. This will load the ResNet50 model architecture, along with a set of weights from a version of the model that was trained using the ImageNet dataset. We'll also specify False for the include_top parameter, which will remove the final dense layer used to perform classification. We will not need this, since we are not using the ImageNet classes.

Listing 5-21. Load a pretrained model using Keras applications

```
# Load model.
model = tf.keras.applications.resnet50.ResNet50(
        weights='imagenet',
        include_top=False
        )
```

Once the model has been loaded, we may apply the summary() method to explore its architecture. Doing this, you will notice two things. First, there are many layers and more than 25,000,000 parameters. Additionally, nearly all of those parameters fall under the "trainable params" category, which means they'll be trained if you compile the model and apply the fit() method. And second, some of the layers may be unfamiliar.

Next, we need to set the convolutional base, which is the part of the model we have loaded, to be untrainable, which we do in Listing 5-22. This will ensure that we only train the classification head and that the rest of the model is simply used to extract features from the input images. After this, we'll define an input layer, which we'll pass to the model, setting the training parameter to False, since this is not a layer with trainable parameters. The model will now be able to accept image tensors of shape (80, 80, 3) and output a set of feature maps.

Since we want the model to yield predicted class probabilities, rather than feature maps, we'll need to reshape the feature map into a vector. We can do this using a global average pooling layer, which is similar to the max pooling operation we described earlier, but computes an average, rather than a maximum. We can now define a dense output layer and a functional model that accepts input images and outputs class probabilities. Finally, we'll compile and fit the model.

Listing 5-22. Train the classification head of a pretrained model in Keras

```
# Set convolutional base to be untrainable.
model.trainable = False

# Define input layer.
inputs = tf.keras.Input(shape=(80, 80, 3))
x = model(inputs, training=False)

# Define pooling and output layers, and model.
x = tf.keras.layers.GlobalAveragePooling2D()(x)
outputs = tf.keras.layers.Dense(1)(x)
model = tf.keras.Model(inputs, outputs)

# Compile and train the model.
model.compile(loss='binary_crossentropy', optimizer="adam",
        metrics=['accuracy'])

model.fit(X_train, y_train, epochs = 10,
        class_weight = class_weights,
        batch_size = 32,
        validation_split = 0.20)
```

Just as we did with the convolutional base, we can apply the `summary()` method to the full model. If we were to do this, we'd see that the total parameters is similar, but the number of trainable parameters dropped from over 25,000,000 to slightly over 2000. This will make it feasible to train a highly accurate classifier without having a large number of images on which to train. It will also prevent overfitting by reducing the size of the trainable model dramatically.

Model Fine-Tuning

A final and optional step is to perform model fine-tuning. The purpose of fine-tuning is to make slight adjustments to the convolutional filters, so that they capture features more relevant to your classification problem. This step is relatively simple and involves setting the convolutional base to be trainable, recompiling the model, and then training on a low learning rate, as shown in Listing 5-23.

If you apply the `summary()` method to the model one last time, you'll notice that it now has more than 23,000,000 trainable parameters. For this reason, we have to train on a low learning rate to prevent the model from overfitting by making substantial changes to the pretrained convolutional filters. Note that such modifications can also degrade or "un-learn" the information embedded in the pretrained parameters.

Listing 5-23. Fine-tune a pretrained model in Keras

```
# Set convolutional base to be untrainable.
model.trainable = True

# Compile model with a low learning rate.
model.compile(loss='binary_crossentropy',
        optimizer=tf.keras.optimizers.Adam(
        learning_rate=1e-5),
```

```
        metrics=['accuracy'])

# Perform fine-tuning.
model.fit(X_train, y_train, epochs = 10,
        class_weight = class_weights)
```

Summary

While computer vision once required the use of sophisticated models and domain knowledge, it can now be performed using convolutional neural networks with standard architectures. Furthermore, we have reached a point at which convolutional neural networks tend to outperform models that rely feature engineering, making it sufficient to master CNNs for most tasks.

The use of image classification remains underexploited in academic economics and finance, but has gained broader use in economic applications in industry. In this chapter, we gave an example of using satellite imagery to identify ships, which could be used to measure ship traffic at ports at a high frequency. The same approach could also be used to measure traffic on highways, count cars parked at malls, measure the pace of building construction, or identify changes in land cover.

In this chapter, we demonstrated how to construct neural networks using dense layers, which could be used for a variety of different regression and classification tasks. We also discussed how to define and train convolutional neural networks, which make use of special layers that take advantage of the properties of images. We saw that this resulted in a considerable reduction in the number of parameters needed relative to a model with only dense layers.

Finally, we discussed how to load pretrained models and use them in our classification problem. We used a ResNet50 model that was pretrained using ImageNet data to extract features from images of ships. We then used those features to train a dense classifier layer. As a final step, we also showed how the entire network could be fine-tuned by training the convolutional layers at a low learning rate.

Bibliography

Addison, D., and B. Stewart. 2015. "Night time lights revisited: The use of night time lights data as a proxy for economic variables." *World Bank Policy Research Working Paper No. 7496.*

Bickenbach, F., E. Bode, P. Nunnenkamp, and M. Söder. 2016. "Night lights and regional GDP." *Review of World Economics* 152 (2): 425–447.

Bluhm, R., and M. Krause. 2018. "Top lights - bright cities and their contribution to economic development." *CESifo Working Paper No. 7411.*

Borgshulte, M., M. Guenzel, C. Liu, and U. Malmendier. 2019. "CEO Stress and Life Expectancy: The Role of Corporate Governance and Financial Distress." *Working Paper.*

Chen, X., and W. Nordhaus. 2011. "Using luminosity data as a proxy for economic statistics." *Proceedings of the National Academy of Sciences* 108 (21): 8589–8594.

Cheng, H.T., and et al. 2016. "Wide & Deep Learning for Recommender Systems." *arXiv.*

Donaldson, D., and A. Storeygard. 2016. "The view from above: Applications of satellite data in economics." *Journal of Economic Perspectives* 30 (4): 171–198.

Gibson, J., S. Olivia, and G. Boe-Gibson. 2020. "Night Lights in Economics: Sources and Uses." *CSAE Working Paper Series 2020-01* (Centre for the Study of African Economies, University of Oxford).

Goldblatt, R., K. Heilmann, and Y. Vaizman. 2019. "Can medium resolution satellite imagery measure economic activity at small geographies? Evidence from Landsat in Vietnam." *The World Bank Economic Review* Forthcoming.

Grodecka, A., and I. Hull. 2019. "The Impact of Local Taxes and Public Services on Property Values." *Sveriges Riksbank Working Paper Series No. 374.*

Henderson, V., A. Storeygard, and D. Weil. 2012. "Measuring economic growth from outer space." *American Economic Review* 102 (2): 994–1028.

LeNail, A. 2019. "NN-SVG: Publication-Ready Neural Network Architecture Schematics." *Journal of Open Source Software* 4 (33).

Mitnik, O.A., P. Yañez-Pagans, and R. Sanchez. 2018. "Bright investments: Measuring the impact of transport infrastructure using luminosity data in Haiti. *IZA Discussion Paper No. 12018.*

Naik, N., S.D. Kominers, R. Raskar, E.L. Glaeser, and C.A. Hidalgo. 2017. "Computer vision uncovers urban change predictors." *Proceedings of the National Academy of Sciences* 114 (29): 7571–7576.

Nordhaus, W., and X. Chen. 2015. "A sharper image? Estimates of the precision of night time lights as a proxy for economic statistics." *Journal of Economic Geography* 15 (1): 217–246.

CHAPTER 6

Text Data

The economics and finance disciplines have been generally reluctant to integrate forms of unstructured data. One exception to this is text, which has been applied to a wide variety of empirical problems. This may have arisen, in part, as a consequence of early successful applications in economics, such as Romer and Romer (2004), which demonstrated the empirical value of measuring internal central bank narratives.

The more widespread adoption of text may also be attributable to its many natural applications within economics and finance. It can, for instance, be used to extract latent variables, such as economic policy uncertainty from newspapers,[1] consumer inflation expectations from social media content (Angelico, et al. 2018), and central bank and private firm sentiment from announcements and filings.[2] It can also be used to predict bank distress (Cerchiello et al. 2017), measure the impact of news media on the business cycle (Chahrour et al. 2019), identify descriptions

---

[1]See Baker et al. (2016) and Bloom et al. (2019) for an overview of the construction of Economic Policy Uncertainty (EPU) indices and the current state of the literature. EPU indices for different countries are posted and updated at www.policyuncertainty.com.

[2]Measuring sentiment in central bank statements and in financial filings are two of the most common uses of text-based data in economics. Loughran and McDonald (2011) was one of the earliest applications for financial filings. As a by-product of their work, they introduced a financial sentiment dictionary, which has gained widespread use in economics and finance, including for problems in central banks. Apel and Blix Grimaldi (2014) later introduced a sentiment dictionary that made use of terms specific to central banking.

© Isaiah Hull 2021
I. Hull, *Machine Learning for Economics and Finance in TensorFlow 2,*
https://doi.org/10.1007/978-1-4842-6373-0_6

of fraud in consumer financial complaints (Bertsch et al. 2020), analyze financial stability (Born et al. 2013; Correa et al. 2020), forecast economic variables (Hollrah et al. 2018; Kalamara et. al 2020), and study central bank decision-making.[3]

The focus on textual data in economics gained renewed emphasis when Robert Shiller gave a presidential address to the American Economic Association entitled "Narrative Economics" (Shiller 2017). He argued that academic work in economics and finance has failed to account for the rise and decline of popular narratives, which have the capacity to drive macroeconomic and financial fluctuations, even if the narratives themselves are wrong. He then suggested that the discipline should begin the long project of correcting this deficiency through the exploration of text-based datasets and methods.

This chapter will discuss how text can be prepared and applied in the context of economics and finance. Throughout, we'll use TensorFlow for modeling purposes, but will also make use of the Natural Language Toolkit (NLTK) to pre-process the data. We will also frequently refer to and use conventions from Gentzkow et al. (2019), which provides a comprehensive overview of many text analysis topics in economics and finance.

Data Cleaning and Preparation

The first step in any text analysis project is to clean and prepare the data. If, for instance, we want to use newspaper articles about a company to forecast its stock market performance, we'll need to start by assembling a collection or "corpus" of newspaper articles and then converting the text in those articles to a numerical format.

---

[3]See, for example, Hansen and McMahon (2016), Hansen et al. (2018), Acosta (2019), and Armelius et al. (2020).

The way in which we convert from text to numbers will determine what types of analysis we can perform. For this reason, the data cleaning and preparation step will be an important part of the pipeline for any such project. We will cover it in this subsection, focusing on its implementation using the Natural Language Toolkit (NLTK).

We'll start by installing NLTK. We'll then import it and download its models and datasets. You can use nltk.download('book') to download book-related data, nltk.download('popular') to download the most popular packages, or nltk.download('all') to download all available datasets and models, which is what we do in Listing 6-1.

Listing 6-1. Install, import, and prepare NLTK

```
# Install nltk.
!pip install nltk

# Import nltk.
import nltk

# Download all datasets and models
nltk.download('all')
```

Now that we've installed NLTK and have downloaded all of the datasets and models, we can make use of its basic data cleaning and preparation tools. Before we can do that, though, we'll need to prepare a dataset and introduce some notation.

Collecting the Data

The data we'll use comes from US Securities and Exchange Commission (SEC) filings, which are available through their online system, EDGAR.[4] The EDGAR interface, shown in Figure 6-1, allows users to perform a variety of queries. We'll first pull up the interface for company filings. Here, we can search for documents by company name or specify search parameters that will return documents for all companies that fit that criteria. Let's assume that we want to create a project to monitor SEC filings about the metal mining industry. In that case, we'll search by standard industrial classification (SIC) code.

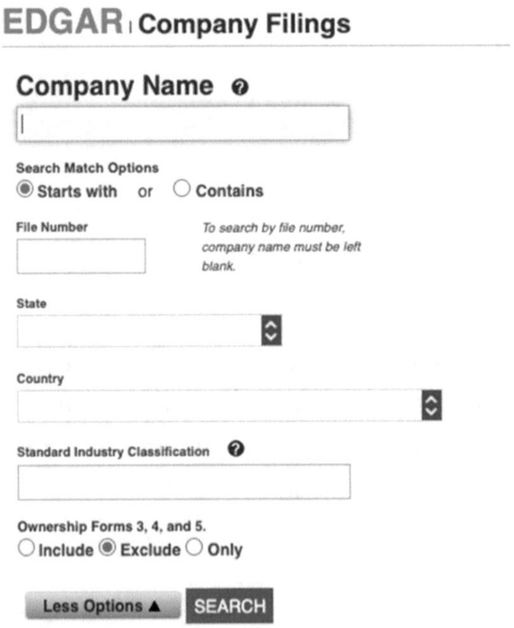

Figure 6-1. The EDGAR search interface for company filings. Source: SEC.gov

---

[4]You can perform queries and download files from EDGAR at the following URL: www.sec.gov/edgar/search-and-access.

Pulling up the SEC's list of SIC codes, we can see that metal mining has been assigned the code 1000 and falls under the responsibility of the Office of Energy and Transportation, as is shown in Figure 6-2. We can now search for all filings by companies with the 1000 SIC code, yielding the results given in Figure 6-3. Each page lists companies, the state or country associated with the filing, and the Central Index Key (CIK), which can be used to identify a filing individual or corporation.

In our case, we'll select the filings for "Americas Gold and Silver Corp," which you can locate by searching for 0001286973 in the CIK field. From there, we'll look at the text of Exhibit 99.1 from the 6-K financial filing on 2020-05-15. We show the title and some text from this filing in Figure 6-4.

Division of Corporation Finance:
Standard Industrial Classification (SIC) Code List

The Standard Industrial Classification Codes that appear in a company's disseminated EDGAR filings indicate the company's type of business. These codes are also used in the Division of Corporation Finance as a basis for assigning review responsibility for the company's filings. For example, a company whose business was Metal Mining (SIC 1000) would have its filings reviewed by staffers in the Office of Energy & Transportation.

SIC Code	Office	Industry Title
100	Office of Life Sciences	AGRICULTURAL PRODUCTION-CROPS
200	Office of Life Sciences	AGRICULTURAL PROD-LIVESTOCK & ANIMAL SPECIALTIES
700	Office of Life Sciences	AGRICULTURAL SERVICES
800	Office of Life Sciences	FORESTRY
900	Office of Life Sciences	FISHING, HUNTING AND TRAPPING
1000	Office of Energy & Transportation	METAL MINING
1040	Office of Energy & Transportation	GOLD AND SILVER ORES
1090	Office of Energy & Transportation	MISCELLANEOUS METAL ORES
1220	Office of Energy & Transportation	BITUMINOUS COAL & LIGNITE MINING
1221	Office of Energy & Transportation	BITUMINOUS COAL & LIGNITE SURFACE MINING
1311	Office of Energy & Transportation	CRUDE PETROLEUM & NATURAL GAS
1381	Office of Energy & Transportation	DRILLING OIL & GAS WELLS
1382	Office of Energy & Transportation	OIL & GAS FIELD EXPLORATION SERVICES
1389	Office of Energy & Transportation	OIL & GAS FIELD SERVICES, NEC

Figure 6-2. *A partial list of SIC classification codes. Source: SEC.gov*

As we can see in Figure 6-4, the filing corresponds to the first quarter of 2020 and appears to contain information about the company that could be useful for assessing its value. We can see, for instance, that there is information about the firm's acquisitions. It also discusses mining production plans at specific sites. Now that we know how to retrieve filing information from the EDGAR system and have identified a specific filing of interest, we'll introduce notation to describe such textual information. We'll then return to the cleaning and preparation tasks in NLTK.

Companies for SIC 1000 - METAL MINING
Click on CIK to view company filings

Items 1 - 40

CIK	Company	State/Country
0000825171	37 CAPITAL INC	A1
0001011903	ABACUS MINERALS CORP	A1
0001071832	ACCORD VENTURES INC	A6
0001194506	ACREX VENTURES LTD	
0001171008	ADAMANT DRI PROCESSING & MINERALS GROUP	F4
0001050602	ADASTRA MINERALS INC	X0
0000830821	Advanced Mineral Technologies, Inc	ID
0001318196	ALASKA GOLD CORP.	NV
0001360903	Alaska Pacific Resources Inc	NV
0001142462	ALBERTA STAR DEVELOPMENT CORP	A1
0001484457	Alderon Iron Ore Corp.	A1
0001015647	ALMADEN MINERALS LTD	A1
0001442999	ALTEROLA BIOTECH INC.	CA
0001402279	AMCA RESOURCES, INC.	A6
0001576873	AMERICAN BATTERY METALS CORP	NV
0001072019	American Bonanza Gold Corp.	A1
0000948341	AMERICAN BULLION MINERALS LTD	A1
0000891713	AMERICAN CONSOLIDATED MANAGEMENT GROUP INC	SC
0001282613	AMERICAN EAGLE ENERGY Corp	CO
0000949055	AMERICAN GEM CORP	MT
0001356371	AMERICAN LITHIUM MINERALS, INC.	NV
0001137239	AMERICAS ENERGY Co - AECO	TN
0001286973	Americas Gold & Silver Corp	A6

Figure 6-3. *A partial list of metal mining company search results. Source: SEC.gov*

Operational and First Quarter Financial Highlights

- Relief Canyon continues to ramp-up following first gold pour in February and the Company is focused on achieving commercial production by late Q2-2020 or early Q3-2020.
- Subsequent to Q1-2020, the Company closed a bought deal public offering for gross proceeds of approximately C$28.75 million which provides the Company with available capital to address working capital needs including bringing Relief Canyon into commercial production, particularly in the COVID-19 environment.
- As a result of Relief Canyon being in pre-commercial production, the Cosalá Operations producing for less than a month during the quarter, and the exclusion of operating metrics from the Galena Complex during the Galena recapitalization plan ("Recapitalization Plan"), Q1-2020 revenue was $7.3 million resulting in a net loss of $4.1 million or ($0.03) per share.
- Cosalá production for the first 26 days of Q1-2020 yielded 420 gold equivalent ounces[1] or 0.3 million silver equivalent ounces[2] at cost of sales of $7.19/oz equivalent silver, by-product cash cost[3] of negative ($11.32/oz) silver, and all-in sustaining cost[3] of negative ($0.83/oz) silver.
- The Galena Recapitalization Plan is proceeding better than expected with the Company seeing both increased production and encouraging exploration results.
- Outlook for 2021 continues to be 90,000 to 110,000 gold equivalent ounces at expected all-in sustaining costs[4] of $900 to $1,100 per gold equivalent ounce.
- At March 31, 2020, the Company had a cash balance of approximately $16.4 million.
- The Company has chosen not to host a conference call to discuss the Q1-2020 results given the limited production and the extensive operations update released on May 4, 2020. The Company will resume the quarterly conference calls following its Q2-2020 results.

Figure 6-4. A partial 6-K financial filing for a metal mining company. Source: SEC.gov

Text Data Notation

The notation we'll use follows Gentzkow et al. (2019). We'll let D to denote a collection of N documents or a "corpus." C will denote a numerical array, which contains observations on K features for each document, $D_j \in D$. In some cases, we'll predict outcomes, V, using C or we'll use fitted values, $\hat{V}$, in a two-step casual inference problem.

Before we can apply NLTK to clean and prepare the data, we have to answer the following two questions:

1. What is D?

2. What features of D should be embodied in C?

If we're working with only one 6-K filing, then D_j might be a paragraph or sentence in that filing. Alternatively, if we have many 6-K filings, then D_j is likely to represent a single filing. For the sake of fixing an example, we'll assume that D is the collection of sentences in a single 6-K filling – namely, the one we discussed earlier.

What, then, is C? It depends on the features or "tokens" we wish to extract from each sentence of the filing. In many cases, we'll use word counts as features; and we'll do that in this example too. The expression for C, which is commonly referred to as the "document-feature" or "document-term" matrix is given in Equation 6-1.

Equation 6-1. Document-feature matrix.

$$C = \begin{pmatrix} c_{11} & \cdots & c_{1k} \\ \vdots & \ddots & \vdots \\ c_{n1} & \cdots & c_{nk} \end{pmatrix}$$

Each element, c_{ij}, is the frequency with which word j appears in sentence i. A natural question we might ask is *which* words are included in the matrix? Should we include all words in a given dictionary? Or should we restrict it to words that appear at least once in the corpus?

Data Preparation

In practice, we'll select a maximum number of words, K, based on some filtering criteria. In addition to this, we'll also usually remove all non-word symbols, such as numbers and punctuation, during the cleaning and data preparation process. This will typically consist of four steps, which we outline as follows and then implement in an example using NLTK:

1. **Convert to lowercase:** Text data is inherently high dimensional, which will force us to use dimensionality reduction strategies wherever possible. One simple way in which we can do this is to ignore capitalization. Instead of treating "gold" and "Gold" as separate features, we'll convert all characters to lowercase and treat them as the same word.

2. **Remove stop words and rare words**: Many words do not contain meaningful content, such as articles, conjunctions, and prepositions. For this reason, we will often compile a list of "stop words," which will be removed from texts during the cleaning process. If our C matrix consists of word counts, knowing how many times the words "the" and "and" were used will not tell us much about our topic of interest. Similarly, when we exclude words from the document-term matrix, we will often exclude rare words, which do not appear frequently enough to allow a model to discern their meaning.

3. **Stem or lemmatize**: The need to reduce data dimensionality further will often lead us to perform "stemming" or "lemmatization." Stemming entails converting a word to its stem. That is, we might map the verb "running" to "run." Since many words will map to the same stem, this will reduce the dimensionality of the problem, just as converting to lowercase letters did. Removing a word stem may result in non-word, which could be undesirable when the objective of a project is to yield interpretable outputs. In this case, we will want to consider using lemmatization instead, which maps many words to one, but uses the "base" or "dictionary" version of the word, rather than a stem.

4. **Remove non-word elements**: In most problems we'll encounter in economics and finance, it will not be possible to make use of punctuation, numbers, and special characters and symbols. For this reason, we will discard them, rather than including them in the document-term matrix.

We'll now step through these cleaning and preparation steps in NLTK. For the sake of completeness, we'll start by downloading the 6-K filing from SEC's website using urllib and BeautifulSoup in Listing 6-2. Understanding these libraries will not be necessary for understanding the remainder of the chapter.

Listing 6-2.   Download HTML and extract text

```
from urllib.request import urlopen
from bs4 import BeautifulSoup

# Define url string.
url = 'https://www.sec.gov/Archives/edgar/
data/1286973/000156459020025868/d934487dex991.htm'

# Send GET request.
html = urlopen(url)

# Parse HTML tree.
soup = BeautifulSoup(html.read())

# Identify all paragraphs.
paragraphs = soup.findAll('p')

# Create list of the text attributes of paragraphs.
paragraphs = [p.text for p in paragraphs]
```

To briefly explain the content of Listing 6-2, we first imported two submodules: urlopen from urllib.request and BeautifulSoup from bs4. The urlopen submodule allowed us to send GET requests, which is a way of requesting a file from a server. In this case, we requested the HTML document located at the specified url. We then used BeautifulSoup to create a parse tree from the HTML, so that we could make use of its structure, searching it by tag. Next, we searched for all instances of the "p" or paragraph tag. Using a list comprehension, we'll step through each instance, returning its text attribute, which we'll collect in a list of strings.

Recall that we decided to use sentences, rather than paragraphs, as our units of analysis. This means we'll need to join the paragraphs together into a single string and then determine how to identify sentences within that string. We'll start by merging and printing the paragraphs in Listing 6-3.

Listing 6-3. Join paragraphs into single string

```
# Join paragraphs into single string.
corpus = " ".join(paragraphs)

# Print contents.
print(corpus)

Darren Blasutti VP, Corporate Development & Communications
President and CEO Americas Gold and Silver Corporation Americas
Gold and Silver Corporation 416-874-1708 Cautionary Statement
on Forward-Looking Information: This news release contains
"forward-looking information" within\n      the meaning of
applicable securities laws. Forward-looking information
includes,\n  ...
```

Upon printing the corpus, we can see that it requires cleaning. It contains punctuation, stop words, line breaks, and special characters, all of which will need to be removed before computing the document-feature matrix. Now, we might be tempted to start with the cleaning step, but doing so would remove indicators of what constitutes a sentence in the text. For this reason, we'll first split the text into sentences.

While we could write a function to perform the splitting based on the location of punctuation, this is a solved problem in natural language processing and is implemented in the NLTK toolbox. In Listing 6-4, we import NLTK, instantiate a "sentence tokenizer," which splits a text into individual sentences, and then apply it to the corpus we constructed in the previous step.

Listing 6-4. Tokenize text into sentences using NLTK

```
import nltk

# Instantiate sentence tokenizer.
sentTokenizer = nltk.sent_tokenize

# Identify sentences.
sentences = sentTokenizer(corpus)

# Print the number of sentences.
print(len(sentences))

50

# Print a sentence.
print(sentences[7])
```

The Company continues to target commercial production by late Q2-2020 or early Q3-2020 and will be providing more regular updates regarding the operation between now and then.

The next step is to perform the previously discussed cleaning tasks. While it will generally make sense to define a single function for this purpose, we'll divide it into three steps for the sake of clarity. We'll start by converting all characters to lowercase and removing stop words in Listing 6-5. For now, we will leave rare words in the corpus.

Listing 6-5. Convert characters to lowercase and remove stop words

```
from nltk.corpus import stopwords

# Convert all characters to lowercase.
sentences = [s.lower() for s in sentences]

# Define stop words as a set.
```

```
stops = set(stopwords.words('english'))

# Instantiate word tokenizer.
wordTokenizer = nltk.word_tokenize

# Divide corpus into list of lists.
words = [wordTokenizer(s) for s in sentences]

# Remove stop words.
for j in range(len(words)):
        words[j] = [w for w in words[j] if
        w not in stops]

# Print first five words in first sentence.
print(words[0][:5])

['americas', 'gold', 'silver', 'corporation', 'reports']
```

In the next step, we'll apply a stemmer to reduce the dimensionality of the dataset by collapsing each word into its stem. In Listing 6-6, we import the Porter stemmer (Porter 1980), instantiate it, and then apply it to each word in each sentence. We again print the first five words in the first sentence. We can see that the stemmer mapped "corporate" to "corpor" and "reports" to "report." Recall that a word stem will not always be a word.

Listing 6-6. Replace words with their stems

```
from nltk.stem.porter import PorterStemmer

# Instantiate Porter stemmer.
stemmer = PorterStemmer()

# Apply Porter stemmer.
for j in range(len(words)):
        words[j] = [stemmer.stem(w) for w in words[j]]
```

```
# Print first five words in first sentence.
print(words[0][:5])
```

```
['america', 'gold', 'silver', 'corpor', 'report']
```

The last step in the cleaning process is to remove special characters, punctuation, and numbers. We'll do this using regular expressions, which are commonly referred to as "regexes." A regular expression is a short string that encodes a pattern that can be identified in texts. In our case, the string is [^a-z]+. The brackets indicate that the pattern is over a range of characters – namely, all the characters of the alphabet. We use the caret symbol, ^, to negate this pattern, indicating that the regex should only match characters not contained in it. This, of course, includes special symbols, punctuation, and numbers. Finally, the + symbol indicates that we allow for such symbols to be repeated in a sequence.

Listing 6-7 implements this final step in the cleaning process. We first import the library, re, which is used to implement regular expressions. Next, we iterate through each word in each sentence and substitute an empty string for any pattern matches. This leaves us with a list of sentences, each broken down into a list of words. Since the process will have left some empty strings, we'll rejoin the words in each sentence. We'll also remove any white space at the start and end of the sentence.

Listing 6-7. Remove special characters and join words into sentences

```
import re

# Remove special characters, punctuation, and numbers.
for j in range(len(words)):
        words[j] = [re.sub('[^a-z]+', '', w)
        for w in words[j]]

# Rejoin words into sentences.
```

```
for j in range(len(words)):
        words[j] = " ".join(words[j]).strip()
```

```
# Print sentence.
print(words[7])
```

```
compani continu target commerci product late q earli q provid
regular updat regard oper
```

Printing the same sentence once again, we can see that it now looks quite different from its original form. Rather than a sentence, it looks like a collection of word stems. Indeed, in the following section, we will apply a form of text analysis that treats documents as a collection of words and ignores the order in which they appear. This is often referred to as the "bag-of-words" model.

The Bag-of-Words Model

In the previous section, we suggested that one possible construction of the document-term (DT) matrix, C, would use word counts as features. This representation would not allow us to account for grammar or word order, but it would permit us to capture word frequency. There are many problems in economics and finance in which we will be able to achieve our objective under such constraints.

The model we've described is called the "bag-of-words" (BoW) model, which was introduced in the information retrieval literature by Salton and McGill (1983). The term bag-of-words appears to have originated in a linguistic context in Harris (1954):

> *we build a stock of utterances each of which is a particular combination of particular elements. And this stock of combinations of elements becomes a factor ... for language is not merely a bag of words but a tool with particular properties which have been fashioned in the course of its use.*

203

In this section, we'll see how to construct a BoW model, starting with the cleaned and prepared data from the previous section. In addition to NLTK, we'll also use submodules from sklearn to construct the DT matrix. While there are routines to perform such tasks in NLTK, they are not part of the core module and are generally less efficient.

Recall that words contained the 50 sentences we extracted from a 6-K filing for a metal mining company. We'll use this list of lists to construct the document-term matrix in Listing 6-8, where we start by importing text from sklearn.feature_extraction. We'll then instantiate a CounterVectorizer(), which will compute the frequency of words in each sentence and then construct the C matrix based on some constraints, which can be supplied as parameters. For the sake of illustration, we'll set max_features to 10. This will constrain the maximum number of columns in the document-term matrix to be no higher than 10.

Next, we'll apply fit_transform() to words, transforming it into a document-term matrix, C. Since C will be large for many problems, sklearn saves it as a sparse matrix. You can convert it to an array using the toarray() method. We can also apply the get_feature_names() of vectorizer() to recover the terms that correspond to each of the columns.

Listing 6-8. Construct the document-term matrix

```
from sklearn.feature_extraction import text

# Instantiate vectorizer.
vectorizer = text.CountVectorizer(max_features = 10)

# Construct C matrix.
C = vectorizer.fit_transform(words)

# Print document-term matrix.
print(C.toarray())
[[3 1 0 2 0 0 1 0 2 2]
 [1 2 0 1 0 0 0 0 0 1]
```

```
    • • •
    • • •
    • • •
 [0 1 0 0 0 1 0 0 0 0]
 [0 0 0 0 0 0 0 1 1 0]]
```

```
# Print feature names.
print(vectorizer.get_feature_names())
```

```
['america', 'compani', 'cost', 'gold', 'includ',
 'inform', 'oper', 'product', 'result', 'silver']
```

Printing the document-term matrix and feature names, we can see that we recovered counts for ten different features. While this was useful for the sake of illustration, we will typically want to use considerably more features in actual applications; however, allowing more features may result in the inclusion of less useful features, which will necessitate the use of filtering.

Sklearn provides us with two additional parameters we can use to perform filtering: max_df and min_df. The max_df parameter determines the maximum number or proportion of documents that a term may appear in before it is removed from the term matrix. Similarly, the minimum threshold is given by min_df. In both cases, specifying an integer value, such as 3, indicates a document count, whereas specifying a float, such as 0.25, indicates a proportion of documents.

The value of specifying a maximum threshold is that it will remove all terms that appear too frequently to provide meaningful variation. If, for instance, a term appears in more than 50% of documents, we may want to remove it by specifying a max_df of 0.50. In Listing 6-9, we compute the document-term matrix again, but this time allow for up to 1000 terms and also apply filtering to remove terms that appear in either more than 50% or fewer than 5% of documents.

If we print the shape of the C matrix, we can see that it does not appear that the document-term matrix was constrained by the maximum feature limit of 1000, since only 109 feature columns were returned. This may have been a consequence of our selection of maximum document frequency and minimum document frequency parameters, which eliminated terms that were unlikely to be useful for our purposes.

Another way in which we can perform filtering is to use the term-frequency inverse-document frequency (tf-idf) metric, which is shown in Equation 6-2.

Equation 6-2. Computing the term-frequency inverse-document frequency for column j.

$$tfidf_j = \sum_i c_{ij} * log\left(\frac{N}{\sum_i 1_{[c_{ij} > 0]}}\right)$$

The tf-idf is computed for each feature, j, in the document-term matrix, C. It consists of the product of two components: (1) the frequency with which term j appears across all documents in the corpus, $\sum_i c_{ij}$, and (2) the natural logarithm of the document count, divided by the number of documents in which term j appears at least once, $N / \sum_i 1_{[c_{ij} > 0]}$. The tf-idf metric is increasing in the number of times j appears across the entire corpus and decreasing in the share of documents in which j appears. If j isn't used frequently or is used in too many documents, the tf-idf score will be low.

Listing 6-9. Adjust the parameters of CountVectorizer()

```
# Instantiate vectorizer.
vectorizer = text.CountVectorizer(
        max_features = 1000,
        max_df = 0.50,
        min_df = 0.05
)
```

```
# Construct C matrix.
C = vectorizer.fit_transform(words)

# Print shape of C matrix.
print(C.toarray().shape)
```

```
(50, 109)
```

```
# Print terms.
print(vectorizer.get_feature_names()[:10])
```

```
['abil', 'activ', 'actual', 'affect', 'allin', 'also',
 'america', 'anticip', 'approxim', 'avail']
```

In Listing 6-10, we repeat the same steps as in Listing 6-8, but we use a TfidfVectorizer(), rather than CountVectorizer(). This allows us to access the idf_ parameter, which contains the inverse document frequency scores. We can then optionally perform filtering by dropping columns with a tf-idf score below a certain threshold.

Listing 6-10. Compute inverse document frequencies for all columns

```
# Instantiate vectorizer.
vectorizer = text.TfidfVectorizer(max_features = 10)

# Construct C matrix.
C = vectorizer.fit_transform(words)

# Print inverse document frequencies.
print(vectorizer.idf_)
```

```
[2.36687628 1.84078318 3.14006616 2.2927683  2.44691898
 2.22377543 1.8873032  2.22377543 2.22377543 2.2927683 ]
```

In some applications, we may want to use several words in a sequence (n-grams) – rather than individual words (unigrams) – as our features. We can do this by setting the ngram_range parameter of TfidfVectorizer() or CountVectorizer(). In Listing 6-11, we set the parameter to (2, 2), which means we only permit two-word sequences (bigrams). Note that the first value in the tuple is the minimum number of words and the second value is the maximum. We can see that the set of feature names returned is now different from the unigrams we generated in Listing 6-9.

In general, applying the bag-of-words model and computing a document-term matrix will be only the first step in a natural language processing project; however, it should be straightforward to see how such a matrix could be combined with standard tools from econometrics to perform analysis. If, for instance, we had a dependent variable associated with each document, such as stock returns for a firm on the same days as SEC filings, we could combine the two to train a predictive model or to test a hypothesis.

Listing 6-11. Compute the document-term matrix for unigrams and bigrams

```
# Instantiate vectorizer.
vectorizer = text.TfidfVectorizer(
        max_features = 10,
        ngram_range = (2,2)
)

# Construct C matrix.
C = vectorizer.fit_transform(words)

# Print feature names.
print(vectorizer.get_feature_names())
```

```
['america gold', 'cosal oper', 'forwardlook inform', 'galena
complex', 'gold silver', 'illeg blockad', 'oper result',
'recapit plan', 'relief canyon', 'silver corpor']
```

Dictionary-Based Methods

In the previous sections, we cleaned and prepared data and then explored it using the bag-of-words model. This yielded a NxK document-term matrix, C, which consisted of word counts for each document. We filtered certain words of the document-term matrix, but otherwise remained agnostic about what features we wished to find in the text.

An alternative to this approach is to use a pre-selected "dictionary" of words, which is constructed to capture some latent feature in the text. Such approaches are often referred to as "dictionary-based methods" and are the most commonly used form of text analysis in economics.

An early application of dictionary-based methods in economics made use of latent "sentiment" in *Wall Street Journal* articles to study the relationship between news and stock market performance (Tetlock 2007). Later work, such as Loughran and McDonald (2011) and Apel and Blix Grimaldi (2014), introduced dictionaries that were designed to measure specific latent variables, which lead to their widespread use in the literature. Loughran and McDonald (2011) introduced a dictionary for 10-K financial filings, which was ultimately used to measure negative and positive sentiment in many contexts. Apel and Blix Grimaldi (2014) introduced a dictionary that measured "hawkishness" and "dovishness" in central bank communication.

Gentzkow et al. (2019) argue that economics and the social sciences should expand the set of tools they use for performing text analysis. Rather than using dictionary-based methods as a default choice, they should instead only be considered when the following two criteria are satisfied:

1. The prior information you have about the latent variable and how it is represented in text is strong and reliable.

2. The information about the latent variable in the text is weak and diffuse.

An ideal example of this is the Economic Policy Uncertainty (EPU) index introduced by Baker et al. (2016). The latent variable they wanted to measure was a theoretical object, which they captured in text by identifying the joint use of words that referred to the economy, policy, and uncertainty. Without specifying a dictionary for such an object, it is unlikely that it would emerge from a model as a common feature or topic. Additionally, having specified a dictionary, they demonstrated that it captured the underlying theoretical object by comparing EPU index scores with human ratings of the same newspaper articles.

Since dictionary-based methods are simple to implement and do not require the use of TensorFlow, we'll demonstrate how they work with a single example involving the Loughran-McDonald (LM) dictionary. We'll start by using pandas to load the LM dictionary in Listing 6-12.[5] We'll use the read_excel submodule from pandas and will specify the file path and the sheet name. Note that we've specified the "Positive" sheet, since we will exclusively make use of the dictionary of positive words in this example.

Listing 6-12. Compute the Loughran-McDonald measure of positive sentiment

```
import pandas as pd
```

---

[5]The LM dictionary is currently available for download on the following page: https://sraf.nd.edu/textual-analysis/resources/#LM%20Sentiment%20 Word%20Lists.

```
# Define data directory path.
data_path = '../data/chapter6/'

# Load the Loughran-McDonald dictionary.
lm = pd.read_excel(data_path+'LM2018.xlsx',
        sheet_name = 'Positive',
        header = None)

# Convert series to DataFrame.
lm = pd.DataFrame(lm.values, columns = ['Positive'])

# Convert to lower case.
lm = lm['Positive'].apply(lambda x: x.lower())

# Convert DataFrame to list.
lm = lm.tolist()

# Print list of positive words.
print(lm)

['able',
 'abundance',
 'abundant',
        ...
 'innovator',
        ...
 'winners',
 'winning',
 'worthy']
```

Next, we'll convert the pandas Series into a DataFrame and use the column header "Positive" for the dictionary. We'll then use a lambda function to convert all of the words to lowercase, since they are uppercase in the LM dictionary. Finally, we'll convert the DataFrame to a list object and then print. Looking at the last three terms, we can see that two of them – winners and winning – are likely to have the same word stem.

In general, we will typically either want to stem the dictionary and stem the corpus or stem neither. Since we have already stemmed the corpus – namely, the sentences from a 6-K filling – we'll stem the dictionary too, dropping duplicate stems in the process. We do this in Listing 6-13.

Listing 6-13. Stem the LM dictionary

```
from nltk.stem.porter import PorterStemmer

# Instantiate Porter stemmer.
stemmer = PorterStemmer()

# Apply Porter stemmer.
slm = [stemmer.stem(word) for word in lm]

# Print length of list.
print(len(slm))
```

354

```
# Drop duplicates by converting to set.
slm = list(set(slm))

# Print length of list.
print(len(slm))
```

151

Following the steps we took earlier in the chapter, we'll first instantiate a Porter stemmer and then apply it to each word in the dictionary using a list comprehension. The original list contains 354 words. If we then convert that list to a set, this will drop duplicate stems, reducing the number of dictionary terms to 151.

The next step is to take the words list, which contains the 50 sentences we extracted from a document, and count the instances of positive word stems. Recall that we cleaned and stemmed each of the words in a sentence – and then stored them as strings. We'll need to iterate through each string, counting the number of times each of the positive words appears. We'll do this in Listing 6-14.

Listing 6-14. Count positive words

```
# Define empty array to hold counts.
counts = []

# Iterate through all sentences.
for w in words:
        # Set initial count to 0.
        count = 0
        # Iterate over all dictionary words.
        for i in slm:
                count += w.count(i)
        # Append counts.
        counts.append(count)
```

In Listing 6-14, we started by defining an empty list to hold the counts. We then iterated over all strings that are contained in the words list in the outer loop. Whenever we started a new sentence, we set the positive word count to 0. We then stepped through the inner loop, which iterates over all words in the stemmed LM dictionary, counting the number of times they appear in the string and adding that to the total. We appended the total for each sentence to counts.

Figure 6-5 shows a histogram of the positive word counts. We can see that most sentences have none, whereas one sentence has more than ten. If we were to perform this analysis at the document level, as we typically will, we would most likely find a non-zero value for most 6-K filings.

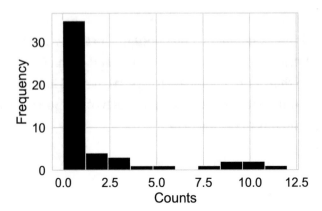

Figure 6-5. *The distribution of positive word counts across sentence in a 6-K filling*

In principle, we could take our positivity counts and include them as a feature in a regression. In practice, however, we will typically use a transformation of the count variable that has a more natural interpretation. If we did not have zero counts, we might use the natural logarithm of the count, allowing us to interpret the estimated effect as the impact on the percentage change in positivity. Alternatively, we could use the ratio of positive words to all words.

Finally, in economics and finance applications, it is common to use a net index, combining both positivity and negativity or "hawkishness" and "dovishness," as is shown in Equation 6-3. Often, we will take the difference between the positive and negative word counts and then divide by a normalization factor. This factor may be the total word count for the document or the sum of the positive and negative terms.

Equation 6-3. Net positivity index.

$$net\ positivity = \frac{positivity - negativity}{normalization\ factor}$$

Word Embeddings

So far, we have used one-hot encoding (dummy variables) to construct numerical representations of words. One potential downside to this approach is that we implicitly assume that each pair of words is orthogonal. The words "inflation" and "prices," for instance, are assumed to have no relationship to each other.

An alternative to using words as features is to instead use embeddings. In contrast to word vectors, which have a high-dimensional, sparse representation, word embeddings use a low-dimensional, dense representation. This dense representation allows us to identify the degree to which words are related.

Figure 6-6 provides a simple comparison of one-hot encoded words and dense word embeddings. The statement "...inflation rose sharply..." – which might appear in a central bank announcement – could be encoded using either approach. If we use the one-hot encoded approach, shown on the left of the diagram, each word will be translated into a sparse, high-dimensional vector. And each such vector will be orthogonal to all others. If, on the other hand, if we use embeddings, each word will be associated with a lower-dimensional, dense representation, shown on the right of Figure 6-6. The relationship between two such vectors is measurable and can be captured, for instance, using their inner product. The formula for the inner product of two vectors of dimension n – x and z – is given in Equation 6-4.

Equation 6-4. The inner product of two vectors, x and z.

$$x^T z = x_0 z_0 + \ldots + x_n z_n$$

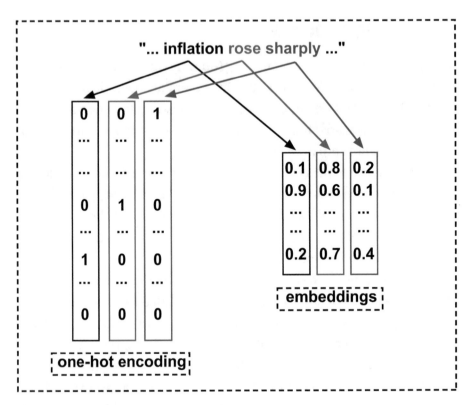

Figure 6-6. *Comparison of one-hot encoding and word embeddings*

While the inner product may give us a compact summary of the relationship between the two words, it does not provide more granular information about how two embedding vectors are related. For this, we can directly compare elements in the same position for a pair of vectors. Such elements provide a measurement for the same feature. While we might not be able to identify what the underlying feature is, we know that having similar values in the same position indicates two words are related along that dimension.

In contrast to one-hot encoding, we will need to use some supervised or unsupervised method to train embeddings. Since embeddings need to capture meaning in words and the relationships between words, it will often not make sense to do the training ourselves. Among other things, the embedding layer will need to learn the language in which you are performing your analysis, and the corpus you provide will almost certainly be insufficient for that task.

For this reason, you will often instead use pretrained word embeddings. Common choices include Word2Vec (Mikolov et al. 2013) and Global Vector for Word Representation (Pennington et al. 2014).

Notice that there is a strong analogy between word embeddings and convolutional layers. With convolutional layers, we said that they included general vision filters. For this reason, it often made sense to use convolutional layers from a model pretrained on millions of images. Additionally, we said that it was possible to "fine-tune" the training of such models to improve local performance on your particular image classification task. The same is also true with word embeddings.

Topic Modeling

The purpose of a topic model is to uncover a latent set of topics in a corpus and to determine the extent to which those topics are present in individual documents. The first topic model, the latent Dirichlet allocation (LDA), was introduced to the machine learning literature in Blei et al. (2003) and has since found applications in many areas, including economics and finance.

While TensorFlow does not provide an implementation for standard workhorse topic models, it is the framework of choice for many sophisticated topic models. In general, a topic model will be more likely to be implemented in TensorFlow if it makes use of deep learning.

Since topic modeling is seeing increased use in economics, we will provide a brief introduction in this section, even though we will not make use of TensorFlow. We'll start with a theoretical overview of the static LDA model Blei et al. (2003), followed by a description of how to implement and tune it using sklearn. We'll will close the section by discussing recently-introduced variants of the model.

In Blei et al. (2003), the LDA model is described as follows:

a generative probabilistic model of a corpus. The basic idea is that documents are represented as random mixtures over latent topics, where each topic is characterized by a distribution over words.

There are a few concepts worth explaining, since they will reappear throughout this chapter and text. First, the model is "generative" because it generates a novel output – the topic distribution – rather than performing a discriminative task, such as learning a classification for a document. Second, it is "probabilistic" because the model is explicitly grounded in probability theory and yields probabilities. And third, we say that topics are "latent" in that they are not explicitly measured or labeled, but are assumed to be an underlying feature of documents.

While we won't discuss the details of solving an LDA model, we'll briefly summarize the assumptions underlying the model in Blei et al. (2003), starting with notation. First, they assume that words are drawn from a fixed vocabulary of length V and represent them using one-hot encoded vectors. Next, they define a document as a sequence of N words, $w = (w_1, w_2, ..., w_N)$. Finally, they define a corpus as collection of documents, $D = \{w_1, w_2, ..., w_M\}$.

The model makes three assumptions about the underlying process that generates a document, w, in a corpus, D:

1. The number of words, N, in each document, w, is drawn from a Poisson distribution.

2. The latent topics are drawn from a k-dimensional random variable, θ, which has a Dirichlet distribution: $\theta \sim Dir(\alpha)$.

3. For each word, n, a topic, z_n, is drawn from a multinomial distribution that is conditional on θ.

The word itself is then drawn from a multinomial distribution, conditional on the topic, z_n.

The authors argue that the Poisson distribution of word counts is not an important assumption and that it would be better to use a more realistic assumption. The choice of the Dirichlet distribution constrains θ to a *(k-1)*-dimensional simplex. It also provides a multivariate generalization of the beta distribution and is parameterized by a k-vector of positive-valued weights, α. Blei et al. (2003) choose the Dirichlet distribution for three reasons: "*...it is in the exponential family, has finite dimensional sufficient statistics, and is conjugate to the multinomial distribution.*" They argued that this would ensure its suitability in estimation and inference algorithms.

The probability density of the topic distribution, θ, is given in Equation 6-5.

Equation 6-5. The distribution of topics.

$$p(\theta|\alpha) = \frac{\Gamma\left(\sum_i \alpha_i\right)}{\Pi_i \Gamma(\alpha_i)} \theta_1^{\alpha_1-1} \cdots \theta_k^{\alpha_k-1}$$

In Figure 6-7, we provide a visual illustration of 100 random draws from the Dirichlet distribution in the case where $k = 2$. In the left panel of Figure 6-7, we set $\alpha = [0.9, 0.1]$, and in the right panel, we set $\alpha = [0.5, 0.5]$. In both cases, all points are located on the simplex. That is, summing the coordinates associated with any point will yield 1. Additionally, we can see that choosing identical values of α_0 and α_1 yields evenly distributed points along the simplex, whereas increasing the relative value of α_0 results in a skew toward the horizontal axis (i.e., topic θ_k).

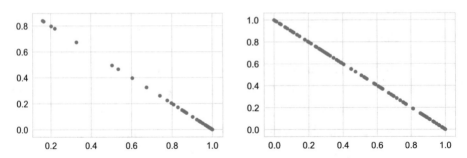

Figure 6-7. *Plot of random draws from Dirichlet distribution with k=2 and parameter vectors [0.9, 0.1] (left) and [0.5, 0.5] (right)*

We'll next implement an LDA model, making use of the document corpus we constructed earlier by dividing a 6-K filing into sentences. Recall that we defined a document-term matrix, *C*, using `CountVectorizer`. We'll make use of both in these in Listing 6-15, where we start by importing `LatentDirichletAllocation` from `sklearn.decomposition`. Next, we instantiate a model with our preferred parameter values. In this case, we will only set the number of topics, `n_components`. This corresponds to the *k* parameter in the theoretical model.

We can now train the model on the document-term matrix and recover the output, `wordDist`, using `lda.components_`. Note that `wordDist` has shape (3, 109). The rows correspond to latent topics, and the columns correspond to weights. The higher the weight, the more important a word is for defining a topic.[6]

We'll next make use of the output, `wordDist`, to identify the words with the highest weights to for each topic. We'll define an empty list, `topics`, to hold the topics. Within a list comprehension, we'll step through each topic array and apply `argsort()` to recover the indices that would sort the array. We'll then recover the last five indices and reverse their order.

---

[6]`lda.components_` returns unnormalized results that do not sum to 1. For this reason, we'll refer to them as weights, rather than probabilities.

For each index, we'll identify the associated term by making use of feature_names, which we recovered from vectorizer. We'll then print the list of topics.

A complete description of a topic consists of a vector of weights over the vocabulary. We can choose how such a topic is described by determining which words have weights that are sufficiently high to justify their inclusion in the topic's description. In this case, we have simply used the five words with the highest weights; however, in principle, we could have used a threshold value or some other criterion.

Listing 6-15. Perform LDA on 6-K filing text data

```
from sklearn.decomposition import LatentDirichletAllocation

# Set number of topics.
k = 5

# Instantiate LDA model.
lda = LatentDirichletAllocation(n_components = k)

# Recover feature names from vectorizer.
feature_names = vectorizer.get_feature_names()

# Train model on document-term matrix.
lda.fit(C)

# Recover word distribution for each topic.
wordDist = lda.components_

# Define empty topic list.
topics = []

# Recover topics.
for i in range(k):
        topics.append([feature_names[name] for
        name in wordDist[i].argsort()[-5:][::-1]])
```

```
# Print list of topics.
print(topics)
```

```
[['inform', 'america', 'gold', 'forwardlook', 'result'],
 ['oper', 'compani', 'product', 'includ', 'relief'],
 ['silver', 'lead', 'cost', 'ounc', 'galena']]
```

Now that we have identified topics, the next step is to determine what those topics describe. In our simple example, we recovered three topics. The first appears to reference forward-looking information related to gold. The second appears to involve company operations and production. And the third topic is concerned with the cost of metals.

Finally, we complete the exercise by using the transform() method of our model to assign topic probabilities to sentences in Listing 6-16.

Listing 6-16. Assign topic probabilities to sentences

```
# Transform C matrix into topic probabilities.
topic_probs = lda.transform(C)
```

```
# Print topic probabilities.
print(topic_probs)
```

```
array([[0.0150523 , 0.97172408, 0.01322362],
       [0.02115127, 0.599319  , 0.37952974],
       [0.33333333, 0.33333333, 0.33333333],
                       . . .
       [0.93766165, 0.03140632, 0.03093203],
       [0.08632993, 0.82749933, 0.08617074],
       [0.95509882, 0.02178363, 0.02311755]])
```

The output, as we can see in Listing 6-16, is a matrix of shape (3, 50), which contains topic probabilities that sum to one for each sentence. If, for instance, we had collected separate 6-K filings for each date, rather than looking at sentences within a filing, we'd now have the time series of topic proportions.

We've also plotted the topic proportions in Figure 6-8. We can see that there appears to be persistence in topics across sentences in the document document. For instance, topic 1 is dominant at the start and end of the document, and topic 3 rises in importance in the middle.

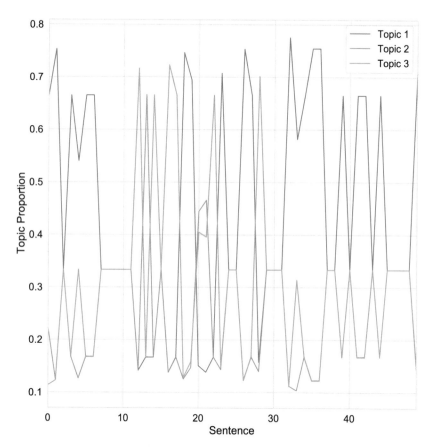

Figure 6-8. *Topic proportions by sentence*

While we considered a simple example that did not require a careful choice of model or training parameters, the LDA implementation in sklearn does, in fact, permit the choice of a variety of different parameters. We consider six of those parameters in the following:

1. **Topic prior**: By default, the LDA model will use
   1/n_components as the prior for all elements in
   α. You can, however, supply a different prior by
   explicitly providing a topic distribution for the
   parameter doc_topic_prior.

2. **Learning method**: By default, the LDA model in
   sklearn will use variational Bayes to train the model
   and will make use of the full sample to perform each
   update. It is, however, possible to train in mini-
   batches by setting the learning_method parameter
   to 'online'.

3. **Batch size**: Conditional on using online training,
   you will also have the option to change the mini-
   batch size from its default value of 128. You can do
   this using the batch_size parameter.

4. **Learning decay**: When using the online learning
   method, the learning_decay parameter can be
   used to adjust the learning rate. A higher value
   of decay lowers the information we retain from
   previous iterations. The default value is 0.7, and the
   documentation recommends selecting a decay in
   the (0.5, 1] interval.

5. **Maximum number of iterations**: Setting a
   maximum number of iterations will terminate
   the training process after that threshold has been
   reached. By default, the max_iter parameter is set to
   128. If the model does not appear to converge within
   128 iterations, you may want to set a higher value for
   this parameter.

Finally, two limitations of the standard LDA model introduced by Blei et al. (2003) merit discussion. First, neither the number nor content of topics may vary over the corpus. For many problems, this is not an issue; however, for applications in economics and finance that involve a time series dimension, this can be quite problematic, as we will expand on in the following paragraph. And second, the LDA model does not provide any meaningful control over the topics extracted. If we wish to track specific types of events in the data, we may not be able to do that using an LDA model, since there is no guarantee that it will identify those events.

With respect to the first problem – namely, using an LDA in time series contexts – two issues may arise. First, the model will censor topics that appear only briefly, such as financial crises, even if they are quite important during the period in which they appear. And second, it will introduce a "look-ahead" bias in the topic distribution by forcing topics that emerge in the future to also be topics in the entire sample. This can create the impression that the LDA model would have predicted events that it would not have if the sample were truncated at the date of the event.

With respect to the second problem, LDA presents two issues. The first is that we do not have the possibility to guide the model toward topics of interest. We cannot, for instance, submit topic queries to the LDA model. The second issue is that the topics the model does generate are often challenging to interpret. This is because a topic is simply a distribution over all words in the vocabulary. We will often be unable to determine what exactly a topic is without studying the distribution and examining the documents in which it is determined to be dominant.

There are, however, more recently developed models that attempt to overcome the limitations of the static LDA model. Blei and Lafferty (2006), for instance, introduce a dynamic version of the topic model. Additionally, Dieng et al. (2019) extend this further by introducing a dynamic embedded topic model (D-ETM). This model is dynamic, permits the use of a large vocabulary, and tends to generate more interpretable topics. This solves both of the issues related to the original static LDA model.

Text Regression

As Gentzkow et al. (2019) discuss, most text analysis within economics and finance centers around the bag-of-words model and dictionary-based methods. While these techniques are useful under certain circumstances, they are not the best tool for all research questions. Consequently, many projects that involve text analysis in economics could likely be improved by making use of different methods from natural language processing.

One option is to use a text regression, which is simply a regression model that includes text features, such as columns from the term-document matrix, as regressors. Gentzkow et al. (2019) argue that text regression is a good candidate method for economists to adopt. This is because economists primarily use linear regression for empirical work and often have familiarity with penalized linear regression. Thus, learning how to perform a text regression is mostly about constructing the document-term matrix, not learning how to estimate a regression.

We'll start this section by performing a simple text regression in TensorFlow. To do this, we'll need to construct the document-term matrix and a continuous dependent variable. Rather than using sentences within a 6-K filing, we'll use all 8-K filings for Apple in the SEC's system to construct the document-term matrix.[7] We'll then use the daily percentage change in Apple's stock price on the day of the filing as the dependent variable.

For the sake of brevity, we'll omit the details of the data collection process other than to say that we performed the same steps discussed earlier in the chapter to produce a document-term matrix, x_train, and stored the stock returns data as y_train. In total, we made use of 144 filings and extracted 25 unigram counts to construct x_train.

---

[7]The most commonly used SEC documents for research in economics and finance are 10-K, 10-Q, and 8-K filings. 10-K and 10-Q filings are submitted annually and quarterly and contain a high volume of text. 8-K filings are "press releases" that are submitted irregularly to comply with information disclosure rules. Apart from ownership information, 8-K filings are the most numerous, which is why we have selected them for this project.

Recall from Chapter 3 that a linear model with k regressors has the form given in Equation 6-6. In this case, the k regressors are the feature counts from the document-term matrix. Note that we index documents using t, since we are using a time series of filings and returns.

Equation 6-6. A linear model.

$$Y_t = \alpha + \beta_0 X_{t0} + \ldots + \beta_{k-1} X_{tk-1}$$

We could, of course, make use of OLS and solve for the parameter vector with an analytical expression. However, for the sake of building toward models that are not analytically tractable, we'll instead make use of a LAD regression. In Listing 6-17, we import tensorflow and numpy, initialize a constant term (alpha) and the vector of coefficients (beta), transform x_train and y_train into numpy arrays, and then define a function (LAD), which transforms the parameters and data into predictions.

Recall that we must define the parameters we wish to train using tf.Variable() and can use either np.array() or tf.constant() to define data.

Listing 6-17. Prepare the data and model for a LAD regression in TensorFlow

```
import tensorflow as tf
import numpy as np

# Draw initial values randomly.
alpha = tf.random.normal([1], stddev=1.0)
beta = tf.random.normal([25,1], stddev=1.0)

# Define variables.
alpha = tf.Variable(alpha, tf.float32)
beta = tf.Variable(beta, tf.float32)

# Convert data to numpy arrays.
```

```
x_train = np.array(x_train, np.float32)
y_train = np.array(y_train, np.float32)

# Define LAD model.
def LAD(alpha, beta, x_train):
        prediction = alpha + tf.matmul(x_train, beta)
        return prediction
```

The next steps are to define a loss function and perform minimization, which we do in Listing 6-18. We will use a mean absolute error (MAE) loss, since we're performing a LAD regression. We'll then instantiate an Adam() optimizer with default parameter values. Finally, we'll perform 1000 training iterations.

Listing 6-18. Define an MAE loss function and perform optimization

```
# Define number of observations.
N = len(x_train)

# Define function to compute MAE loss.
def maeLoss(alpha, beta, x_train, y_train):
        y_hat = LAD(alpha, beta, x_train)
        y_hat = tf.reshape(y_hat, (N,))
        return tf.losses.mae(y_train, y_hat)

# Instantiate optimizer.
opt = tf.optimizers.Adam()

# Perform optimization.
for i in range(1000):
        opt.minimize(lambda: maeLoss(alpha, beta,
        x_train, y_train),
        var_list = [alpha, beta])
```

Now that we've trained a model, we can feed arbitrary inputs into the LAD function, which will yield predicted values. We'll do that using x_train to generate predictions, y_pred, for y_train in Listing 6-19.

Listing 6-19. Generate predicted values from model

```
# Generate predicted values.
y_pred = LAD(alpha, beta, x_train)
```

We plot the predicted values against the true values in Figure 6-9. The constant term matches the mean return, and the predictions appear to capture the direction of most changes correctly; however, the model generally fails to explain much of the variation in the data.

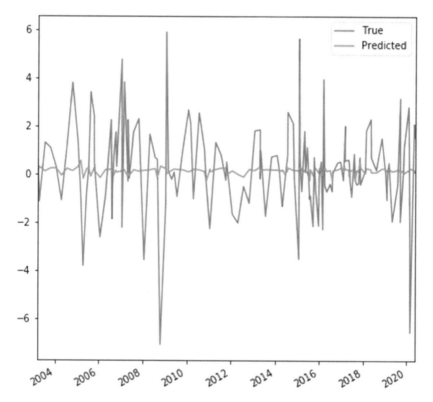

Figure 6-9. *True and predicted values of Apple stock returns*

There are several reasons that are unrelated to natural language processing that are likely to explain our inability to explain much of the variation in the data using the model. First, the 1-day time window could be too large and may capture developments unrelated to the announcement effect. Indeed, much of the literature in economics on the subject has moved to concentrating on narrower windows around announcements, such as 30 minutes. Second, we didn't include any non-text features in the regression, such as lagged returns, returns from the entire tech sector, or data releases from statistical agencies. And third, predicting surprise returns is challenging and even good models will typically fail to explain most of the variation in the data.

For the sake of this exercise, however, let's put all of that aside and consider how we might improve prediction purely from NLP on announcements. A good place to start might be to question whether we selected unigrams that contained meaningful content for explaining returns. Given that we uncritically accepted the 25 features selected by the CountVectorizer(), it is possible that a more thoughtful selection of features could lead to an improvement. Recall that we can extract the features from vectorizer using the get_feature_names() method. In Listing 6-20, we do this and then print the unigrams extracted from texts.

Listing 6-20. Generate predicted values from model

```
# Get feature names from vectorizer.
feature_names = vectorizer.get_feature_names()

# Print feature names.
print(feature_names)

['act', 'action', 'amend', 'amount', 'board',
'date', 'director', 'incom', 'law', 'made',
'make', 'net', 'note', 'offic', 'order',
'parti', 'price', 'product', 'quarter', 'refer',
'requir', 'respect', 'section', 'state', 'term']
```

Many terms, as we can see in Listing 6-20, appear to be neutral. Depending on how they are modified in the text, they could predict either a positive or a negative return. If the model were able to treat the uses in their proper contexts, it might assign a large magnitude to the correctly signed feature.

We might try to fix this by expanding the set of features, performing more extensive filtering to determine the features we include, or changing the model specification to allow for non-linearities, such as feature interactions. Since we have already covered cleaning and filtering, we'll focus on the expansion of features and the inclusion of non-linearities.

Given that the training set only contains 144 observations, we might be concerned that including more features will lead to training sample improvements, but through overfitting. This is a valid concern, and we will overcome it by using a penalized regression model. The penalty will be such that including more parameters with non-zero values will lower the value of the loss function. Thus, if the parameters do not provide considerable predictive value, we will zero them out or assign low magnitudes to them.

Gentzkow et al. (2019) define a general penalized estimator as the solution to the minimization problem in Equation 6-7.

Equation 6-7. The minimization problem for a penalized estimator.

$$\min\left\{l(\alpha,\beta)+\lambda\sum_{j}\kappa_{j}\left(\left|\beta_{j}\right|\right)\right\}$$

Note that $l(\alpha, \beta)$ is a loss function, such as the MAE loss for a linear regression, λ scales the magnitude of the penalty, and $\kappa_{j}(\cdot)$ is an increasing penalty function that could, in principle, differ by parameter; however, in practice, we will often assume it is identical for all regressors.

There are three types of penalized regression we will often encounter, each of which is defined by the associated choice of $\kappa(\cdot)$:

1. **LASSO regression**: The least absolute shrinkage and selection parameter (LASSO) model uses the L_1 norm of β, reducing κ to an absolute value or $|\beta_j|$ for all j. The functional form of the penalty in a LASSO regression will force certain parameter values to 0, yielding a sparse parameter vector.

2. **Ridge regression**: A ridge regression uses the L_2 norm of β, yielding $\kappa(\beta_j) = \beta_j^2$. Unlike a LASSO regression, a ridge regression will yield a dense representation of β with coefficients not set precisely to zero. Since the penalty term of a ridge regression is a convex function, it will yield a unique minimum.

3. **Elastic net regression**: An elastic net regression combines both the LASSO and ridge regression penalties. That is, $\kappa(\beta_j) = \kappa_1|\beta_j| + \kappa_2\beta_j^2$ for all j.

The minimization problems for LASSO, ridge, and elastic net regressions are given in Equations 6-8, 6-9, and 6-10, respectively.

Equation 6-8. The minimization problem for a LASSO regression.

$$\min\left\{l(\alpha,\beta) + \lambda\sum_j |\beta_j|\right\}$$

Equation 6-9. The minimization problem for a ridge regression.

$$\min\left\{l(\alpha,\beta) + \lambda\sum_j \beta_j^2\right\}$$

Equation 6-10. The minimization problem for an elastic net regression.

$$\min\left\{l(\alpha,\beta)+\lambda\sum_{j}\left[\kappa_1\left|\beta_j\right|+\kappa_2\beta_j^2\right]\right\}$$

We will return to the Apple stock returns prediction problem, but will now make use of a LASSO regression, which will yield a sparse coefficient vector. In our case, there were many neutral terms that likely added minimal value in a linear model, where they couldn't be modified by adjectives. By using a LASSO regression, we'll allow the model to decide whether to ignore them entirely by assigning a zero weight.

Before we modify the model, we'll first apply CountVectorizer() again, but this time, we'll construct a document-term matrix for 1000 terms, rather than 25. For the sake of brevity, we'll omit the details and will instead start at the end of the process, where feature_names contains 1000 elements and x_train has the shape (144, 1000).

Next, in Listing 6-21, we'll re-define beta; set the magnitude of the penalty, lam; and re-define the loss function, which we'll now call lassoLoss(). Notice that the only difference is that we've added a term that consists of lam, multiplied by the L_1 norm of beta. Beyond that, nothing else changed. We still use the LAD function to make predictions, just as we did with the linear regression model.

Listing 6-21. Convert a LAD regression into a LASSO regression

```
# Re-define coefficient vector.
beta = tf.random.normal([1000,1], stddev=1.0)

# Set value of lambda parameter.
lam = tf.constant(0.10, tf.float32)

# Modify the loss function.
def lassoLoss(alpha, beta, x_train, y_train,
lam = lam):
        y_hat = LAD(alpha, beta, x_train)
```

```
y_hat = tf.reshape(y_hat, (N,))
loss = tf.losses.mae(y_train, y_hat) +
lam * tf.norm(beta, 1)
return loss
```

In Listing 6-22, we'll repeat the steps to train the model using the modified loss function and generate predictions on the training set.

Listing 6-22. Train a LASSO model

```
# Perform optimization.
for i in range(1000):
        opt.minimize(lambda: lassoLoss(alpha, beta,
        x_train, y_train),
        var_list = [alpha, beta])

# Generate predicted values.
y_pred = LAD(alpha, beta, x_train)
```

Now that we have the predicted values from the LASSO model, we can perform a comparison with the true returns. Figure 6-10 depicts this comparison, providing an update to Figure 6-9, which conducted the same exercise, but for the LAD model without a penalty term and with only 25 features.

We can see that performance has substantially improved under the LASSO model with 1000 features; however, we might worry that the penalty magnitude we selected wasn't sufficiently severe and that the model is overfitting. To evaluate this, we can adjust lam to higher values and check the model's performance. Furthermore, we can perform cross-validation using a test set; however, this will be somewhat more challenging in a time series context with only 144 observations.

For now, we recall that a LASSO regression returns a sparse coefficient vector and will examine how many coefficients have non-zero values. Figure 6-11 plots the histogram of the coefficient magnitudes. From this, we can see that over 800 features were assigned values of approximately zero. While we still have enough features to be concerned about overfitting, this is less concerning, given that most of the 1000 features were ignored by the model as a consequence of the penalty function.

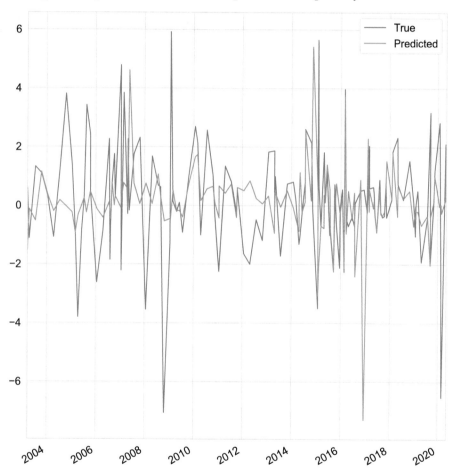

Figure 6-10. *True and predicted values of Apple stock returns using a LASSO model*

We've now seen that we can make use of additional features in a regression by employing a form of regularization (i.e., a penalty function). The penalty function prevents us from simply adding more parameters to improve fit. Doing this will increase the penalty, which will force parameter values to justify their inclusion in the model by substantially improving fit. This also means that we'll be able to include many more features and allow the model to sort out which should be assigned non-zero magnitudes.

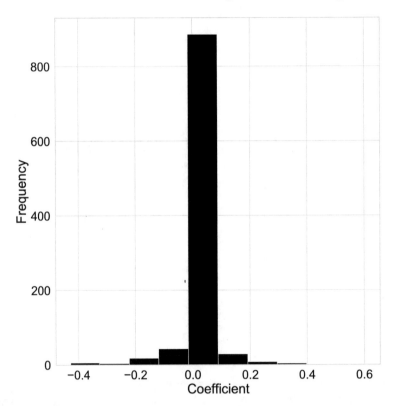

Figure 6-11. *True and predicted values of Apple stock returns using a LASSO model*

We mentioned earlier that using a LASSO model allowed us to expand the feature set, which was one way to improve performance. Another option we mentioned was to allow for dependence between words. We can do this by permitting non-linearities in the model. In principle, we could engineer these features. We could also make use of any non-linear model to perform such a task. Furthermore, we could couple this with a penalty term, just as we did with the LASSO model, to avoid overfitting.

While these are viable strategies and can be implemented with relative ease in TensorFlow, we'll instead make use of a more general option: deep learning. We have already discussed deep learning in the context of images in Chapter 5, but we return to it here because it provides a flexible and potent modeling strategy for most text regression problems.

The distinction between "deep learning" (e.g., neural networks) and "shallow learning" (e.g., linear regression) is that shallow learning models require us to perform feature engineering. For instance, in a linear text regression, we must decide which features are in the document-term matrix (e.g., unigrams or bigrams). We must also decide how many features to allow in the model. The model will determine which are most important for explaining variation in the data, but we must choose which to include.

Recall, again, that this was not the case with images. We input pixel values into convolutional neural networks and those networks identified successive layers of increasingly complex features. First, the networks identified edges. In the next layer, they identified corners. Each successive layer built on the previous one to identify new features that were useful for the classification task.

Deep learning can also be used in the same way for text. Rather than deciding how terms relate to each other through the use of feature engineering, we can allow a neural network to uncover these relationships for us. Just as we did in Chapter 5, we'll make use of the high-level Keras API in TensorFlow.

In Listing 6-23, we define a neural network with dense layers that we'll use to predict stock returns for Apple. There is only one substantive difference between this network and the dense layer-based image networks we defined in Chapter 5: the use of dropout layers. Here, we have included two such layers, each of which has a rate of 0.20. During the training phase, this will randomly drop 20% of the nodes, forcing the model to learn robust relationships, rather than using the high number of model parameters to memorize output values.[8]

In addition to this, notice that we've defined the model to accept an input with 1000 feature columns, which is the number we've included in our document-term matrix. We also use relu activation functions for all hidden layers. Additionally, we use a linear activation function in the outputs layer, since we have a continuous target (stock returns).

Listing 6-23. Define a deep learning model for text using the Keras API

```
import tensorflow as tf

# Define input layer.
inputs = tf.keras.Input(shape=(1000,))

# Define dense layer.
dense0 = tf.keras.layers.Dense(64,
        activation="relu")(inputs)

# Define dropout layer.
dropout0 = tf.keras.layers.Dropout(0.20)(dense0)

# Define dense layer.
dense1 = tf.keras.layers.Dense(32,
        activation="relu")(dropout0)

# Define dropout layer.
dropout1 = tf.keras.layers.Dropout(0.20)(dense1)
```

---

[8]While we did not use dropout layers in the dense neural network models we discussed in Chapter 5, we will typically make use of them in image-related problems to perform regularization.

```
# Define output layer.
outputs = tf.keras.layers.Dense(1,
        activation="linear")(dropout1)
```

```
# Define model using inputs and outputs.
model = tf.keras.Model(inputs=inputs,
        outputs=outputs)
```

The architecture we've selected will require us to train many parameters. Recall that we can check this using the summary() method of a keras model, which we do in Listing 6-24. In total, the model has 66,177 trainable parameters.

With the LASSO model, we were already concerned about overfitting, even though the model only had 1001 parameters and the penalty function effectively forced 850 of them to be zero. We now have a model with 66,177 parameters, which should make us even more concerned about overfitting. This is why we've used a form of regularization (dropout) and why we'll also use a training and validation sample.

Listing 6-24. Summarize the architecture of a Keras model

```
# Print model architecture.
print(model.summary())
```

Layer (type)	Output Shape	Param #
input_3 (InputLayer)	[(None, 1000)]	0
dense_5 (Dense)	(None, 64)	64064
dropout_1 (Dropout)	(None, 64)	0
dense_6 (Dense)	(None, 32)	2080

dropout_2 (Dropout)	(None, 32)	0
dense_7 (Dense)	(None, 1)	33

```
=====================================================
Total params: 66,177
Trainable params: 66,177
Non-trainable params: 0
```

Recall that, in addition to defining a model, we'll need to compile it. We'll do that and train the model in Listing 6-25. Notice that we use the Adam optimizer, the mean absolute error (MAE) loss, and a validation split of 30% of the sample. We'll also use 20 epochs.

Listing 6-25. Compile and train the Keras model

```
# Compile the model.
model.compile(loss="mae", optimizer="adam")

# Train the model.
model.fit(x_train, y_train, epochs=20,
batch_size=32, validation_split = 0.30)

Epoch 1/20
100/100 [==============================] - 0s 5ms/sample -
loss: 2.6408 - val_loss: 2.5870

...


Epoch 10/20
100/100 [==============================] - 0s 117us/sample -
loss: 1.7183 - val_loss: 1.3514

...
```

```
Epoch 15/20
100/100 [==============================] - 0s 110us/sample -
loss: 1.6641 - val_loss: 1.2014

...

Epoch 20/20
100/100 [==============================] - 0s 113us/sample -
loss: 1.5932 - val_loss: 1.2536
```

As we can see in Listing 6-25, training initially reduces the loss for both the training and validation split; however, by the 15th epoch, the loss on the training split continues to decline while the loss on the validation split begins to increase slightly. This suggests that we might be starting to overfit.

Figure 6-12 repeats the prediction exercise for the returns, using the predict() method of model. While the predictions appear to be an improvement over the linear and LASSO regressions, it is likely that part of this gain is attributable to overfitting.

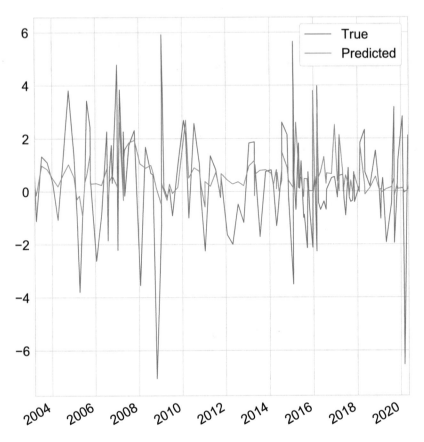

Figure 6-12. *True and predicted values of Apple stock returns using a neural network*

If we want to reduce the risk of overfitting even further, we could increase the rates in our two dropout layers or decrease the number of nodes in the hidden layers.

Finally, note that making use of word sequences, rather than ignoring the order in which words appear, can lead to substantial improvements in model performance. This will require the use of recurrent neural networks and their variants, including the long short-term memory (LSTM) model. Since we will use the same family of models to perform time series analysis, we'll delay their introduction to Chapter 7.

Text Classification

In the previous section, we discussed how TensorFlow could be used to perform text regression. Once we had constructed the document-term matrix, we saw that it was relatively simple to perform a LAD regression and a LASSO regression and to train a neural network. In some cases, however, we will have a discrete target and will want to perform classification instead. Fortunately, TensorFlow provides us with the flexibility to perform classification tasks by making minor adjustments to models we have already defined.

Listing 6-26, for instance, shows how we can define a logistic model to perform classification. We'll assume we're using the same document-term matrix, x_train, but have now replaced y_train with hand-classified labels that we produced by reading the individual 8-K filings and then classifying them as "positive" or "negative" based on our perception of the content. A positive score will be indicated by a 0 and a negative by a 1.

Listing 6-26. Define a logistic model to perform classification in TensorFlow

```
# Define a logistic model.
def logitModel(x_train, beta, alpha):
        prediction = tf.nn.softmax(tf.matmul(
        x_train, beta) + alpha)
        return prediction
```

In addition to the changes to model definition, we'll also need to modify the loss function to use the binary cross-entropy loss, which we do in Listing 6-27. After that, we'll only need to change the function handle when we perform optimization. Everything else will work as it did for the linear regression example.

Listing 6-27. Define a loss function for the logistic model to perform classification in TensorFlow

```
# Define number of observations.
N = len(x_train)
```

```
# Define function to compute MAE loss.
def logisticLoss(alpha, beta, x_train, y_train):
        y_hat = LogitModel(alpha, beta, x_train)
        y_hat = tf.reshape(y_hat, (N,))
        loss = tf.losses.binary_crossentropy(
        y_train, y_hat)
        return loss
```

Similarly, if we want to perform classification with the neural network we defined in Listing 6-23, we'll only need to modify two lines of code, as is shown in Listing 6-28.

Listing 6-28. Modify a neural network to perform classification

```
# Change output layer to use sigmoid activation.
outputs = tf.keras.layers.Dense(1,
        activation="sigmoid")(dropout1)
```

```
# Use categorical cross entropy loss in compilation.
model.compile(loss="binary_crossentropy", optimizer="adam")
```

We changed two things: the activation function used in the outputs layer and loss function. First, we needed to use a sigmoid activation function, since we're performing classification with two classes. And second, we used the binary_crossentropy loss, which is standard for classification problems with two classes. If we instead had a problem with multiple classes, we'd use a softmax activation function and a categorical_crossentropy loss.

For an extended overview of classification with neural networks, see Chapter 5, which covers similar material, but in the context of image classification problems. Additionally, for information about sequential models, which are commonly used for text classification problems, see Chapter 7, which makes use of the same models for time series analysis.

Summary

This chapter provided an extended overview of how text analysis is currently used in economics and finance and how it might be used in the future. The part of the process that is likely to be least familiar for economists is the data cleaning and preparation step, which transforms text into numerical data. The simplest version of this was the bag-of-words model, which stripped words from their context and summarized the content of a document using word counts alone. While this method is relatively simple to implement, it is powerful and remains one of the more commonly used methods in economics.

Dictionary-based methods also work on the bag-of-words model. However, rather than counting all terms in a document, we instead construct a dictionary that measures a latent variable. Such methods are frequently used in text analysis in economics, but are not always the best tool for many research applications, as Gentzkow et al. (2019) discuss. The EPU index (Baker, Bloom and Davis 2016) is arguably an ideal use case for dictionary-based methods in economics, since the measure is interesting for theoretical purposes, but is unlikely to emerge as a dominant topic from a corpus.

We also discussed word embeddings and saw how to implement topic models, text regression models, and text classification models. This included an overview of using deep learning models for text. We did, however, defer the discussion of sequential models to Chapter 7, which uses them for time series analysis.

Bibliography

Acosta, M. 2019. "A New Measure of Central Bank Transparency and Implications for the Effectiveness of Monetary Policy." *Working Paper.*

Angelico, C., J. Marcucci, M. Miccoli, and F. Quarta. 2018. "Can We Measure Inflation Expectations Using Twitter?" *Working Paper.*

Apel, M., and M. Blix Grimaldi. 2014. "How Informative Are Central Bank Minutes?" *Review of Economics* 65 (1): 53–76.

Ardizzi, G., S. Emiliozzi, J. Marcucci, and L. Monteforte. 2020. "News and Consumer Card Payments." *Bank of Italy Economic Working Paper.*

Armelius, H., C. Bertsch, I. Hull, and X. Zhang. 2020. "Spread the Word: International Spillovers from Central Bank Communication." *Journal of International Money and Finance* (103).

Athey, S., and G.W. Imbens. 2019. "Machine Learning Methods that Economists Should Know About." *Annual Review of Economics* 11: 685–725.

Baker, S.R., N. Bloom, and S.J. Davis. 2016. "Measuring Economic Policy Uncertainty." *Quarterly Journal of Economics* 131 (4): 1593–1636.

Bertsch, C., I. Hull, Y. Qi, and X. Zhang. 2020. "Bank Misconduct and Online Lending." *Journal of Banking and Finance* 116.

Blei, D.M., A.Y. Ng, and M.I. Jordan. 2003. "Latent Dirichlet Allocation." *Journal of Machine Learning Research* 3: 993–1022.

Blei, D.M., and J.D. Lafferty. 2006. "Dynamic Topic Models." *ICML '06: Proceedings of the 23rd international conference on Machine Learning.* 113–120.

Bloom, N., S.R. Baker, S.J. Davis, and K. Kost. 2019. "Policy News and Stock Market Volatility." *Mimeo.*

Born, B., B. Ehrmann, and M. Fratzcher. 2013. "Central Bank Communication on Financial Stability." *The Economic Journal* 124.

Cerchiello, P., G. Nicola, S. Ronnqvist, and P. Sarlin. 2017. "Deep Learning Bank Distress from News and Numerical Financial Data." *arXiv.*

Chahrour, R., K. Nimark, and S. Pitschner. 2019. "Sectoral Media Focus and Aggregate Fluctuations." *Working Paper.*

Correa, R., K. Garud, J.M. Londono, and N. Mislang. 2020. "Sentiment in Central Banks' Financial Stability Reports." *International Finance Discussion Papers 1203, Board of Governors of the Federal Reserve System (U.S.).*

Dieng, A.B., F.J.R. Ruiz, and D.M. Blei. 2019. " The Dynamic Embedded Topic Model." *arXiv preprint.*

Gentzkow, M., B. Kelly, and M. Taddy. 2019. "Text as Data." *Journal of Economic Literature* 57 (3): 535–574.

Hansen, S., and M. McMahon. 2016. "Shocking Language: Understanding the Macroeconomic Effects of Central Bank Communication." *Journal of International Economics* 99.

Hansen, S., M. McMahon, and A. Prat. 2018. "Transparency and Deliberation within the FOMC: A Computational Linguistics Approach." *Quarterly Journal of Economics* 133: 801–870.

Harris, Z. 1954. "Distributional Structure." *Word* 10 (2/3): 146–162.

Hollrah, C.A., S.A. Sharpe, and N.R. Sinha. 2018. "What's the Story? A New Perspective on the Value of Economic Forecasts." *Finance and Economics Discussion Series 2017-107, Board of Governors of Federal Reserve System (U.S.).*

Kalamara, E., A. Turrell, C. Redl, G. Kapetanios, and S. Kapadia. 2020. "Making Text Count: Economic Forecasting Using Newspaper Text." *Bank of England Staff Working Paper No. 865.*

LeNail, A. 2019. "NN-SVG: Publication-Ready Neural Network Architecture Schematics." *Journal of Open Source Software* 4 (33).

Loughran, T., and B. McDonald. 2011. "When is a Liability Not a Liability? Textual Analysis, Dictionaries, and 10-Ks." *Journal of Finance* 66 (1): 35–65.

Mikolov, T., K. Chen, G. Corrado, and J. Dean. 2013. "Efficient Estimation of Word Representations in Vector Space." (arXiv).

Nimark, K.P., and S. Pitschner. 2019. "News Media and Delegated Information Choice." *Journal of Economic Theory* 181: 160–196.

Pennington, J., R. Socher, and C. Manning. 2014. "GloVe: Global Vectors for Word Representation." *Proceedings of the 2014 Conference on Empirical Methods in Natural Language Processing (EMNLP).* Doha: Association for Computational Linguistics. 1532–1543.

Pitschner, S. 2020. "How Do Firms Set Prices? Narrative Evidence from Corporate Filings." *European Economic Review* 124.

Porter, M.F. 1980. "An Algorithm for Suffix Stripping." *Program* 14 (3): 130–137.

Romer, C.D., and D.H. Romer. 2004. "A New Measure of Monetary Shocks: Derivation and Implications." *American Economic Review* 94: 1055–1084.

Salton, G., and M.J. and McGill. 1983. *Introduction to Modern Information Retrieval.* New York, NY: McGraw-Hill.

Shapiro, A.H., and D. Wilson. 2019. "Taking the Fed at its Word: A New Approach to Estimating Central Bank Objectives using Text Analysis." *Federal Reserve Bank of San Francisco Working Paper 2019-02.*

Shiller, R.J. 2017. "Narrative Economics." *American Economic Review* 107 (4): 967–1004.

Tetlock, P. 2007. "Giving Content to Investor Sentiment: The Role of Media in the Stock Market. " *Journal of Finance* 62 (3): 1139–1168.

CHAPTER 7

Time Series

Empirical work in economics is typically concerned with causal inference and hypothesis testing, whereas machine learning is centered around prediction. There is, however, a clear intersection between objectives when it comes to forecasting in economics and finance. Consequently, there has been increasing interest in using methods from machine learning to produce and evaluate economic forecasts.

In Chapter 2, we discussed Coulombe et al. (2019), which evaluated the usefulness of machine learning for time series econometrics. They identified non-linear models, regularization, cross-validation, and alternative loss functions as potentially valuable tools that could be imported for use in time series econometric contexts.

In this chapter, we'll discuss the value of machine learning for time series forecasting. Since we'll concentrate on a TensorFlow implementation, our focus will diverge from Coulombe et al. (2019) and instead concentrate on deep learning models. In particular, we will make use of neural network models with specialized layers that are used to process sequential data.

Throughout the chapter, we'll build on a forecasting exercise (Nakamura 2005), which was one of the first applications of neural networks in time series econometrics. Nakamura (2005) used a dense neural network to demonstrate gains over a univariate autoregressive model for forecasting inflation.

© Isaiah Hull 2021
I. Hull, *Machine Learning for Economics and Finance in TensorFlow 2*,
https://doi.org/10.1007/978-1-4842-6373-0_7

Sequential Models of Machine Learning

Thus far, we have discussed several specialized layers for neural networks, but have not explained how to handle sequential data. As we will see, there are robust frameworks for handling such data in neural networks, which were largely developed for the purpose of natural language processing (NLP), but are equally useful in time series contexts. We will also briefly return to their use in NLP contexts at the end of the chapter.

Dense Neural Networks

We have already used dense neural networks in Chapters 5 and 6; however, we have not explained how they can be adapted for use with sequential data. So far, all of our uses of neural networks involved exercises that lacked or did not exploit a time dimension.

We'll start this section by examining how to make use of sequence data to predict quarterly inflation in a setting similar to Nakamura (2005). To conduct this exercise, we'll use quarterly inflation for the United States over the period between 1947:Q2 and 2020:Q2,[1] which is plotted in Figure 7-1. Additionally, following Nakamura (2005), we'll consider univariate models, where we do not include any additional explanatory variables beyond lags of inflation.

When we worked with text and image data in earlier chapters, we often needed to perform pre-processing tasks to transform the raw inputs into something suitable for use in a neural network. With sequential data, we will also need to transform the time series into sequences of fixed length.

---

[1]The Consumer Price Index (CPI) and measures of inflation derived from it are computed by the Bureau of Labor Statistics: www.bls.gov. The series we use in this exercise is available under ID number CUSR0000SA0 on the BLS's website.

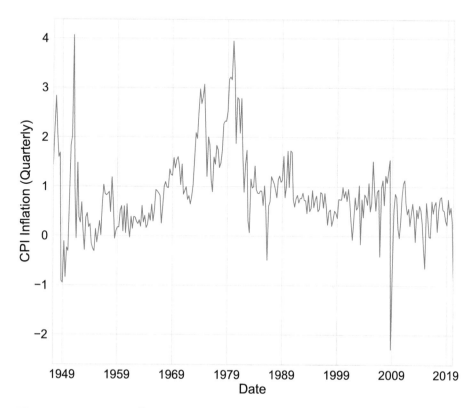

Figure 7-1. *CPI inflation over the period between 1947:Q2 and 2020:Q2. Source: US Bureau of Labor Statistics*

We'll start by deciding the sequence length, which is the number of lags we'll use as inputs to the neural network. If, for instance, we select a sequence length of three, then the network will predict inflation in period *t+h* using the realizations in periods *t*, *t-1*, and *t-3*. Figure 7-2 illustrates the pre-processing step, where we split a single time series into overlapping sequences of three consecutive observations. The left side of the diagram shows the original input series. The right side shows two examples of sequences. The dashed rectangles connect the sequences with the value they would predict if we use a single quarter as the forecast horizon (*h=1*).

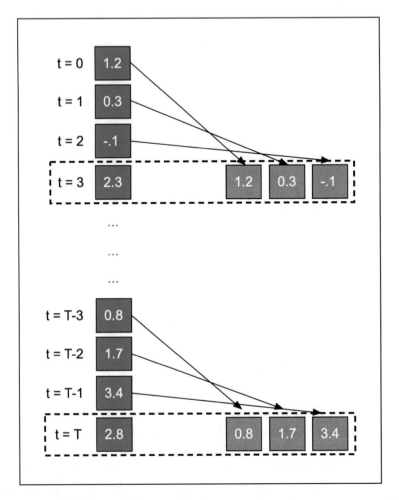

Figure 7-2. *Division of time series into overlapping sequences of three consecutive observations*

We'll assume the data has been downloaded and saved as `inflation.csv` in a directory located at `data_path`. We'll start by loading it with `pandas` in Listing 7-1 and then converting it into a `numpy array`. Next, we'll define a generator object using `TimeseriesGenerator()` from the `tensorflow.keras.preprocessing.sequence` submodule. As inputs, it will take the network's features and target, the length of the sequence, and the batch size.

In this case, we'll perform a univariate regression, where the feature and target are both `inflation`. We'll use a sequence length of 4, which we can set using the `length` parameter. Finally, we'll use a `batch_size` of 12, which means that our generator will yield 12 sequences and 12 target values each iteration.

Listing 7-1. Instantiate a sequence generator for inflation

```
import numpy as np
import tensorflow as tf
from tensorflow.keras.preprocessing.sequence import
TimeseriesGenerator

# Set data path.
data_path = '../data/chapter7/'

# Load data.
inflation = pd.read_csv(data_path+'inflation.csv')

# Convert to numpy array.
inflation = np.array(inflation['Inflation'])

# Instantiate time series generator.
generator = TimeseriesGenerator(inflation, inflation,
    length = 4, batch_size = 12)
```

We now have a generator object that we can use to create batches of data. A Keras model can use the generator, rather than data, as an input. In Listing 7-2, we'll define a model and then train it using the generator. Note that we use a `Sequential()` model. This enables us to construct a model by stacking layers in sequence and does not have anything to do with the use of sequential data.

We first instantiate the model using the sequential API. We then set the number of input nodes to match the sequence length, define a single hidden layer with two nodes, and define an output layer that uses a linear activation function, since we have a continuous target. Finally, we'll compile the model using the mean squared error loss and an adam optimizer.

When we trained models previously, we used np.array() or tf. constant() objects as input data. In Listing 7-2, we've used a generator, which will require us to use the fit_generator() method, rather than fit(), as we have previously.

Listing 7-2. Train a neural network using generated sequences

```
# Define sequential model.
model = tf.keras.models.Sequential()

# Add input layer.
model.add(tf.keras.Input(shape=(4,)))

# Define dense layer.
model.add(tf.keras.layers.Dense(2, activation="relu"))

# Define output layer.
model.add(tf.keras.layers.Dense(1, activation="linear"))

# Compile the model.
model.compile(loss="mse", optimizer="adam")

# Train the model.
model.fit_generator(generator, epochs=100)

Train for 25 steps
Epoch 1/100
25/25 [==============================] - loss: 4.3247
```

```
...
Epoch 100/100
25/25 [==============================] - loss: 0.3816
```

Between epochs 1 and 100, the model makes considerable progress in
reducing mean squared error, lowering it from 4.32 to 0.38. Importantly,
we have not used regularization, such as dropout, and have not created
a test sample split, so it is possible that there is substantial overfitting.
In Listing 7-3, we use the summary() method of model to examine its
architecture. We can see that it has only 13 trainable parameters, which is
small in comparison to the models we have worked with previously.

Listing 7-3. Summarize model architecture

```
# Print model architecture.
print(model.summary())
```

Layer (type)	Output Shape	Param #
dense_1 (Dense)	(None, 2)	10
dense_1 (Dense)	(None, 1)	3

```
Total params: 13
Trainable params: 13
Non-trainable params: 0
```

We can now use model.predict_generator(generator) to generate
a series of predicted values for inflation. Figure 7-3 plots the true values of
inflation against our model's prediction. While model performance looks
compelling, we have not yet taken the proper precautions to ensure that
we are not overfitting.

In Figure 7-4, we examine whether overfitting is an issue for this by using the post-2000 period as the test sample. To do this, we need to construct a separate generator, which only uses the pre-2000 values to train. We then use our original generator to make predictions for the entire sample, including the post-2000 values.

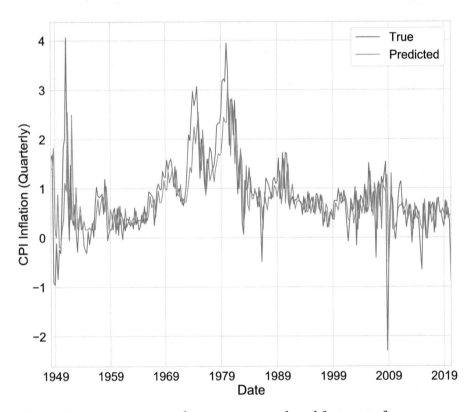

Figure 7-3. *Dense network one-quarter-ahead forecast of inflation*

We can see that Figure 7-4 does not look substantially different from Figure 7-3 post 2000. In particular, there does not appear to be a performance degradation after 2000, which is what we would expect if the model were overfitting on the pre-2000 data. This is not too surprising, since the model has relatively few parameters, making it more difficult to overfit.

In the remainder of this section, we will make use of the same pre-processing steps, but will add specialized layers to our model that are designed to handle input sequences. These layers will exploit the temporal information encoded in the lag structure, rather than treating all features the same, as we are currently doing with the dense model.

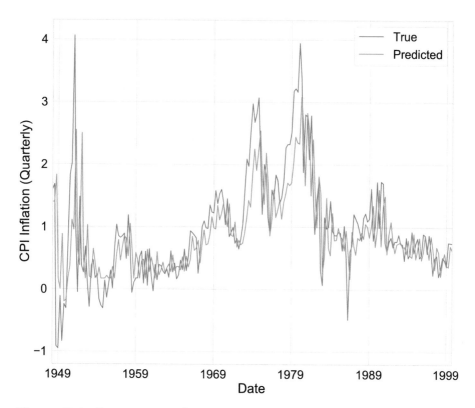

Figure 7-4. *Dense network one-quarter-ahead forecast of inflation in model trained on data from 1947 to 2000*

Recurrent Neural Networks

A recurrent neural network accepts a sequence of inputs and processes them using a combination of dense layers and specialized recurrent layers

(Rumelhart et al. 1986).[2] This sequence of inputs could be word vectors, word embeddings, musical notes, or, as we will consider in this chapter, inflation measurements at different points in time.

We will follow the treatment of recurrent neural networks (RNNs) given in Goodfellow et al. (2017). The authors describe a recurrent layer as consisting of cells that each take an input value, $x(t)$, and a state, $h(t-1)$, and produce an output value, $o(t)$. The process by which the output value is produced for a recurrent cell is given by Equations 7-1, 7-2, and 7-3.

In Equation 7-1, we take the state of the series, $h(t-1)$, and multiply it by weights, W. We then take the input value, $x(t)$, and multiply it by a separate set of weights, U. Finally, we sum both terms together, along with a bias term, b.

Equation 7-1. Performing the multiplication step for an RNN cell.

$$a(t) = b + Wh(t-1) + Ux(t)$$

We next take the output of the multiplication step and pass it to a hyperbolic tangent activation function, as shown in Equation 7-2. The output of this step is the updated state of the system, $h(t)$.

Equation 7-2. Applying an activation function in an RNN cell.

$$h(t) = tanh(a(t))$$

In the final step, given in Equation 7-3, we multiply the updated state by a separate set of weights, V, and add a bias term.

Equation 7-3. Generating the output value from an RNN cell.

$$o(t) = c + Vh(t)$$

In the example we're working with in this chapter, inflation is the only feature. This means that $x(t)$ is a scalar and W, U, and V are also scalars.

---

[2]In a natural language processing context, RNNs will also often contain an embedding layer.

Additionally, notice that these weights are shared for all time periods, which reduces the model size relative to what would be needed with a dense network. In our case, we will only need five parameters for a layer with one RNN cell.

Figure 7-5 provides a complete illustration of an RNN. The pink nodes indicate input values, which are lags of inflation in our example. The orange node indicates the target variable, which is inflation in the following quarter. The blue nodes are individual RNN cells, which form an RNN layer. The network we've illustrated has four inputs and two RNN cells.

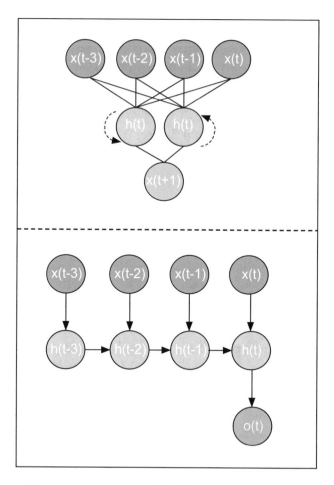

Figure 7-5. *Illustration of a RNN (top) and unrolled RNN cell (bottom)*

The bottom panel of Figure 7-5 shows an "unrolled" RNN cell, where the cell's iterative structure has been broken down into a sequence. In each individual step, the state is combined with an input to yield the next state. The final step yields an output, $o(t)$, which is an input to a final dense layer – along with the outputs of the other cells – that yields a prediction for inflation one quarter ahead.

We've now seen that an RNN makes use of sequential data by retaining a state, which it updates at each step of the sequence. It also reduces the number of parameters through the use of weight sharing. Furthermore, since it is not necessary to apply time-specific weights, it will also be possible to use RNN cells with sequences of arbitrary and variable length.

We have now discussed how an RNN differs from a dense network. Let's construct a simple RNN for our inflation forecasting example. We'll start by loading the data in Listing 7-4. Here, we've repeated the steps from Listing 7-1, but with two important differences. First, we use `np.expand_dims()` to add a dimension to the `inflation` array. This will allow our time series data to conform to the input shape requirements of RNN cells in Keras. And second, we've defined a train generator, which exclusively uses data prior to 2000 by slicing the `inflation` array, retaining only the first 211 observations.

Once we have loaded and prepared our data, the next step is to define the model, which we do in Listing 7-5. As we can see, the model requires no more lines of code than did the dense network we used to predict inflation. All we do is define a sequential model, add an RNN layer, and define a dense output layer with a `linear` activation function.

Notice that the `SimpleRNN` layer we used required two arguments: the number of RNN cells and the shape of the input layer. For the first argument, we selected two cells to keep the network simple at the potential risk of underfitting the data. We needed to provide the second argument because we defined the RNN layer as the first in our network. We set the input_shape to be (4, 1) because the sequence length is four and the number of features is one.

Listing 7-4. Instantiate a sequence generator for inflation

```
import numpy as np
import tensorflow as tf
from tensorflow.keras.preprocessing.sequence import
TimeseriesGenerator

# Load data.
inflation = pd.read_csv(data_path+'inflation.csv')

# Convert to numpy array.
inflation = np.array(inflation['Inflation'])

# Add dimension.
inflation = np.expand_dims(inflation, 1)

# Instantiate time series generator.
train_generator = TimeseriesGenerator(
        inflation[:211], inflation[:211],
        length = 4, batch_size = 12)
```

Listing 7-5. Define an RNN model in Keras.

```
# Define sequential model.
model = tf.keras.models.Sequential()

# Define recurrent layer.
model.add(tf.keras.layers.SimpleRNN(2, input_shape=(4, 1)))

# Define output layer.
model.add(tf.keras.layers.Dense(1, activation="linear"))
```

The final steps are to compile the model and to use the fit_ generator() method to train it, along with the train_generator we constructed earlier. As we can see in Listing 7-6, the model achieves a lower mean squared error (0.2594) than we were able to achieve in the dense network with 100 epochs of training. Additionally, as shown in Figure 7-6, test sample performance (post-2000) does not appear to degrade in any noticeable way.

Listing 7-6. Compile and train an RNN model in Keras

```
# Compile the model.
model.compile(loss="mse", optimizer="adam")

# Fit model to data using generator.
model.fit_generator(train_generator, epochs=100)

Epoch 1/100
18/18 [==============================] - 1s 31ms/step - loss:
0.9206

...

Epoch 100/100
18/18 [==============================] - 0s 2ms/step - loss:
0.2594
```

We also mentioned that the RNN model has the benefit of requiring fewer parameter values than a dense network. When we stepped through the operations performed in an RNN cell, we saw that only five parameters were needed for a layer with a single RNN cell. In Listing 7-7, we'll use the summary() method of model to explore the model's architecture. We can see that it has eight parameters in the RNN layer and three in the dense output layer. In total, it has 11 parameters, which is fewer than the dense network we used earlier. The contrast is not particularly large here, of course, since both networks are quite small.

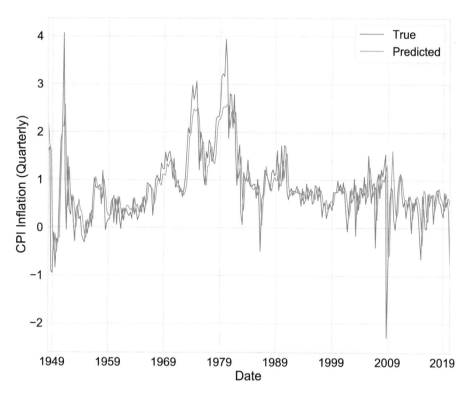

Figure 7-6. *One-quarter-ahead forecast of inflation for RNN model trained on data from 1947 to 2000*

Listing 7-7. Summarize RNN architecture in a Keras model

```
# Print model summary.
print(model.summary())
```

Layer (type)	Output Shape	Param #
simple_rnn_1 (SimpleRNN)	(None, 2)	8

dense_1 (Dense)	(None, 1)	3

===

Total params: 11
Trainable params: 11
Non-trainable params: 0

In practice, we will not typically use an RNN model without modification. At a minimum, there are at least two things we will want to consider adjusting. The first is related to a technical problem – the "vanishing gradient problem" – which makes it challenging to train deep networks. This is also a problem with the original RNN model and long sequences of data. Another problem with the original RNN model is that it does not allow for the possibility that objects far apart in time or within the sequence are more closely related than objects nearer together. In the following two subsections, we'll make some minor adjustments to the RNN model that will allow us to deal with both problems.

Long Short-Term Memory (LSTM)

The first problem with RNNs is that they suffer from the vanishing gradient problem when long sequences of data are used as inputs. The most effective solution to this problem is to make use of a gated RNN cell. There are two such cells that are commonly used: (1) long short-term memory (LSTM) and (2) gated recurrent units (GRUs). We will concentrate on the former in this subsection.

The LSTM model was introduced by Hochreiter and Schmidhuber (1997) and functions through the use of operators that limit the follow of information in long sequences. We will again follow Goodfellow et al. (2017) in describing the operations performed in an LSTM.

Equations 7-4, 7-5, and 7-6 define the "forget gate," "external input gate," and "output gate," all of which play a role in controlling the follow of information through an LSTM cell.

Equation 7-4. Definition of trainable weights called forget gates.

$$f(t) = \sigma\left(b^f + W^f h(t-1) + U^f x(t)\right)$$

Equation 7-5. Definition of trainable weights called external input gates.

$$g(t) = \sigma\left(b^g + W^g h(t-1) + U^g x(t)\right)$$

Equation 7-6. Definition of trainable weights called output gates.

$$q(t) = \sigma\left(b^q + W^q h(t-1) + U^q x(t)\right)$$

Notice that each gate has the same functional form and uses a sigmoid activation function, but has its own separate weights and biases. This allows the gating procedure to be learned, rather than applied from a fixed rule.

The internal states are updated using the expression in Equation 7-7, where the forget gate, external input gate, input sequence, and state are all applied.

Equation 7-7. Expression for updating the internal state.

$$s(t) = f^t s(t-1) + g(t)\sigma\left(b + Wh(t-1) + Ux(t)\right)$$

Finally, we update the hidden state, making use of the internal state and the output gate, as in Equation 7-8.

Equation 7-8. Expression for updating the hidden state.

$$h(t) = tanh(s(t))q(t)$$

While the use of gates increases the number of parameters in the model, it also yields substantial improvements in the handling of long sequences in many practical applications. For this reason, we will typically use an LSTM model as the baseline in time series analysis, rather than the original RNN model.

In Listing 7-8, we define and train an LSTM model using 100 epochs. The only difference was that we used tf.keras.layers.LSTM(), rather than tf.keras.layers.SimpleRNN(). We can see that mean squared error is higher for the LSTM than it was for the RNN after 100 epochs. This is because the model must train more weights, which will require additional training epochs. Additionally, the LSTM is likely to be most useful in settings with longer sequences.

Listing 7-8. Train an LSTM model in Keras

```
# Define sequential model.
model = tf.keras.models.Sequential()

# Define recurrent layer.
model.add(tf.keras.layers.LSTM(2, input_shape=(4, 1)))

# Define output layer.
model.add(tf.keras.layers.Dense(1, activation="linear"))

# Compile the model.
model.compile(loss="mse", optimizer="adam")

# Train the model.
model.fit_generator(train_generator, epochs=100)
```

```
Epoch 1/100
18/18 [==============================] - 1s 62ms/step - loss:
3.1697

...

Epoch 100/100
18/18 [==============================] - 0s 3ms/step - loss:
0.5873
```

Finally, in Listing 7-9, we summarize the model's architecture. When we discussed the additional operations an LSTM cell required, we mentioned that it introduced a forget gate, an external input gate, and an output gate. All of these required their own set of parameters. As we can see from Listing 7-9, the LSTM layer uses 32 parameters, which is four times as many as the RNN.

Listing 7-9. Summarize LSTM architecture in a Keras model

```
# Print model architecture.
print(model.summary())
```

Layer (type)	Output Shape	Param #
lstm_1 (LSTM)	(None, 2)	32
dense_1 (Dense)	(None, 1)	3

```
Total params: 35
Trainable params: 35
Non-trainable params: 0
```

Intermediate Hidden States

By convention, the LSTM model only makes use of the final value of the hidden state. In Figure 7-5, for instance, the model uses $h(t)$ and not $h(t-1)$, $h(t-2)$, and $h(t-3)$, even though we computed them. Recent work, however, has shown that using the intermediate hidden states can lead to considerable improvements in modeling long-term dependencies, especially in natural language processing problems (Zhou et al. 2016). This is typically done in the context of an attention model.

We will not discuss the attention model here, but will explain how to make use of hidden states in an LSTM model. Let's start by naively setting the LSTM cells in our model from Listing 7-8 to return hidden states by setting return_sequences to True. We'll do that in Listing 7-10 and then check the model's architecture using the summary() method.

Listing 7-10. Incorrect use of LSTM hidden states

```
# Define sequential model.
model = tf.keras.models.Sequential()

# Define recurrent layer to return hidden states.
model.add(tf.keras.layers.LSTM(2, return_sequences=True,
          input_shape=(4, 1)))

# Define output layer.
model.add(tf.keras.layers.Dense(1, activation="linear"))

# Summarize model architecture.
model.summary()
```

```
Layer (type)          Output Shape              Param #
=======================================================
lstm_1 (LSTM)         (None, 4, 2)                  32

_____

dense_1 (Dense)       (None, 4, 1)                   3
=======================================================
Total params: 35
Trainable params: 35
Non-trainable params: 0
```

As we can see, there's something unusual about the model's architecture: rather than outputting a scalar prediction for each observation in the batch, it instead outputs a 4x1 vector. This appears to be a consequence of the LSTM layer, which is now outputting 4x1 vectors, rather than scalars, from each of its two LSTM cells.

There are several ways in which we can make use of the LSTM output. One such method is called a stacked LSTM (Graves et al. 2013). This works by passing the full sequence hidden states to a second LSTM layer, creating depth in the network that allows for more than one level of representation.

In Listing 7-11, we define such a model. In the first LSTM layer, we use a layer with three LSTM cells and an input shape of (4, 1). We set return_sequences to True, which means that each cell will return a 4x1 sequence of hidden states, rather than a scalar. We'll then pass this 3-tensor (4x1x3) to a second LSTM layer with two cells, which only returns the final hidden states and not intermediate state values.

Listing 7-11. Define a stacked LSTM model

```
# Define sequential model.
model = tf.keras.models.Sequential()

# Define recurrent layer to return hidden states.
model.add(tf.keras.layers.LSTM(3, return_sequences=True,
        input_shape=(4, 1)))

# Define second recurrent layer.
model.add(tf.keras.layers.LSTM(2))

# Define output layer.
model.add(tf.keras.layers.Dense(1, activation="linear"))
```

The model's architecture is summarized in Listing 7-12. We can see that it now outputs a scalar prediction, which is what we want for the inflation forecast. We will omit an analysis of model performance, but will point out that the use of such models for time series forecasting remains underexplored. It is possible that using stacked LSTM models, the attention model, or the transformer model could lead to improvements in time series forecasting in cases where modeling long-run dependencies is important.

Listing 7-12. Summarize stacked LSTM architecture

```
# Summarize model architecture.
model.summary()
```

Layer (type)	Output Shape	Param #
lstm_1 (LSTM)	(None, 4, 3)	60

```
lstm_2 (LSTM)        (None, 2)                     48

dense_1 (Dense)    (None, 1)                        3
=========================================================
Total params: 111
Trainable params: 111
Non-trainable params: 0
```

Multivariate Forecasts

So far, we have focused on the mechanics of different methods and have structured all examples around the univariate inflation forecasting exercise in Nakamura (2005). The methods we have discussed all carry over to a multivariate setting. For the sake of completeness, we will provide a brief multivariate forecasting example, making use of both the LSTM model and gradient boosted trees, which we discussed in Chapter 4. We will, again, attempt to forecast inflation, but will do so at a monthly frequency and using five features, rather than one.

We'll start by loading and previewing the data in Listing 7-13. We'll then discuss how to implement a multivariate forecast model using an LSTM and gradient boosted trees. The four features we've added are unemployment, hours worked in the manufacturing sector, hourly earnings in the manufacturing sector, and a measure of the money supply (M1). Unemployment is measured in first differences, whereas all level variables transformed using percentage changes from the previous period.

Listing 7-13. Load and preview inflation forecast data

```
import pandas as pd

# Load data.
macroData = pd.read_csv(data_path+'macrodata.csv',
        index_col = 'Date')

# Preview data.
print(macroData.round(1).tail())
```

	Inflation	Unemployment	Hours	Earnings	M1
Date					
12/1/19	-0.1	0.1	0.5	0.2	0.7
1/1/20	0.4	0.6	-1.7	-0.1	0.0
2/1/20	0.3	-0.2	0.0	0.4	0.8
3/1/20	-0.2	0.8	-0.2	0.4	6.4
4/1/20	-0.7	9.8	-6.8	0.5	12.9

LSTM

As we saw earlier in the chapter, we can prepare the data for use in an LSTM model by instantiating a generator. We'll first convert the target and features to np.array() objects. We'll then create one generator for training data and another for test data. In the previous example, we used quarterly data and four-quarter sequence lengths. In this case, we'll use monthly data and 12-month sequence lengths in Listing 7-14.

Listing 7-14. Prepare data for use in LSTM model

```
import numpy as np
import tensorflow as tf
from tensorflow.keras.preprocessing.sequence import
TimeseriesGenerator
```

```
# Define target and features.
target = np.array(macroData['Inflation'])
features = np.array(macroData)

# Define train generator.
train_generator = TimeseriesGenerator(features[:393],
        target[:393], length = 12, batch_size = 6)

# Define test generator.
test_generator = TimeseriesGenerator(features[393:],
        target[393:], length = 12, batch_size = 6)
```

With the generators defined, we can now train the model in Listing 7-15. We'll use two LSTM cells. Additionally, we'll need to change the input shape, since we now have 12 elements in each sequence and five features. Over 20 epochs of training, the model reduces the mean squared error from 0.3065 to 0.0663. If you've done macroeconomic forecasting using econometric models, you might worry about the number of model parameters, since we're using longer sequences and more variables; however, for the reasons we discussed earlier, the longer sequence length does not increase the number of parameters. In fact, the model has only 67 parameters.

Listing 7-15. Define and train LSTM model with multiple features

```
# Define sequential model.
model = tf.keras.models.Sequential()

# Define LSTM model with two cells.
model.add(tf.keras.layers.LSTM(2, input_shape=(12, 5)))

# Define output layer.
model.add(tf.keras.layers.Dense(1, activation="linear"))

# Compile the model.
model.compile(loss="mse", optimizer="adam")
```

```
# Train the model.
model.fit_generator(train_generator, epochs=100)

Epoch 1/20
64/64 [==============================] - 2s 26ms/step - loss:
0.3065

...

...

Epoch 20/20
64/64 [==============================] - 0s 6ms/step - loss:
0.0663
```

Finally, in Listing 7-16, we'll evaluate the model by comparing the training sample results to the test sample results. We can see that the training set performance appears to be better than test set performance, which is common; however, if the disparity becomes sufficiently large, we should consider using regularization or terminating the training process after fewer epochs.

Listing 7-16. Use MSE to evaluate train and test sets

```
# Evaluate training set using MSE.
model.evaluate_generator(train_generator)

0.06527029448989197

# Evaluate test set using MSE.
model.evaluate_generator(test_generator)

0.15478561431742632
```

Gradient Boosted Trees

As a final example, we'll consider performing the same forecasting exercise, but using gradient boosted trees, which we discussed in Chapter 4. Within the set of tools TensorFlow offers, gradient boosted trees and deep learning are most suitable for time series forecasting tasks.

Just as LSTM models require us to prepare data by splitting it into sequences, gradient boosting with trees will require us to prepare the data in a format usable in the Estimator API. This will involve defining feature columns for each of the five features, as we do in Listing 7-17.

The next step is to define functions that generate data. We'll do this separately for train and test functions, so that we can evaluate overfitting, just as we did for the LSTM example. Listing 7-18 defines the two functions. Again, we use the same sample split: the train set will cover the years prior to 2000, and the test set will cover the years afterward.

Listing 7-17. Define feature columns

```
# Define lagged inflation feature column.
inflation = tf.feature_column.numeric_column(
        "inflation")

# Define unemployment feature column.
unemployment = tf.feature_column.numeric_column(
        "unemployment")

# Define hours feature column.
hours = tf.feature_column.numeric_column(
        "hours")

# Define earnings feature column.
earnings = tf.feature_column.numeric_column(
        "earnings")
```

275

```
# Define M1 feature column.
m1 = tf.feature_column.numeric_column("m1")

# Define feature list.
feature_list = [inflation, unemployment, hours,
        earnings, m1]
```

In Listing 7-19, we train a `BoostedTreeRegressor` using 100 epochs and `train_data`. We then perform evaluation on both the training and test sets and print the results.

Listing 7-18. Define the data generation functions

```
# Define input function for training data.
def train_data():
        train = macroData.iloc[:392]
        features = {"inflation": train["Inflation"],
        "unemployment": train["Unemployment"],
        "hours": train["Hours"],
        "earnings": train["Earnings"],
        "m1": train["M1"]}
        labels = macroData["Inflation"].iloc[1:393]
        return features, labels

# Define input function for test data.
def test_data():
        test = macroData.iloc[393:-1]
        features = {"inflation": test["Inflation"],
        "unemployment": test["Unemployment"],
        "hours": test["Hours"],
        "earnings": test["Earnings"],
        "m1": test["M1"]}
        labels = macroData["Inflation"].iloc[394:]
        return features, labels
```

The results indicate that the model may be overfitting. The average training loss is 0.01, and the average test loss is 0.14. This suggests that we should try to train the model again using fewer epochs and then see whether the gap between the two closes. If we do not see convergence between the two, then we will want to perform additional model tuning to reduce overfitting. For a review of what parameters we can tune, see Chapter 4.

Listing 7-19. Train and evaluate model. Print results

```
# Instantiate boosted trees regressor.
model = tf.estimator.BoostedTreesRegressor(feature_columns =
feature_list, n_batches_per_layer = 1)

# Train model.
model.train(train_data, steps=100)

# Evaluate train and test set.
train_eval = model.evaluate(train_data, steps = 1)
test_eval = model.evaluate(test_data, steps = 1)

# Print results.
print(pd.Series(train_eval))
print(pd.Series(test_eval))

average_loss           0.010534
label/mean             0.416240
loss                   0.010534
prediction/mean        0.416263
global_step          100.000000
dtype: float64

average_loss           0.145123
label/mean             0.172864
loss                   0.145123
prediction/mean        0.286285
global_step          100.000000
dtype: float64
```

Summary

One of the challenges of applying machine learning to economics and finance is that machine learning is concerned with prediction, whereas much of the research in economics and finance is concerned with causal inference and hypothesis testing. There are, however, several areas in which machine learning has considerable overlap with economics, and forecasting is a case where the two coincide exactly.

In this chapter, we examined how to make use of time series forecasting tools from machine learning, focusing primarily on deep learning models, but also covering gradient boosted trees, which are also available in TensorFlow. We structured examples around one of the earliest uses of a neural network in economics for the purpose of time series forecasting (Nakamura 2005). We then covered modern models, including RNNs, LSTMs, and stacked LSTMs, which have largely been developed for other sequential data processing tasks, such as NLP.

Readers who have an interest in learning more about macroeconomic time series forecasting with deep learning models may wish to read Cook and Hall (2017). For recent work in finance on stock return and bond premium forecasting, see Heaton et al. (2016), Messmer (2017), Rossi (2018), and Chen et al. (2019). For recent work on high-dimensional time series regression and nowcasting with sparse group LASSO models, see Babii, Ghysels, and Striaukas (2019, 2020).

Bibliography

Babii, A., E. Ghysels, and J. Striaukas. 2019. "Inference for High-Dimensional Regressions with Heteroskedasticity and Auto-correlation." *arXiv preprint.*

Babii, A., E. Ghysels, and J. Striaukas. 2020. "Machine Learning Time Series Regressions with an Application to Nowcasting." *arXiv preprint.*

Bianchi, D., M. Büchner, and A. Tamoni. 2020. "Bond Risk Premia with Machine Learning." *WBS Finance Group Research Paper No. 252.*

Chen, L., M. Pelger, and J. Zhu. 2019. "Deep Learning in Asset Pricing." (arXiv).

Cook, T.R., and A.S. Hall. 2017. "Macroeconomic Indicator Forecasting with Deep Neural Networks." *Federal Reserve Bank of Kansas City, Research Working Paper 17-11.*

Coulombe, P.G., M. Leroux, D. Stevanovic, and S. Surprenant. 2019. "How is Machine Learning Useful for Macroeconomic Forecasting?" *CIRANO Working Papers.*

Goodfellow, I., Y. Bengio, and A. Courville. 2017. *Deep Learning.* Cambridge, MA: MIT PRESS.

Graves, A., A.-r. Mohamed, and G. Hinton. 2013. "Speech Recognition with Deep Recurrent Neural Networks." *arXiv.*

Guanhao, F, J. He, and N.G. Polson. 2018. "Deep Learning for Predicting Asset Returns." *arXiv.*

Heaton, J.B., N.G. Polson, and J.H. Witte. 2016. "Deep Learning for Finance: Deep Portfolios." *Applied Stochastic Models in Business and Industry* 33 (1): 3–12.

Hochreiter, S., and J. Schmidhuber. 1997. "Long Short-term Memory." *Neural Computation* 9 (8): 1735–1780.

Messmer, M. 2017. "Deep Learning and the Cross-Section of Expected Returns." *SSRN Working Paper.*

Nakamura, Emi. 2005. "Inflation Forecasting Using a Neural Network." *Economics Letters* 85: 373–378.

Rossi, A.G. 2018. "Predicting Stock Market Returns with Machine Learning." *Working Paper.*

Rumelhart, D., G. Hinton, and R. Williams. 1986. "Learning Representations by Back-Propagating Errors." *Nature* 533–536.

Zhou, P., W. Shi, J. Tian, Z. Qi, B. Li, H. Hao, and B. Xu. 2016. "Attention-Based Bidirectional Long Short-Term Memory Networks for Relation Classification." *Proceedings of the 54th Annual Meeting of the Association for Computational Linguistics.* Berlin: Association for Computational Linguistics.

CHAPTER 8

Dimensionality Reduction

Many problem classes in machine learning are inherently high dimensional. Natural language processing problems, for instance, often involve the extraction of meaning from words, which can appear in an intractably large number of potential sequences in writing. Even if we limit ourselves to parsing only the 1000 most common words in texts, a short paragraph of 50 words will have 10^{150} possible permutations, which is more than the number of atoms of the observable universe. We are unlikely to make progress in such a setting without reframing the problem or reducing its dimensionality.

Research in economics and finance often makes use of dimensionality-reduction techniques, such as principal component analysis (PCA) and factor analysis (FA). This is typically done in cases where the number of covariates (features) is large enough that it risks the possibility of overfitting or explicitly violates an assumption of the econometric model. PCA and FA are also sometimes used when there is an interest in reducing data down to a small number of factors of interest.

© Isaiah Hull 2021
I. Hull, *Machine Learning for Economics and Finance in TensorFlow 2*,
https://doi.org/10.1007/978-1-4842-6373-0_8

In this chapter, we will briefly discuss two methods used in both machine learning and economics: PCA and partial least squares (PLS). We will then introduce the concept of autoencoders, which are used in machine learning. Autoencoders perform a combination of both "upsampling" and "downsampling" or "compression" and "decompression." A by-product of this process is a latent state that encodes the information needed to recover the original input state. We can think of autoencoders as providing – among other things – a flexible, deep learning-based approach to dimensionality reduction.

Dimensionality Reduction in Economics

Throughout this section, we'll follow the notation in Gentzkow et al. (2019), which discusses dimensionality reduction in the context of text analysis. Additionally, we'll use a combination of sklearn and tensorflow to perform the dimensionality-reduction tasks commonly used in economics. While everything can be done in tensorflow, it lacks many of the convenience methods for PCA and PLS that sklearn offers.

We will also use a common dataset through much of the chapter: GDP growth in 25 countries over the period between 1961:Q2 and 2020:Q1, which is produced by the OECD. A plot of the data is shown in Figure 8-1. We omit a legend, since individual country series are not distinguishable.

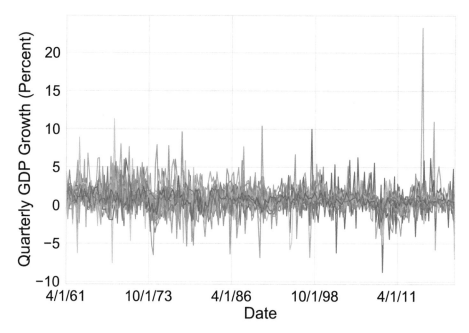

Figure 8-1. *GDP growth for 25 countries from 1961:Q2 to 2020:Q1*

In most exercises, we'll attempt to extract common components of growth across all countries included in the sample. Techniques such as PCA will enable us to determine what share of the variance in growth is explained by a handful of common components. We'll also see how those components relate to individual country series, giving a sense of which countries may be responsible for driving growth internationally.

Principal Component Analysis

The most common method for dimensionality reduction in economics and finance is principal component analysis. PCA maps a collection of features to k principal components, where k is set by the econometrician. The components are ordered by the share of the variance they explain in the data. The first principal component, for instance, explains the largest share of variance in the data. Additionally, they are constructed to be orthogonal.

In many cases, we will perform PCA with the intention of reducing the dimensionality of the dataset, so that we can use a small number of principal components in a regression. The properties we've described earlier make it particularly attractive for that purpose.

Using the notation in Gentzkow et al. (2019), we may write down PCA as the solution to the minimization problem given in Equation 8-1.

Equation 8-1. Principal component analysis minimization problem.

$$\min_{\{G,B\}} trace\left[\left(C-GB\right)\left(C-GB'\right)'\right]$$

$$s.t.\ \ rank\left(G\right)=rank\left(B\right)=k$$

In Listings 8-1 and 8-2, we sketch out how such an optimization problem could be solved in tensorflow; however, for our purposes, it will be more convenient to use the implementation in sklearn, which we will do for the remainder of the chapter.

Listing 8-1. Define variables for PCA in TensorFlow

```
import tensorflow as tf
import pandas as pd
import numpy as np

# Define data path.
data_path = '../data/chapter8/'

# Load data.
C = pd.read_csv(data_path+'gdp_growth.csv',
        index_col = 'Date')

# Convert data to constant object.
C = tf.constant(np.array(C), tf.float32)
```

```
# Set number of principal components.
k = 5

# Get shape of feature matrix.
n, p = C.shape

# Define variable for gamma matrix.
G = tf.Variable(tf.random.normal((n, k)), tf.float32)

# Define variable for beta matrix.
B = tf.Variable(tf.random.normal((p, k)), tf.float32)
```

Listing 8-1 loads the data as the feature matrix, C. It then converts the matrix to a tf.constant() object, sets the number of principal components to five, and then constructs the G and B matrices. Notice that G is an n x k matrix and B is a p x k matrix, where n is the number of time periods and p is the number of countries.

In our case, the G matrix captures the size of the impact of the factors in each period. Additionally, B measures the degree to which each factor is related to each country.

In Listing 8-2, we define a loss function, pcaLoss, which takes C, G, and B as inputs and returns a loss value, constructed according to Equation 8-1. We then instantiate an optimizer and train the model over 1000 epochs. Recall that only G and B are trainable and should be supplied to var_list.

Listing 8-2. Perform PCA in TensorFlow

```
# Define PCA loss.
def pcaLoss(C, G, B):
        D = C - tf.matmul(G, tf.transpose(B))
        DT = tf.transpose(D)
        DDT = tf.matmul(D, DT)
        return tf.linalg.trace(DDT)
```

```
# Instantiate optimizer.
opt = tf.optimizers.Adam()

# Perform train model.
for i in range(1000):
        opt.minimize(lambda: pcaLoss(C, G, B), var_list = [G, B])
```

Now that we've seen how tensorflow could be used to construct a solution method for PCA, let's see how the same task can be done using sklearn. Listing 8-3 imports the PCA method from sklearn.decomposition and loads and prepares the data. We'll use the data in np.array() format.

In Listing 8-4, we set the number of principal components, instantiate a PCA model, and apply the fit() method. We can now recover matrices that were equivalent to those we trained in tensorflow. In particular, we can recover B using the components_ method and G using pca.transform(C). In addition to this, we can recover the share of the variance explained by each principal component, S.

Listing 8-3. Import the PCA library from sklearn and prepare the data

```
from sklearn.decomposition import PCA

# Load data.
C = pd.read_csv(data_path+'gdp_growth.csv',
        index_col = 'Date')

# Transform feature matrix into numpy array.
C = np.array(C)
```

Listing 8-4. Perform PCA with sklearn

```
# Set number of components.
k = 25

# Instantiate PCA model with k components.
pca = PCA(n_components=k)

# Fit model.
pca.fit(C)

# Return B matrix.
B = pca.components_.T

# Return G matrix.
G = pca.transform(C)

# Return variance shares.
S = pca.explained_variance_ratio_
```

Notice that we've computed 25 principal components, which is the number of GDP growth series we had initially. Since our objective is dimensionality reduction, we will want to lower this number. A common visual approach to selecting a number of principal components is called the "elbow method." This entails plotting the explained share of the variance, *S*, to identify a sharp reduction in the magnitude of the slope – an "elbow" – which indicates that the next principal component explains much less than does the one that preceded it in importance. This is visualized in Figure 8-2.

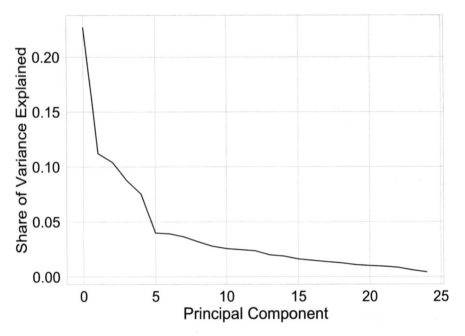

Figure 8-2. *Plot of explained variance share by principal component*

Based on Figure 8-2, the most pronounced "elbow" appears at the fifth principal component. Subsequent principal components appear to explain a considerably smaller share of GDP growth. Consequently, we may wish to exclusively make use of the first five principal components in subsequent exercises.

Beyond this, we may also want to visualize the association strengths between the principal components and the original country series. These values are given in the B matrix. Figure 8-3 plots them for the first principal component, given by the first column of B. This appears to be a component of growth that is associated with small open economies, such as Greece and Iceland.

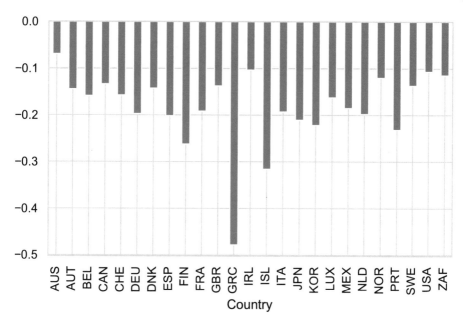

Figure 8-3. *Strength of associations between country series and first principal component*

In general, when we perform PCA or another form of dimensionality reduction, we will do so in the context of broader problem. One common application is a principal component regression (PCR), which is a two-step procedure that involves the use of PCA, followed by the inclusion of selected principal components in a regression. A variant of this is used, for instance, in Bernanke et al. (2005) to perform factor-augmented vector autoregressions (FAVAR), which they use to identify the monetary transmission mechanism.[1]

We'll consider a simple problem of the form of Equation 8-2, where we want to predict Canada's GDP growth using growth data from other countries. We may want to do this to impute values for GDP growth in

---

[1]Using a FAVAR allows Bernanke et al. (2005) to dramatically expand the set of variables included in the VAR, so that they can properly account for the information sets that the central bank and private actors can access.

periods where the country is missing a value. Alternatively, we may be interested in recovering the coefficient estimates themselves, so we can see how GDP growth in one country is affected by different global components of growth.

Equation 8-2. Principal component regression.

$$gdp\_growth_t^{CAN} = \alpha + \beta_o PC_{t0} + \ldots + \beta_{p-1} C_{tp-1} + \epsilon_t$$

In Listing 8-5, we load the data using pandas, extract the column for Canada from the DataFrame, create a copy of the DataFrame, delete the column for Luxembourg from that copy, and then convert both to np.array() objects.

Listing 8-5. Prepare data for use in a principal component regression

```
import tensorflow as tf
import numpy as np
import pandas as pd

# Load data.
gdp = pd.read_csv(data_path+'gdp_growth.csv',
         index_col = 'Date')

# Copy Canada from C.
Y = gdp['CAN'].copy()

# Copy gdp to C and drop LUX.
C = gdp.copy()
del C['CAN']

# Convert data to numpy arrays.
Y = np.array(Y)
C = np.array(C)
```

In Listing 8-6, we perform PCA on *C* and recover the principal components, *G*, which we use as an input to a PCR regression of *Y* on *G* in tensorflow.

Listing 8-6. Perform PCA and PCR

```
# Set number of components.
k = 5

# Instantiate PCA model with k components.
pca = PCA(n_components=k)

# Fit model and return principal components.
pca.fit(C)
G = tf.cast(pca.transform(C), tf.float32)

# Initialize model parameters.
beta = tf.Variable(tf.random.normal([k,1]),
tf.float32)
alpha = tf.Variable(tf.random.normal([1,1]),
tf.float32)

# Define prediction function.
def PCR(G, beta, alpha):
        predictions = alpha + tf.reshape(
        tf.matmul(G, beta), (236,))
        return predictions

# Define loss function.
def mseLoss(Y, G, beta, alpha):
        return tf.losses.mse(Y, PCR(G, beta, alpha))

# Instantiate an optimizer and minimize loss.
opt = tf.optimizers.Adam(0.1)
for j in range(100):
```

```
opt.minimize(lambda: mseLoss(Y, G, beta, alpha),
    var_list = [beta, alpha])
```

Now that we've trained a model, we can use it to predict the series for Canada's GDP growth. We plot this series against the true series in Figure 8-4. Prior to the Great Moderation period, which begins in the mid-1980s, we can see that GDP growth is more volatile and the model fit is worse. After 1980, however, much of Canada's GDP growth appears to be explained by five factors that were present in the GDP growth series of 24 other countries.

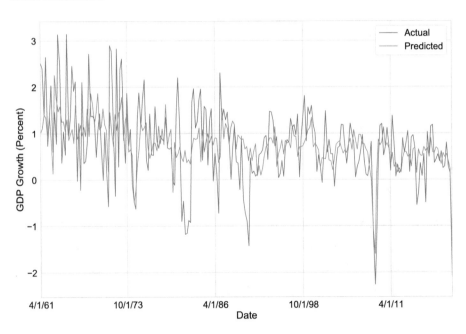

Figure 8-4. *Actual and PCR-predicted GDP growth in Canada*

Our finding suggests that there are common global factors that are associated with growth. If we wanted to examine this further, we might try to determine what those factors are by examining their relationship to different countries using the *B* matrix. For example, it could be the case that growth in North America is particularly important for growth in

Canada. PCA will help us to reduce the dimensionality of the problem, but will also give us the tools to try to tell plausible stories about what we're left with after the reduction is done.

Partial Least Squares

PCR managed to satisfactorily explain quarterly variation in Canadian GDP growth using only five principal components. While the two-step procedure we described is convenient to implement and performs serviceably for a wide variety of tasks, it does not account for the relationship between C and Y in the first stage, which we might think is suboptimal if our goal is ultimately to perform prediction.

Indeed, PCA is performed exclusively using C. We then take the principal components from C and use them in a regression with Y as the dependent variable. It could, however, be the case that the components we select explain a high share of the variation in GDP growth for many countries, but not for Canada.

There are, however, alternatives to PCR that account for the strength of comovement between Y and the feature columns of C. We'll consider one of those – partial least squares (PLS) – in this brief subsection. Our description follows Gentzkow et al. (2019) and consists of the following steps:

1. Compute $\hat{Y} = \dfrac{\sum_j \psi_j C_j}{\sum_j \psi_j}$, where C_j is the jth feature column and ψ_j is the univariate covariance between Y and C_j.

2. Orthogonalize Y and C with respect to $\hat{Y}$.

3. Repeat step 1.

4. Repeat steps 2 and 1 to generate the desired number of components.

In contrast to PLR, PLS makes use of the covariance between Y and C to generate components that are best suited to the prediction of Y. In principle, this should lead us to select components that have greater predictive value than we would generate using PCA on C and then performing a linear regression in a second step.

In Listing 8-7, we implement a PLS regression using sklearn. We will assume that C and Y have been defined as they were in Listing 8-5. For the sake of comparability to the PLR results, we'll again use five components. We will then instantiate and train a PLS model and then use the predict() method to generate a time series of predictions for Canada.

Listing 8-7. Perform PLS

```
from sklearn.cross_decomposition import PLSRegression

# Set number of components.
k = 5

# Instantiate PLS model with k components.
pls = PLSRegression(n_components = k)

# Train PLS model.
pls.fit(C, Y)

# Generate predictions.
pls.predict(C)
```

In Figure 8-5, we compare actual and PLS-predicted GDP growth in Canada for the duration of the sample. As expected, PLS achieves a mild improvement over what we were able to do with a two-step PCA procedure. This is because it allowed us to exploit the relationship between our target variable and feature matrix.

Note that both PCR and PLS take many forms. While we performed PCR using OLS in the second step, we could have, in principle, used any model to capture the relationship between the principle components extracted from the feature matrix and Canada's GDP growth. This is one of the benefits of performing the second step in tensorflow, rather than sklearn.

For a deeper treatment of the econometric theory of PLS, see Kelly and Pruitt (2013, 2015). Additionally, for a rigorous treatment of forecasting with PCA, see Stock and Watson (2002). For an application of the method to weekly GDP growth forecasting during the COVID-19 outbreak, see Lewis et al. (2020).

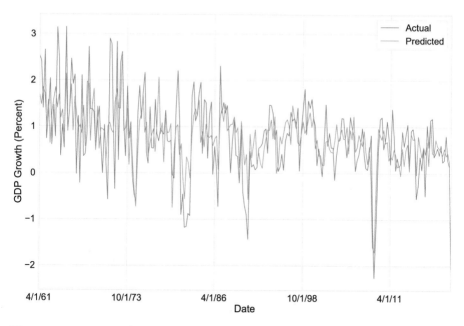

Figure 8-5. *Actual and PLS-predicted GDP growth in Canada*

The Autoencoder Model

An autoencoder is a type of neural network that is trained to predict its input values. Such models can be used to generate music, denoise images, and perform a generalized and non-linear version of principal component analysis, which is what we'll focus on in this chapter.

The autoencoder model was developed in LeCun (1987), Bourlard and Kamp (1988), and Hinton and Zemel (1993). Goodfellow et al. (2017) describe an autoencoder as consisting of two functions. The first is an encoder function, $f(x)$, given in Equation 8-3, which takes inputs, x, and produces a latent state, h. The second is a decoder function, given in Equation 8-4, which takes a latent state, h, and produces a reconstruction of the inputs, r.

Equation 8-3. Encoder function.

$$h = f(x)$$

Equation 8-4. Decoder function.

$$r = g(h)$$

In practice, we may train an autoencoder by minimizing a loss function of the form given in Equation 8-5. Notice that $g(f(x))$ is the reconstruction, r, we generate from the encoder and decoder functions and the set of inputs. The less distance there is between r and x, the smaller the loss will be.

Equation 8-5. Autoencoder loss function.

$$L(x, g(f(x)))$$

The encoder part of the network has an architecture that resembles a standard dense neural network. It takes inputs and then passes them through a sequence of dense layers with a decreasing number of nodes.

The encoder performs "downsampling" or "compression." To the contrary, a decoder has the architecture of an inverted neural network. It takes a latent state as the input and then performs "upsampling" or "decompression" to yield a larger output.

The architecture for an example autoencoder is given in Figure 8-6. Here, we have five input nodes, which are reduced to three in the following neural network layer. We then output two nodes from the encoder network. These are used as inputs in the decoder network, which upsamples to three nodes and then five, ultimately providing us with something that is comparable to the inputs. The pink nodes at the top of the image are the model inputs, whereas the pink nodes at the bottom represent the attempted reconstruction of the inputs.

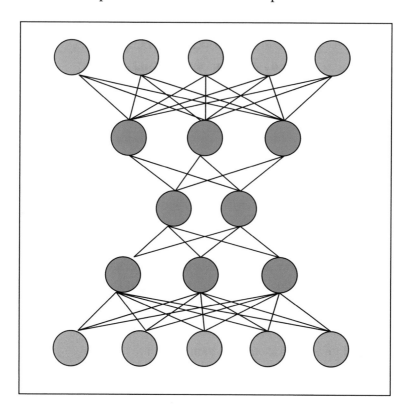

Figure 8-6. *Example architecture for an autoencoder*

While we'll focus on the use of autoencoders to perform dimensionality reduction, they also have two more common uses in machine learning that could also be applied to problems in economics and finance:

1. **Noise reduction**: Both audio and images often contain noise. Autoencoders allow us to filter out the noise by memorizing only large, important features of the image or audio signal. By selecting an architecture with relatively few nodes in the latent state, we can force the network to compress all of the information contained in an image or audio signal into a few numbers. When we attempt to reconstruct the image or audio signal using the decoder, it will not be possible to recover idiosyncratic noise, since that would require more information than is contained in the latent state. This means we'll recover only a denoised version.

2. **Generative machine learning**: In addition to classifying different types of objects, machine learning algorithms can also be used to generate new instances of a class. The decoder of an autoencoder model is trained to reconstruct images from information in a latent state. This means that we can generate entirely new images by randomly generating a latent state and then passing it through the decoder. Additionally, we can extract a latent state from an image using the encoder and modify the latent state it outputs to manipulate the image we'll get when passing it to the decoder.

Based on their use as denoisers and in generative machine learning tasks, two things should be clear. First, we don't typically want to train an autoencoder to recover the inputs exactly. Rather, we want it to learn important relationships in the data, so that it can generalize, not memorize. This is why we use regularization and keep the network sufficiently small. And second, the output layer of the encoder, the latent state, serves as a bottleneck that must summarize the features in a set of inputs. This is precisely why it will be useful as a form of dimensionality reduction.

In the final exercise of this chapter, we'll demonstrate how to train an autoencoder on the same GDP growth data. In Listing 8-8, we'll assume that Y and C have already been loaded and are defined as they have been throughout the chapter. We'll then define the encoder and decoder models, which will share weights, but will also be able to independently accept inputs and produce outputs. We'll set the number of nodes in the latent state, latentNodes, to five, which will give us the equivalent of a five-factor PCR model when we perform a regression in the following step.

Listing 8-8. Train an autoencoder using the Keras API

```
# Set number of countries.
nCountries = 24

# Set number of nodes in latent state.
latentNodes = 5

# Define input layer for encoder.
encoderInput = tf.keras.layers.Input(shape = (nCountries))

# Define latent state.
latent = tf.keras.layers.Input(shape = (latentNodes))
```

```
# Define dense output layer for encoder.
encoded = tf.keras.layers.Dense(latentNodes, activation =
        'tanh')(encoderInput)
```

```
# Define dense output layer for decoder.
decoded = tf.keras.layers.Dense(nCountries, activation =
        'linear')(latent)
```

```
# Define separate models for encoder and decoder.
encoder = tf.keras.Model(encoderInput, encoded)
decoder = tf.keras.Model(latent, decoded)
```

```
# Define functional model for autoencoder.
autoencoder = tf.keras.Model(encoderInput, decoder(encoded))
```

```
# Compile model
autoencoder.compile(loss = 'mse', optimizer="adam")
```

```
# Train model
autoencoder.fit(C, C, epochs = 200)
```

Relative to what we've done so far with neural networks, this model is quite unusual. When we train the model, we can see that the features and target are the same. Additionally, we have an encoder and a decoder model, which are functional on their own, but are also part of a larger autoencoder model, which is the model we actually train. We can also see that we've selected the simplest possible architecture, given that we have a latent state with five nodes. This is summarized in Listing 8-9.

Listing 8-9. Autoencoder model architecture summary

```
# Print summary of model architecture.
print(autoencoder.summary())
```

Layer (type)	Output Shape	Param #
input_11 (InputLayer)	[(None, 24)]	0
dense_8 (Dense)	(None, 5)	125
model_10 (Model)	(None, 24)	144

Total params: 269
Trainable params: 269
Non-trainable params: 0

In total, the model has only 269 parameters, but has been trained to recover 24 GDP growth series, which each consists of 236 quarters of observations. In Figure 8-7, we evaluate the quality of the series construction by plotting the actual and predicted series for the United States, which we can do using the `predict()` method of autoencoder.

The autoencoder appears to have reproduced the series for the United States with a reasonable degree of accuracy. As we discussed earlier, an autoencoder will be forced to discard some of the noise, since the bottleneck layer (latent state) will limit how much information can be passed to the decoder. As a consequence of this, we can see that the series we generated has a lower variance than the original series.

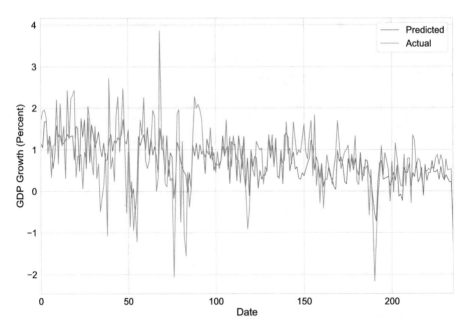

Figure 8-7. *Reconstructed series for US GDP growth using autoencoder*

The next step is to recover the latent state in all periods, which will consist of five output values from the encoder. We can do this using the predict method of the encoder function, as is shown in Listing 8-10.

Listing 8-10. Generate latent state time series

```
# Generate latent state time series.
latentState = encoder.predict(C)

# Print shape of latent state series.
print(latentState.shape)

(236, 5)
```

We can now use these latent state time series in a regression to predict Canada's GDP growth. As we can see from Listing 8-11, nothing of substance has changed from what we did in PCR. Once the latent states have been extracted from the encoder model, the problem reduces to a linear regression.

Listing 8-11. Perform dimensionality reduction in a regression setting with an autoencoder latent state

```
# Initialize model parameters.
beta = tf.Variable(tf.random.normal([latentNodes,1]))
alpha = tf.Variable(tf.random.normal([1,1]))

# Define prediction function.
def LSR(latentState, beta, alpha):
        predictions = alpha + tf.reshape(
        tf.matmul(latentState, beta), (236,))
        return predictions

# Define loss function.
def mseLoss(Y, latentState, beta, alpha):
        return tf.losses.mse(Y, LSR(latentState,
beta, alpha))

# Instantiate an optimizer and minimize loss.
opt = tf.optimizers.Adam(0.1)
for j in range(100):
        opt.minimize(lambda: mseLoss(Y, latentState, beta,
        alpha), var_list = [beta, alpha])
```

In Figure 8-8, we plot the actual and predicted time series for Canadian GDP growth using a regression model built around latent states from an autoencoder. We can see that performance is similar to what we were able to achieve with PLS.

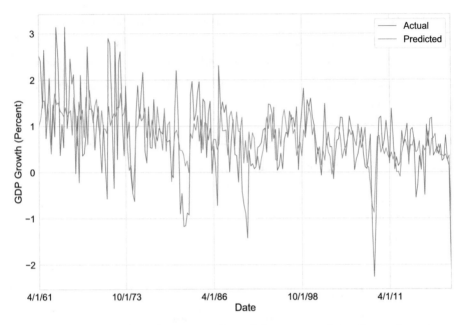

Figure 8-8. *Actual and OLS-predicted GDP growth in Canada using an autoencoder to perform dimensionality reduction on the feature set*

Finally, note that we could have changed at least two things about our approach to this problem. First, we could have modified the autoencoder's architecture. If, for instance, if we thought the model was underfitting and failing to generalize across series, we could have added hidden layers or additional nodes within layers. And second, we could have used an entirely different model in the second step, such as a neural network. Furthermore, using TensorFlow, we could have connected this model directly to the autoencoder, training them jointly to predict Y with a set of five latent features. This would have given us latent states that were more predictive of Y, yielding a PLS-type generalization of the approach.

Summary

Dimensionality reduction is an empirical strategy common to economics and machine learning. In many cases, we'll use dimensionality reduction when the second step of a problem – which may be a supervised learning task – is infeasible using the available feature set. Using principal component analysis or the latent states from an autoencoder, we can compress a high-dimensional set of features into a small number of factors.

In this chapter, we demonstrated how to perform dimensionality-reduction tasks in `tensorflow` and `sklearn`. Concentrating on GDP growth prediction, we saw that a principal component regression performed well, but ultimately used factors that were not selected based on their relationship with the dependent variable. When we used partial least squares, which does exploit comovement between the features and the dependent variable, we found minor improvements in the quality of prediction.

Finally, we explored the possibility of performing dimensionality reduction using an autoencoder. An autoencoder model consists of encoder and decoder networks and is trained to output reconstructions of its inputs. The encoder part of the network outputs a latent state, which can be treated as compressed information about the input features. We showed that regressions that used latent states from an autoencoder for the purpose of dimensionality reduction performed comparably to PLS and could be extended allow for the joint training with the predictive model.

Bibliography

Bernanke, B.S., J. Boivin, and P. Elliasz. 2005. "Measuring the Effects of Monetary Policy: A Factor-Augmented Vector Autoregressive (FAVAR) Approach." *The Quarterly Journal of Economics* 120 (1): 387–422.

Bourlard, H., and Y. Kamp. 1988. "Auto-association by multilayer perceptrons and singular value decomposition." *Biological Cybernetics* 59: 291–294.

Gentzkow, M., B. Kelly, and M. Taddy. 2019. "Text as Data." *Journal of Economic Literature* 57 (3): 535–574.

Goodfellow, I., Y. Bengio, and A. Courville. 2017. *Deep Learning.* Cambridge, MA: MIT Press.

Hinton, G.E., and R.S. Zemel. 1993. "Autoencoders, minimum description length, and Helmholtz free energy." *NIPS'1993.*

Kelly, B., and S. Pruitt. 2013. "Market Expectations in the Cross-Section of Present Values." *Journal of Finance* 68 (5): 1721–1756.

Kelly, B., and S. Pruitt. 2015. "The Three-Pass Regression Filter: A New Approach to Forecasting Using Many Predictors." *Journal of Econometrics* 186 (2): 294–316.

LeCun, Y. 1987. "Modèles connexionistes de l'apprentissage." *Ph.D. thesis, Université de Paris VI.*

Lewis, D., K. Mertens, and J. Stock. 2020. "U.S. Economic Activity during the Early Weeks of the SARS-Cov-2 Outbreak." *Federal Reserve Bank of New York Staff Reports* 920.

Stock, J.H., and M.W. Watson. 2002. "Forecasting Using Principal Components from a Large Number of Predictors." *Journal of the American Statistical Association* 97 (460): 1167–1179.

CHAPTER 9

Generative Models

Machine learning models can be divided into two categories: discriminative and generative. Discriminative models are trained to perform classification or regression. That is, we input a set of features and expect to receive probabilities of class labels or predicted values as outputs. In contrast, generative models are trained to learn the underlying distribution of the data. Once we have trained a generative model, we can use it to produce new examples of a class. Figure 9-1 illustrates the difference between the two categories of model.

Thus far, we have focused on discriminative models in this book; however, there was one exception: the latent Dirichlet allocation (Blei et al. 2003), which we introduced in Chapter 6. The LDA model took a text corpus as an input and returned a set of topics, where each topic was defined as a distribution over the vocabulary.

There has recently been considerable progress in the generative machine learning literature, and much of it has been concentrated in the development of two types of models: variational autoencoders (VAEs) and generative adversarial networks (GANs). With respect to image, text, and music generation, these two categories of model have delivered considerable breakthroughs.

© Isaiah Hull 2021
I. Hull, *Machine Learning for Economics and Finance in TensorFlow 2*,
https://doi.org/10.1007/978-1-4842-6373-0_9

For the most part, this progress hasn't yet reached the economics and finance disciplines; however, some work in economics has begun to make use of GANs. In the final section of the chapter, we will briefly discuss two recent applications of GANs in economics (Athey et. al. 2019 and Kaji et al. 2018) and speculate on potential future uses.

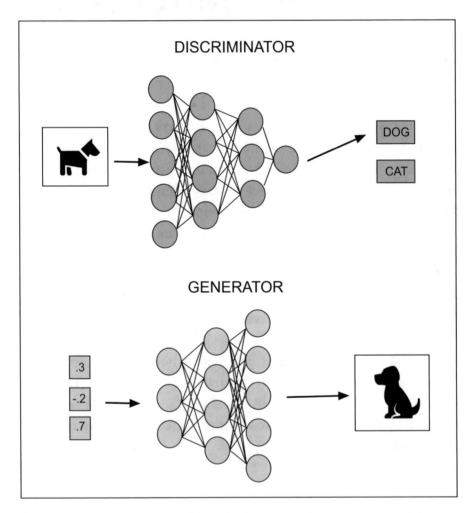

Figure 9-1. *Comparison of discriminator and generator models*

Variational Autoencoders

In Chapter 8, we introduced the concept of an autoencoder, which consisted of two networks with shared weights: an encoder and a decoder. The encoder transformed the model inputs into a latent state. The decoder took the latent state as an input and produced a reconstruction of the features input into the encoder. We trained the model by computing a reconstruction loss, which was a transformation of the difference between the inputs and their predicted values.

We used an autoencoder to perform dimensionality reduction, but discussed other uses of autoencoders, which primarily involved generative tasks, such as the creation of novel images, music, and texts. What we did not mention is that autoencoders suffer from two problems that hinder their performance on such tasks. Both problems, which we discuss as follows, are related to the way in which they generate latent states:

1. **The location and distribution of latent states**:
   The latent states of an autoencoder with N nodes are points in $\mathbb{R}^N$. For many problems, these points will tend to cluster in the same area; however, the autoencoder does not allow us to explicitly determine how and where such points cluster in $\mathbb{R}^N$. This might seem unimportant, but it will ultimately determine what latent states can be fed into the model. If, for instance, we are attempting to generate an image, it would be useful to know what constitutes a valid latent state and, thus, what can be fed into the model. Otherwise, we will use states that are far away from anything the model has observed, which will yield a novel, but perhaps unconvincing image.

2. **The performance of latent states not present in training**: An autoencoder is trained to reconstruct inputs for a set of examples. For the latent state associated with a set of features, the decoder should yield outputs that resemble the input features. If, however, we perturb the latent vector slightly, there's no guarantee that the decoder will have the capacity to generate a convincing example from a point it has never visited.

Variational autoencoders (VAEs) were developed to overcome these limitations. Rather than having a latent state layer, VAEs have a mean layer, a log variance layer, and sampling layer. The sampling layer draws from a normal distribution defined by the mean and log variance parameters in the preceding layers. The output of the sampling layer is then passed to the decoder as the latent state during the training process. Passing the same features to the encoder twice will yield different latent states each time.

Beyond the differences in architecture, VAEs also modify the loss function to include the Kullback-Leibler (KL) divergence for each normal distribution in the sampling layer. The KL divergence penalizes the distance between each of the normal distributions and a normal distribution with both a mean and log variance of zero.

The combination of these features accomplishes three things. First, it eliminates the determinism of latent states. Each set of features will now be associated with a distribution of latent states, rather than a single latent state. This will tend to improve generative performance by forcing the model to treat each individual latent state feature as a continuous variable. Second, it eliminates the sampling problem. We can now draw valid states randomly by making use of the sampling layer. And third, it corrects the issue with the latent distribution in space. The KL divergence component of the loss will push the distribution means close to zero and force them to have similar variances.

The remainder of this section will focus on the implementation of VAEs in TensorFlow. For an extended overview of the development of VAE models and a detailed exploration of their theoretical properties, see Kingma and Welling (2019).

The example we'll use in this chapter makes use of the GDP growth data we introduced in Chapter 8. As a refresher, it consisted of quarterly time series that spanned the period between 1961:Q2 and 2020:Q1 for 25 different OECD countries. In Chapter 8, we used dimensionality-reduction techniques to extract a small number of common components from the 25 series at each point in time.

In this chapter, we will instead use the GDP growth data to train a VAE that is capable of generating similar series. We will start in Listing 9-1 by importing the libraries we'll use in this exercise and will then load and prepare the data. Notice that we transpose the GDP data, so that the columns correspond to a specific quarter and the rows correspond to countries. We'll then convert the data to a `np.array()` and set parameters for the batch size and the number of output nodes in the latent space.

Listing 9-1. Prepare GDP growth data for use in a VAE

```
import tensorflow as tf
import pandas as pd
import numpy as np

# Define data path.
data_path = '../data/chapter9/'

# Load and transpose data.
GDP = pd.read_csv(data_path+'gdp_growth.csv',
        index_col = 'Date').T

# Print data preview.
print(GDP.head())
```

```
Time      4/1/61      7/1/61      10/1/61      1/1/62
AUS   -1.097616  -0.715607    1.139175    2.806800 ...
AUT   -0.349959   1.256452    0.227988    1.463310 ...
BEL    1.167163   1.275744    1.381074    1.346942 ...
CAN    2.529317   2.409293    1.396820    2.650176 ...
CHE    1.355571   1.242126    1.958044    0.575396 ...

# Convert data to numpy array.
GDP = np.array(GDP)

# Set number of countries and quarters.
nCountries, nQuarters = GDP.shape

# Set number of latent nodes and batch size.
latentNodes = 2
batchSize = 1
```

The next step is to define the VAE model architecture, which will consist of an encoder and a decoder, similar to the autoencoder model of Chapter 8. In contrast to the autoencoder, however, latent states will be sampled from a set of independent normal distributions during the training process. We'll start by defining a function that performs the sampling task in Listing 9-2.

Listing 9-2. Define function to perform sampling task in VAE

```
# Define function for sampling layer.
def sampling(params, batchSize = batchSize, latentNodes =
latentNodes):
        mean, lvar = params
epsilon = tf.random.normal(shape=(
        batchSize, latentNodes))
        return mean + tf.exp(lvar / 2.0) * epsilon
```

Notice that the `sampling` layer does not contain any parameters of its own. Rather, it takes a pair of parameters as inputs, draws `epsilon` from a standard normal distribution for each output node in the latent state, and then transforms each draw using the `mean` and `lvar` parameters that correspond to the nodes in that state.

Once we have defined a sampling layer, we can also define an encoder model, which will closely resemble the one we constructed for the autoencoder model. We'll do this in Listing 9-3. The only initial difference is that we'll take the full time series for a country as an input, rather than the cross-section of values across countries at a point in time.

Another difference appears in the `mean` and `lvar` layers, which were not present in the autoencoder. These layers have the same number of nodes as the latent state. This is because they consist of mean and log variance parameter values for normal distributions that are associated with each of the nodes in the latent state.

We next define a `Lambda` layer, which accepts the `sampling` function we defined earlier and passes it the `mean` and `lvar` parameters. We can see that the sampling layer generates an output for each of the features (nodes) in the latent state. Finally, we define a functional model, `encoder`, which takes the input features – quarterly GDP growth observations – and returns a mean layer, a log variance layer, and sampled outputs using the means and log variances to parameterize normal distributions.

Listing 9-3. Define encoder model for VAE

```
# Define input layer for encoder.
encoderInput = tf.keras.layers.Input(shape = (nQuarters))

# Define latent state.
latent = tf.keras.layers.Input(shape = (latentNodes))

# Define mean layer.
mean = tf.keras.layers.Dense(latentNodes)(encoderInput)
```

```
# Define log variance layer.
lvar = tf.keras.layers.Dense(latentNodes)(encoderInput)

# Define sampling layer.
encoded = tf.keras.layers.Lambda(sampling, output_
        shape=(latentNodes,))([mean, lvar])

# Define model for encoder.
encoder = tf.keras.Model(encoderInput, [mean, lvar, encoded])
```

In Listing 9-4, we'll define functional models for the decoder model and the entire variational autoencoder. Similar to the decoder component of an autoencoder, it accepts the latent state as an input from the encoder and then produces a reconstruction of the inputs as an output. The full VAE model also bears similarity to an autoencoder, taking a time series as an input and transforming it into a reconstruction of the same time series.

The final step is to define the loss function, which consists of two components – the reconstruction loss and the KL divergence – and append it to the model, which we do in Listing 9-5. The reconstruction loss is no different from the one we used for the autoencoder. The KL divergence measures how far each of the sampling layer distributions is from a standard normal distribution. The further away they are, the higher the penalty.

Listing 9-4. Define decoder model for VAE

```
# Define output for decoder.
decoded = tf.keras.layers.Dense(nQuarters, activation =
        'linear')(latent)

# Define the decoder model.
decoder = tf.keras.Model(latent, decoded)

# Define functional model for autoencoder.
vae = tf.keras.Model(encoderInput, decoder(encoded))
```

Listing 9-5. Define VAE loss

```
# Compute the reconstruction component of the loss.
reconstruction = tf.keras.losses.binary_crossentropy(
        vae.inputs[0], vae.outputs[0])

# Compute the KL loss component.
kl = -0.5 * tf.reduce_mean(1 + lvar - tf.square(mean) -
        tf.exp(lvar), axis = -1)

# Combine the losses and add them to the model.
combinedLoss = reconstruction + kl
vae.add_loss(combinedLoss)
```

Finally, in Listing 9-6, we compile and train the model. In Listing 9-7, we now have a trained variational autoencoder, which we can use to perform a variety of different generative tasks. We can, for instance, use the predict() method of vae to generate the reconstruction for a given time series input. We can also generate a realization of the latent state for a given input, such as GDP growth for the United States. We can also perturb these latent states by adding random noise and then use the predict() method of decoder to generate an entirely new time series based on the modified latent state.

Listing 9-6. Compile and fit VAE

```
# Compile the model.
vae.compile(optimizer='adam')

# Fit model.
vae.fit(GDP, batch_size = batchSize, epochs = 100)
```

Listing 9-7. Generate latent states and time series with trained VAE.

```
# Generate series reconstruction.
prediction = vae.predict(GDP[0,:].reshape(1,236))

# Generate (random) latent state from inputs.
latentState = encoder.predict(GDP[0,:].reshape(1,236))

# Perturb latent state.
latentState[0] = latentState[0] + np.random.normal(1)

# Pass perturbed latent state to decoder.
decoder.predict(latentState)
```

Finally, in Figure 9-2, we show 25 generated time series that are based on a latent state realization for the US GDP growth series. We then perturb that original state over a 5x5 grid, where the rows add evenly spaced values over the [–1, 1] interval to the first latent state and the columns add equally spaced values over the [–1, 1] interval to the second latent state. The series in the center of the grid, shown in red, adds [0, 0] and, thus, is the original latent state.

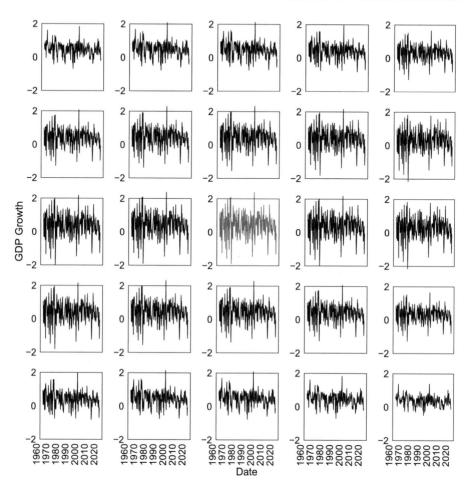

Figure 9-2. *VAE-generated time series for GDP growth for the United States*

While this example was simple and the latent state contained only two nodes for the purpose of demonstration, the VAE architecture can be applied to a wide variety of problems. We can, for instance, add convolutional layers to the encoder and decoder and change the input and output shapes. That will give us a VAE that generates images. Alternatively, we could add LSTM cells to the encoder and encoder, which would give us a VAE that could generate text or music.[1] Furthermore, an LSTM-based architecture could yield some improvements in time series generation over the dense network approach we adopted in this example.

Generative Adversarial Networks

Two families of models have dominated the generative machine learning literature: variational autoencoders and generative adversarial networks. VAEs, as we've seen, provide granular control over the generation of examples through the manipulation of latent states and the features they encode. GANs, in contrast, have been more successful at producing highly convincing examples of classes. For example, some of the most convincing generated images are produced using GANs.

As we discussed in the previous section, VAEs are a combination of two models: an encoder and a decoder, joined by a sampling layer. Similarly, GANs also consist of two models: a generator and a discriminator. The generator takes a random input vector, which we may think of as a latent state, and generates an example of a class, such as a real GDP growth time series (or an image, a sentence, or a musical score).

Once the generator component of a GAN has produced several examples of a class, they are passed to the discriminator, along with an equal number of true examples. In our case, this would be a combination of true and generated real GDP growth series. The discriminator is then trained to differentiate between the real and fake examples.

After the discriminator has finished the classification task, we can train the generator using an adversarial network, which combines both the generator and discriminator models. Just as was the case for the encoder and decoder components of the VAE, an adversarial network will

---

[1]See www.datacamp.com/community/tutorials/using-tensorflow-to-compose-music for an extended tutorial on generative models for music generation.

share weights with both networks. The adversarial network will train the generator to maximize the loss of the discriminator network.

As Goodfellow et al. (2017) discuss, we may view the two networks as trying to maximize their respective payoffs in a zero sum game, where the discriminator receives $v(g, d)$ and the generator receives $-v(g, d)$. The generator chooses samples, g, to trick the discriminator; and the discriminator chooses probabilities, d, for each of those samples. The equilibrium, characterized by a set of generated images, g_*, is given in Equation 9-1.

Equation 9-1. The equilibrium condition for image generation in a GAN.

$$g^* = \arg \min_{g} \max_{d} v(g, d)$$

Consequently, when we train the adversarial part of the network, we must freeze the discriminator weights. This will constrain the network to improve the generation process, rather than weakening the discriminator. Iterating over these steps in the training process will ultimately yield the evolutionary equilibrium described in Equation 9-1.

Figure 9-3 illustrates the generator and discriminator networks of a GAN. To summarize, the generator yields novel examples, which are not drawn from the data. The discriminator combines those examples with true examples and then performs classification. And the adversarial network trains the generator by attaching it to a discriminator, but with frozen weights. Training over the network occurs iteratively.

Following the example from the section on VAEs, we'll again make use of the GDP growth data, which we load and prepare in Listing 9-8. Our intention will be to train a GAN to generate credible GDP growth time series from a randomly drawn vector input. We will follow the approach to GAN construction described in Krohn et al. (2020).

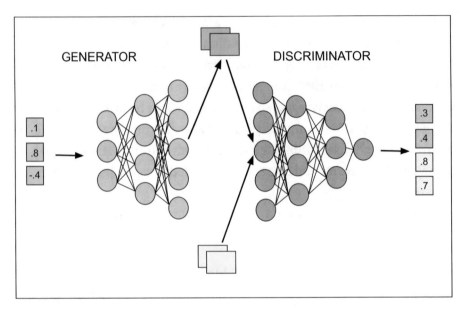

Figure 9-3. *Depiction of the generator and discriminator from a GAN*

Listing 9-8. Prepare GDP growth data for use in a GAN

```
import tensorflow as tf
import pandas as pd
import numpy as np

# Load and transpose data.
GDP = pd.read_csv(data_path+'gdp_growth.csv',
        index_col = 'Date').T

# Convert pandas DataFrame to numpy array.
GDP = np.array(GDP)
```

In Listing 9-9, we define the generative model. We again follow the simple VAE model and draw a vector with two elements as an input to the generator. Since the input to the generator can be seen as an analogy to the latent vector in a VAE, we should view the generator as a decoder.

This means we'll start with a narrow, bottleneck-type layer and will upsample to the output, which will be a generated GDP growth time series.

The simplest version of the generator would consist of an input layer that accepts the latent vector and an output layer, which upsamples the input layer. Since our output layer consists of GDP growth values, we'll use a linear activation function. We'll also include a hidden layer with a relu activation, since the model will otherwise be unable to capture non-linearities.

Listing 9-9. Define the generative model of a GAN

```
# Set dimension of latent state vector.
nLatent = 2

# Set number of countries and quarters.
nCountries, nQuarters = GDP.shape

# Define input layer.
generatorInput = tf.keras.layers.Input(shape = (nLatent,))

# Define hidden layer.
generatorHidden = tf.keras.layers.Dense(16, activation="relu")
(generatorInput)

# Define generator output layer.
generatorOutput = tf.keras.layers.Dense(236,
        activation="linear")(generatorHidden)

# Define generator model.
generator = tf.keras.Model(inputs = generatorInput, outputs =
        generatorOutput)
```

We'll next define the discriminator in Listing 9-10. It will take real and generated GDP growth series as inputs, each of which will have a length of nQuarters. It will then produce a probability of being a real GDP growth series for each of the input series. Note that we did not compile generator, but did compile `discriminator`. This is because we will use an adversarial network to train `generator`.

Listing 9-10. Define and compile the discriminator model of a GAN

```
# Define input layer.
discriminatorInput = tf.keras.layers.Input(shape =
        (nQuarters,))

# Define hidden layer.
discriminatorHidden = tf.keras.layers.Dense(16,
        activation="relu")(discriminatorInput)

# Define discriminator output layer.
discriminatorOutput = tf.keras.layers.Dense(1,
        activation="sigmoid")(discriminatorHidden)

# Define discriminator model.
discriminator = tf.keras.Model(inputs = discriminatorInput,
        outputs = discriminatorOutput)

# Compile discriminator.
discriminator.compile(loss='binary_crossentropy', optimizer=tf.
        optimizers.Adam(0.0001))
```

We have now defined a generator model and a discriminator model. We have also compiled the discriminator. The next step is to define and compile an adversarial model, which will be used to train the generator. The adversarial model will share weights with the generator and will use a frozen version of the weights for the discriminator – that is, the weights will not update when we train the adversarial network, but they will update when we train the discriminator.

Listing 9-11 defines the adversarial network. The input to the adversarial network is a latent vector, so it will have the same size as the input to generator. We will next define the output of the generator model as timeSeries, which will be a fake GDP growth time series. We can then set the trainability of discriminator to False, so that it does not update while we're training the adversarial network. Finally, we'll set the output of the network to be the discriminator's output and define and compile a functional model, adversarial. In Listing 9-12, we'll train discriminator and adversarial.

Listing 9-11. Define and compile the adversarial model of a GAN

```
# Define input layer for adversarial network.
adversarialInput = tf.keras.layers.Input(shape=(nLatent))

# Define generator output as generated time series.
timeSeries = generator(adversarialInput)

# Set discriminator to be untrainable.
discriminator.trainable = False

# Compute predictions from discriminator.
adversarialOutput = discriminator(timeSeries)

# Define adversarial model.
adversarial = tf.keras.Model(adversarialInput,
        adversarialOutput)

# Compile adversarial network.
adversarial.compile(loss='binary_crossentropy', optimizer=tf.
        optimizers.Adam(0.0001))
```

Listing 9-12. Train the discriminator and the adversarial network

```
# Set batch size.
batch, halfBatch = 12, 6

for j in range(1000):
        # Draw real training data.
        idx = np.random.randint(nCountries,
        size = halfBatch)
        real_gdp_series = GDP[idx, :]

        # Generate fake training data.
        latentState = np.random.normal(size=[halfBatch, nLatent])
        fake_gdp_series = generator.predict(latentState)

        # Combine input data.
        features = np.concatenate((real_gdp_series,
        fake_gdp_series))

        # Create labels.
        labels = np.ones([batch,1])
        labels[halfBatch:, :] = 0

        # Train discriminator.
        discriminator.train_on_batch(features, labels)

        # Generate latent state for adversarial net.
        latentState = np.random.normal(size=[batch, nLatent])

        # Generate labels for adversarial network.
        labels = np.ones([batch, 1])

        # Train adversarial network.
        adversarial.train_on_batch(latentState, labels)
```

We start by defining the batch size. We then enter the training loop, which consists of several steps. First, we draw random integers and use them to select rows in the GDP matrix, which each consists of a GDP growth time series. This will be the real samples in the discriminator's training set. Next, we generate the fake data by drawing latent vectors and then passing them to generator. We then combine both types of series and assign them the corresponding labels (i.e., 1 = real and 0 = fake). We can now pass this data to the discriminator to perform a single batch of training.

We next perform an iteration of training for the adversarial network. Here, we'll generate a batch of latent states, input them into generator, and then train with the objective of tricking the discriminator into classifying them as real. Notice that we're iterating over the training of two models and won't use normal stopping criteria for the training process. Rather, we will look for a stable evolutionary equilibrium where neither model appears to be able to gain an advantage.

In Figure 9-4, we plot the model losses over time. We can see that after approximately 500 training iterations, neither model appears to improve substantially, indicating that we have reached a stable evolutionary equilibrium.

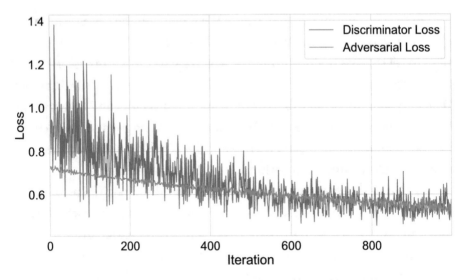

Figure 9-4. *Discriminator and adversarial model losses by training iteration*

Finally, we plot one of the GDP growth series produced by the GAN in Figure 9-5. Taking nothing more than white noise vector inputs and information about the discriminator's performance, the adversarial network managed to train the generator to produce a fairly credible fake GDP growth series after 1000 training iterations. Of course, we could have improved performance considerably by allowing for more latent features and a more advanced model architecture, such as an LSTM.

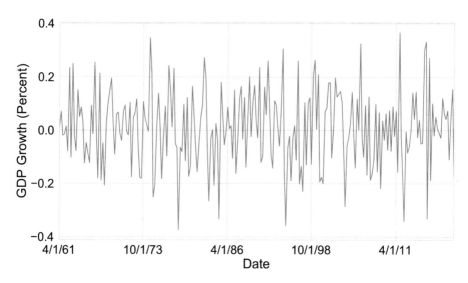

Figure 9-5. *Example fake GDP growth series*

Applications in Economics and Finance

Throughout this chapter, we concentrated on what might seem like an obscure example: generating simulated GDP growth series through the use of generative machine learning models; however, such exercises are common in Monte Carlo simulation studies, which are used to test the small sample properties of estimators in econometrics. Without generating realistic series and adequately capturing interdependencies between series, it is challenging to accurately evaluate the properties of estimators.

In fact, one of the earliest applications of GANs in the economics literature was intended to achieve precisely this objective. Athey et al. (2019) consider the possibility of using Wasserstein GANs to simulate data that appears similar to observations from an existing dataset that is insufficiently large to be used in a Monte Carlo simulation. The value of this is that it allows an econometrician to avoid the two common alternatives to this approach: (1) drawing randomly from the small dataset itself, which will result in many repetitions of the same observations, and (2) generating simulated series that typically fail to accurately capture dependencies between series in the dataset. Athey et al. (2019) demonstrate the value of their approach (and GANs more generally) by evaluating estimators using artificial data generated by a WGAN.

In addition to Athey et al. (2019), recent work in the economics literature (Kaji et al. 2018) examines whether WGANs can be used to perform indirect inference, which is typically used to estimate structural models in economics and finance. In Kaji et al. (2018), they attempt to estimate a model in which workers of different types are choosing from a wage and location menu. The parameters they want to recover are structural and cannot be directly estimated from the data, which requires them to use an indirect inference method. The approach they use is to couple model simulation with a discriminator, training the model until the simulated data is indistinguishable from the true data.

Beyond the existing applications, which are currently focused on model estimation, GANs and VAEs could also be used in off-the-shelf applications to image and text generation. While the use of image data remains limited in economics – even in discriminative models – GANs and VAEs offer the possibility of performing visual counterfactual simulations with economic data. In urban economics, for instance, we could infer how the placement of public infrastructure would have changed depending on the state of public policy and other factors.

Similarly, the growing natural language processing literature in economics and finance could make use of text generation to examine how, for instance, company press releases would differ when the underlying state of the economy or state of the industry changes.

Summary

Prior to this chapter, this book primarily discussed discriminative machine learning models. Such models perform classification or regression. That is, they take features from a training set and attempt to discriminate between different classes or make a continuous prediction for a target. Generative machine learning differs from discriminative machine learning, in that it generates new examples, rather than discriminating among examples.

Outside of the economics and finance disciplines, generative machine learning has been used to create compelling images, music, and text. It has also been used to improve Monte Carlo simulation (Athey et al. 2019) and perform indirect inference for structural models (Kaji et al. 2018) in economics.

In this chapter, we focused on two generative models: the variational autoencoder (VAE) and the generative adversarial network (GAN). The VAE model extended the autoencoder by including mean, variance, and sampling layers. This improved the autoencoder by imposing restrictions on its latent space, forcing states to cluster around the origin and have a log variance of 0.

Similar to autoencoders and VAEs, GANs also consist of multiple component models: a generator model, a discriminator model, and an adversarial model. The generator model creates novel examples. The discriminator model attempts to classify them. And the adversarial model trains the generator to create compelling examples that trick the discriminator. The training process for GANs involves finding a stable evolutionary equilibrium.

Finally, we demonstrated how both VAEs and GANs can be used to generate artificial GDP growth data. We also discussed how they are being applied within economics currently and how they might be applied in the future if they gain more widespread adoption.

Bibliography

Athey, S., G.W. Imbens, J. Metzger, and E. Munro. 2019. "Using Wasserstein Generative Adversarial Networks for the Design of Monte Carlo Simulations." *Working Paper No. 3824.*

Blei, D.M., A.Y. Ng, and M.I. Jordan. 2003. "Latent Dirichlet Allocation." *Journal of Machine Learning Research* 3 (993–1022).

Goodfellow, I., Y. Bengio, and A. Courville. 2017. *Deep Learning.* Cambridge, MA: MIT Press.

Goodfellow, I.J., J. Pouget-Abadie, M. Mirza, B. Xu, D. Warde-Farley, S. Ozair, A. Courville, and Y. Bengio. n.d. "Generative adversarial networks." *NIPS'2014.* 2014.

Kaji, T., E. Manresa, and G. Pouliot. 2018. "Deep Inference: Artificial Intelligence for Structural Estimation." *Working Paper.*

Kingma, D.P., and M. Welling. 2019. "An Introduction to Variational Autoencoders." *Foundations and Trends in Machine Learning* 12 (4): 307–392.

Krohn, J., G. Beyleveld, and A. Bassens. 2020. *Deep Learning Illustrated: A Visual, Interactive Guide to Artificial Intelligence.* Addison-Wesley.

CHAPTER 10

Theoretical Models

Relative to other machine learning packages, TensorFlow requires a substantial time investment to master. This is because it provides users with the capacity to define and solve any graph-based model, rather than providing them with a simple and interpretable set of pre-defined models. This feature of TensorFlow was intended to foster the development of deep learning models; however, it also has secondary value for economists who want to solve theoretical models.

In this chapter, we'll provide a brief overview of TensorFlow's capabilities in this area. We'll start by demonstrating how to define and solve an arbitrary mathematical model in TensorFlow. We'll then apply these tools to solve the neoclassical business cycle model with full depreciation. This model has an analytical solution, which will allow us to evaluate how well TensorFlow performed. However, we will also discuss how to evaluate performance in cases where we do not have analytical solutions.

After we demonstrate how to solve basic mathematical models in TensorFlow, we'll end the chapter by examining deep reinforcement learning, a field that combines reinforcement learning and deep learning. In recent years, it has accumulated several impressive achievements involving the development of robots and networks that play video games with superhuman levels of performance. We'll see how this can be applied to solve otherwise intractable theoretical models in economics.

© Isaiah Hull 2021
I. Hull, *Machine Learning for Economics and Finance in TensorFlow 2*,
https://doi.org/10.1007/978-1-4842-6373-0_10

Solving Theoretical Models

Thus far, we have defined a model by selecting a specific architecture and then training the model's parameters using data. In economics and finance, however, we often encounter a different set of problems that are theoretical, rather than empirical, in nature. These problems require us to solve a functional equation or a system of differential equations. Such problems are derived from a theoretical model that describes optimization problems for households, firms, or social planners.

In such settings, the model's deep parameters – which typically describe technology, constraints, and preferences – are either calibrated or estimated outside of the model and, thus, are known prior to the implementation of the solution method. The role of TensorFlow in such settings is to enable the solution of a system of differential equations.

The Cake-Eating Problem

The cake-eating problem is commonly used as a "hello world" style introduction to dynamic programming.[1] In the problem, an individual is endowed with cake and must decide how much of it to eat in each period. While highly stylized, it provides a strong analogy to the standard consumption-savings problem in economics, where an individual must decide whether to consume more today or delay consumption by allocating more to savings.

As we discussed previously, the deep parameters of such models are typically calibrated or estimated outside of the solution routine. In this case, the individual consuming the cake has a utility function and a

---

[1]Dynamic programming is a method for converting a multi-step optimization problem into a sequence of single-step problems. In economics and finance, dynamic programming is typically used for multi-period dynamic optimization problems. Dynamic programming reduces such problems to sequences of single-period problems.

discount factor. The utility function measures the enjoyment an individual gets from consuming a piece of cake of a certain size. And the discount factor tells us how an individual will value a slice of cake today versus in the future. We will use common values of the parameters in the utility function and for the discount factor.

Formally, the cake-eating problem can be written down as a dynamic, constrained optimization problem. Equation 10-1 defines the instantaneous utility that an individual receives from eating a slice of cake at time t. In particular, we assume that the instantaneous utility received is invariant to the period in which the agent receives it: that is, we place a time subscript on c, but not $u(\cdot)$. We also assume that utility is given by the natural logarithm of the amount of cake consumed. This will ensure that more cake yields more utility, but the incremental gain – the marginal utility – of more cake is decreasing in c. This provides the cake-eater with a natural desire to space consumption out over time, rather than eating the entire cake today.

Equation 10-1. Instantaneous utility of cake consumption.

$$u(c_t) = \log(c_t)$$

The marginal utility of consumption can be expressed as the derivative of $u(c_t)$ with respect to c_t, as given in Equation 10-2. Notice that neither Equation 10-1 nor Equation 10-2 contains parameters. This is one of the benefits of adopting log utility for such problems: it yields simple, parameter-free expressions for utility and marginal utility and satisfies the requirements that we typically place on utility functions in economics and finance.

Equation 10-2. Marginal utility of consumption.

$$u'(c_t) = \frac{du(c_t)}{dc_t} = \frac{1}{c_t}$$

In addition to this, the second derivative is always negative, as can be seen in Equation 10-3.

Equation 10-3. Marginal utility of consumption.

$$u''(c_t) = -\frac{1}{c_t^2}$$

To simplify the problem, we'll normalize the size of the cake to 1, which means that all consumption choices will be between 0 and 1. In Figure 10-1, we plot the level of utility and its first and second derivatives over c values in this interval.

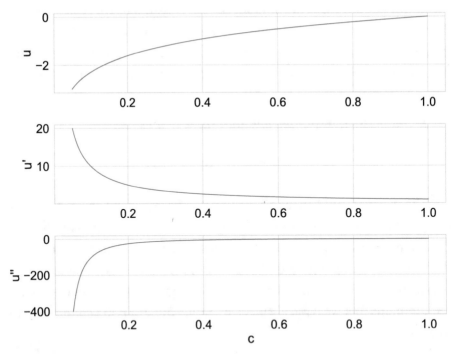

Figure 10-1. *Utility of consumption, along with its first and second derivatives over the (0,1] interval*

We'll start by considering a finite horizon problem, where the agent must divide consumption over T periods. This could be because the cake only remains edible for T periods or because the individual only lives T periods. In this stylized example, the reasoning is not particularly important, but it is, of course, more important for consumption-savings problems.

At time $t = 0$, the agent maximizes the objective function given in Equation 10-4, subject to the budget constraint in Equation 10-5 and a positivity constraint on s_{t+1} in Equation 10-6. That is, the agent must make a sequence of consumption choices, $c_0, \ldots, c_{T-1}$, each of which is constrained by the amount of remaining cake, s_t, and the requirement to carry a positive amount of cake, s_{t+1}, into the following period. Additionally, consumption in all future periods is discounted by $\beta \leq 1$.

In Equation 10-4, we also apply the Principle of Optimality (Bellman 1954) to restate the value of entering period zero with s_0 cake. It will be equal to the discounted sums of utilities along the optimal consumption path, which we will denote as the unknown function, $V(\cdot)$.

Equation 10-4. Objective function for agent at time $t = 0$.

$$V(s_0; 0) = \max_{c_0 \ldots c_{T-1}} \sum_{t \in \{0, \ldots, T-1\}} \beta^t \log(c_t)$$

Equation 10-5. Budget constraint.

$$c_t = s_t - s_{t+1}$$

$$\forall t \in \{0, \ldots, T-1\}$$

Equation 10-6. Positivity constraint.

$$s_{t+1} > 0$$

$$\forall t \in \{0,\dots, T-1\}$$

Bellman (1954) demonstrated that we may re-express the objective function in an arbitrary period using what was later termed the "Bellman equation," given in Equation 10-7. We also substitute the budget constraint into the equation.

Equation 10-7. The Bellman equation for the cake-eating problem.

$$V\left(s_t;t\right) = \max_{s_{t+1}} log\left(s_t - s_{t+1}\right) + \beta V\left(s_{t+1};t+1\right)$$

Rather than choosing a consumption sequence for *T-t+1* periods, we instead choose c_t or the s_{t+1} it implies for the current period. Solving the problem then reduces to solving a functional equation to recover $V(\cdot)$. After doing this, choosing an s_{t+1} will pin down both the instantaneous utility and the discounted flows of utility from future periods, making this a sequence of one-period optimization problems.

For finite horizon problems, such as the one we've set up, we can pin down $V(s_T; T)$ for all s_T. Since the decision problem ends in period $T - 1$, all choices of s_T will yield $V(s_T; T) = 0$. Thus, we'll start by solving Equation 10-8, where it will always be optimal to consume s_{T-1}. We can now step back in time recursively, solving for $V(\cdot)$ in each period until we arrive at $t = 0$.

Equation 10-8. The Bellman equation for the cake-eating problem.

$$V\left(s_{T-1};T-1\right) = \max_{s_T} log\left(s_{T-1} - s_T\right)$$

There are several ways in which we could perform the recursive optimization step. A common one is to use a discrete grid to represent the value function. For the sake of exploiting TensorFlow's strengths and maintaining continuity with the remainder of the chapter, we'll instead focus on a parametric approach. More specifically, we'll parameterize the policy function that maps the state at time t, which is the amount of cake we have at the start of the period, to the state at time t+1, which is the amount of cake we carry into the following period.

To keep things simple, we'll use a linear function for the decision rule that is proportional in the state, as shown in Equation 10-9.

Equation 10-9. Functional form of policy rule for cake-eating.

$$s_{t+1} = \theta_t s_t$$

We will now implement this approach in TensorFlow for the simple case where $T = 2$. That is, we start with a full cake of size 1 and must decide how much to carry forward to period $T - 1$.

In Listing 10-1, we define the constants and parameters need to solve the model. This includes the slope of the policy function, theta, which tells us the share of the cake we carry forward into the following period; the discount factor, beta, which tells us how much the agent values cake in period t relative to $t+1$; and the share of the cake remaining in period zero, s0. Notice that theta is a trainable variable; beta is set to 1.0, indicating that we do not discount cake consumption in period t+1; and we initially have an entire cake (s0= 1).

Listing 10-1. Define the constants and variables for the cake-eating problem

```
import tensorflow as tf

# Define policy rule parameter.
theta = tf.Variable(0.1, tf.float32)

# Define discount factor.
beta = tf.constant(1.0, tf.float32)

# Define state at t = 0.
s0 = tf.constant(1.0, tf.float32)
```

We next define a function for the policy rule in Listing 10-2, which takes values of the parameters and yields s1. Notice that we define s1 as theta*s0. We use tf.clip_by_value() to restrict s1 to the [0.01, 0.99] interval, which imposes the positivity constraint.

Next, in Listing 10-3, we define the loss function, which takes the parameter values as an input and yields the loss. Notice that v1 is pinned down by the choice of s1, since 1 is the terminal period. With v1 determined, we can then compute v0, conditional on the choice of theta. We will choose theta – and, thus, s1 – to maximize v0. However, since we will perform minimization in practice, we'll instead use -v0 as the measure of loss.

Listing 10-2. Define a function for the policy rule

```
# Define policy rule.
def policyRule(theta, s0 = s0, beta = beta):
        s1 = tf.clip_by_value(theta*s0,
        clip_value_min = 0.01, clip_value_max = 0.99)
        return s1
```

Listing 10-3. Define the loss function

```
# Define the loss function.
def loss(theta, s0 = s0, beta = beta):
        s1 = policyRule(theta)
        v1 = tf.math.log(s1)
        v0 = tf.math.log(s0-s1) + beta*v1
        return -v0
```

We next instantiate an optimizer and perform minimization over the course of 500 iterations in Listing 10-4.

Listing 10-4. Perform optimization

```
# Instantiate an optimizer.
opt = tf.optimizers.Adam(0.1)

# Perform minimization.
for j in range(500):
opt.minimize(lambda: loss(theta),
        var_list = [theta])
```

After 100 iterations of training, theta converges to 0.5, as shown in Figure 10-2. The interpretation of theta = 0.5 is that the agent should eat half of the cake in period 0 and half of the cake in period 1, which is exactly what we would expect in the case where the agent does not discount the future.

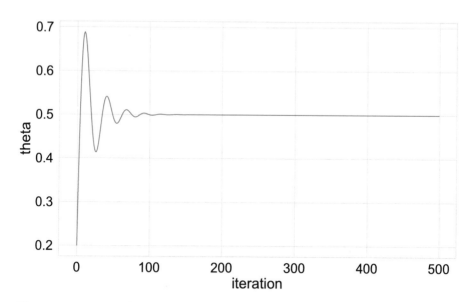

Figure 10-2. *Evolution of policy function parameter over training iterations*

Of course, we will typically assume a beta of less than one. Figure 10-3 plots optimal values of theta for different values of beta. In each case, we re-solve the model. As expected, we see an upward sloping relationship between the two. That is, as we place more value on the future consumption, we also choose to carry more cake forward into the future to consume.

This problem was highly stylized, and focusing on the two-period case trivialized it even further. It did, however, demonstrate the basic template for constructing and solving theoretical models in TensorFlow. In the following subsection, we'll consider a more realistic problem, but will concentrate on a case where we have a closed-form solution. This will make it relatively easy to evaluate the performance of our approach.

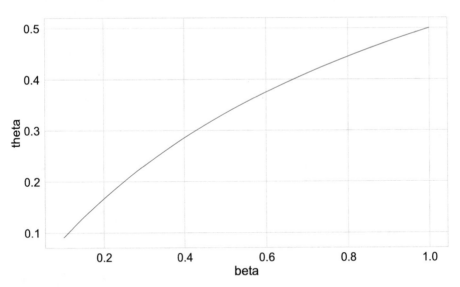

Figure 10-3. *Relationship between the discount factor and the policy rule parameter*

The Neoclassical Business Cycle Model

We will end this section by solving a special form of the neoclassical business cycle model introduced by Brock and Mirman (1972). In the model, a social planner maximizes a representative household's discounted flows of utility from consumption. In each period, t, the planner chooses next period capital, k_{t+1}, which yields output in the following period, y_{t+1}. Under the assumption of log utility and full depreciation, the model has a tractable closed-form solution.

Equation 10-10 is the planner's problem in the initial period, which is subject to the budget constraint in Equation 10-11. The objective is similar to the cake-eating problem, but the household is infinitely lived, so we now have an infinite summation of discounted utility streams from consumption. The budget constraint indicates that the social planner divides output into consumption and capital in each period. Equation 10-12 specifies the production function.

Equation 10-10. The social planner's problem.

$$\max_{c_0} \sum_{t=0}^{\infty} \beta^t \log(c_t)$$

Equation 10-11. The economy-wide budget constraint.

$$y_t = c_t + k_{t+1}$$

Equation 10-12. The production function.

$$y_t = k_t^{\alpha}$$

We also assume that $\beta < 1$, $\alpha \in (0, 1)$, and capital fully depreciates in each period. This means that we recover the output produced using the capital we carried forward from the previous period, but we do not recover any of the capital itself.

One way in which we can solve this problem is by identifying a policy function that satisfies the Euler equation. The Euler equation, given in Equation 10-13, requires that the marginal utility of consumption in period t be equal to the discounted gross return to capital in period $t+1$, multiplied by the marginal utility of consumption in period $t+1$.

Equation 10-13. The Euler equation.

$$\frac{1}{c_t} = \beta \alpha k_{t+1}^{\alpha-1} \frac{1}{c_{t+1}}$$

$$\rightarrow c_{t+1} = \beta \alpha k_{t+1}^{\alpha-1} c_t$$

The Euler equation has an intuitive interpretation: a solution is optimal if the planner can't make the household better off by reallocating a small amount of consumption from period t to period $t+1$ or vice versa. We will find a solution that is consistent with Equations 10-11, 10-12, and 10-13 by defining policy functions for capital and consumption. We will see, though, that the policy function for consumption is redundant.

We'll start by assuming that the solution can be expressed as a policy function that is proportional to output. That is, the planner will choose a share of output to allocate to capital and to consumption. Equation 10-14 provides the policy function for capital, and Equation 10-15 provides the function for consumption.

Equation 10-14. Policy function for capital.

$$k_{t+1} = \theta_k k_t^{\alpha} = \theta_k y_t$$

Equation 10-15. Policy function for consumption.

$$c_t = (1-\theta_k) k_t^{\alpha} = (1-\theta_k) y_t$$

The closed-form expressions for the policy functions are given in Equations 10-16 and 10-17. We will use these to evaluate the accuracy of our results in TensorFlow.

Equation 10-16. Policy rule for capital.

$$k_{t+1} = \alpha\beta k_t^\alpha$$

Equation 10-17. Policy rule for consumption.

$$c_t = (1 - \alpha\beta)k_t^\alpha$$

We have now defined the problem and can implement a solution in TensorFlow. We'll start by defining the parameters and the capital grid in Listing 10-5. We'll use standard values for alpha and beta, the production function parameter and discount factor. Next we'll define thetaK, the share of output that is allocated to capital in the following period. Finally, we'll define a start-of-period capital grid, k0. This is the vector of capital values that a household could hold at the start of period *t*.

Listing 10-5. Define model parameters

```
import tensorflow as tf

# Define production function parameter.
alpha = tf.constant(0.33, tf.float32)

# Define discount factor.
beta = tf.constant(0.95, tf.float32)

# Define params for decision rules.
thetaK = tf.Variable(0.1, tf.float32)

# Define state grid.
k0 = tf.linspace(0.001, 1.00, 10000)
```

In Listing 10-6, we define the loss function. We first compute the policy rule for next period capital and then plug the policy rules into the Euler equation. We then subtract the right-hand side from the left-hand side, yielding error, which is sometimes referred to as the Euler equation residual. We then square the residuals and compute the mean.

Listing 10-6. Define the loss function

```
# Define the loss function.
def loss(thetaK, k0 = k0, beta = beta):
        # Define period t+1 capital.
        k1 = thetaK*k0**alpha

        # Define Euler equation residual.
        error = k1**alpha-
        beta*alpha*k0**alpha*k1**(alpha-1)

        return tf.reduce_mean(tf.multiply(error,error))
```

The final step is to define an optimizer and perform minimization, which we do in Listing 10-7. After performing optimization, we print thetaK and the parameter expression in the closed-form solution, beta*alpha. In both cases, we get 0.3135002, suggesting that our TensorFlow implementation identified the true solution to the model.

Listing 10-7. Perform optimization and evaluate results

```
# Instantiate an optimizer.
opt = tf.optimizers.Adam(0.1)

# Perform minimization.
for j in range(1000):
opt.minimize(lambda: loss(thetaK),
        var_list = [thetaK])

# Print thetaK.
print(thetaK)
```

```
<tf.Variable 'Variable:0' shape=() dtype=float32,
numpy=0.31350002>
```

```
# Compare analytical solution and thetaK.
print(alpha*beta)
```

```
tf.Tensor(0.31350002, shape=(), dtype=float32)
```

Now that we've solved for the policy rules, we can use them to do things like compute transition paths. Listing 10-8 shows how to compute the transitions for consumption, capital, and output using the policy rules and starting from a capital stock value of 0.05. We plot the transition paths in Figure 10-4.

Listing 10-8. Compute transition path

```
# Set initial value of capital.
k0 = 0.05

# Define empty lists.
y, k, c = [], [], []

# Perform transition.
for j in range(10):
        # Update variables.
        k1 = thetaK*k0**alpha
        c0 = (1-thetaK)*k0**alpha

        # Update lists.
        y.append(k0**alpha)
        k.append(k1)
        c.append(c0)

        # Update state.
        k0 = k1
```

Finally, it is worth pointing out that we have used an intentionally trivial example where the solution can be computed analytically. In practice, we will typically encounter problems where this is not the case. In such cases, we will often use Euler equation residuals to evaluate the accuracy of the solution method.

Listing 10-9 demonstrates how we can modify the loss function to compute Euler equation residuals. We'll start by defining a grid over which to compute them. In some cases, we may want to expand the bounds beyond what we used to solve the model to demonstrate that our model also performs well far away from the steady state. In this case, we'll use the same grid that we used to solve the model.

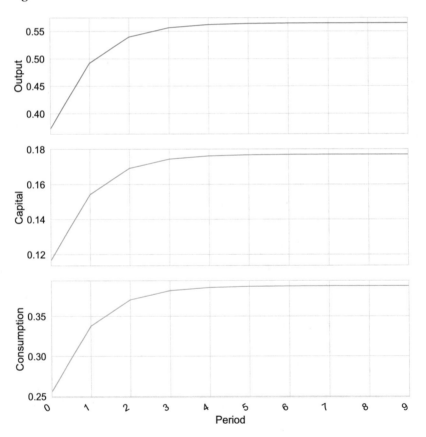

Figure 10-4. *Transition path for output, capital, and consumption*

Perhaps unsurprisingly – since our policy rule matches the analytical solution – the maximum Euler equation residual is negligibly small. While not particularly important for this problem, Euler equation residuals will be helpful whenever we want to determine the extent to which our results are affected by approximation error.

Listing 10-9. Compute the Euler equation residuals

```
# Define state grid.
k0 = tf.linspace(0.001, 1.00, 10000)

# Define function to return Euler equation residuals.
def eer(k0, thetaK = thetaK, beta = beta):
        # Define period t+1 capital.
        k1 = thetaK*k0**alpha

        # Define Euler equation residual.
        residuals = k1**alpha-
        beta*alpha*k0**alpha*k1**(alpha-1)

        return residuals

# Generate residuals.
resids = eer(k0)

# Print largest residual.
print(resids.numpy().max())

5.9604645e-08
```

Deep Reinforcement Learning

Standard theoretical models in economics and finance assume that agents are rational optimizers. This implies that agents form unbiased expectations about the future and achieve their objectives by performing optimization. A rational agent might incorrectly predict the return to capital in every period, but it won't systematically overpredict or unpredict it. Similarly, an optimizer will not always achieve the best results ex-post, but ex-ante, it will have made the best decision given its information set. More explicitly, an optimizer will choose the exact optimum, given their utility function and constraints, rather than using a heuristic or rule of thumb.

As described in Palmer (2015), there are several reasons why we may wish to deviate from the rational optimizer framework. One is that we may want to focus on the process by which agents form policy rules, rather than assuming that they have adopted the one implied by rationality and optimization. Another reason is that breaking either the rationality or optimization requirement will greatly improve the computational tractability of many models.

If we do wish to depart from the standard model, one alternative approach is reinforcement learning, described in Sutton and Barto (1998). Its value within economics has been discussed in Athey and Imbens (2019) and Palmer (2015). Additionally, it was applied in Hull (2015) as a means of solving intractable dynamic programming problems.

Similar to the standard rational optimizer framework in economics, agents in reinforcement learning problems perform optimization, but they do so in an environment where they have limited information about the state of the system. This induces a trade-off between "exploration" and "exploitation" – that is, learning more about the system or optimizing over the part of the system you understand.

In this section, we'll focus on a recently introduced variant of reinforcement learning called "deep Q-learning," which combines deep learning and reinforcement learning. Our objective will be to slacken the computational constraints that prevent us from solving the rational optimizer versions of problems with high-dimensional state spaces, rather than studying the learning process itself. That is, we will still seek a solution for the rational optimizer's problem, but we will do so using deep Q-learning, rather than using more conventional methods in computational economics.

Similar to dynamic programming, Q-learning is often done using a "look-up table" approach. In dynamic programming, this entails constructing a table that represents the value of being in each state. We then iteratively update that table until we achieve convergence. The table itself is the solution for the value function. In contrast, in Q-learning, we instead construct a state-action table. In our neoclassical business cycle model example, which we'll return to here, the state was the capital stock and the action was the level of consumption.

Equation 10-18 demonstrates how the Q-table would be updated in the case where we use temporal difference learning. That is, we update the value associated with the state-action pair (s_t, a_t) in iteration $i+1$ by taking the value in i and adding to it to the learning rate, multiplied by the expected change in value induced by choosing the optimal action.

Equation 10-18. Updating the Q-table.

$$Q_{i+1}(s_t, a_t) \leftarrow Q_i(s_t, a_t) + \lambda \left[r_t + \beta \max_a Q(k_{t+1}, a) - Q_i(s_t, a_t) \right]$$

Deep Q-learning replaces the look-up table with a deep neural network called a "deep Q-network." The approach was introduced in Mnih et al. (2015) and was originally applied to train Q-networks to play video games at superhuman levels of performance.

We will briefly outline how deep Q-learning can be used to solve economic models, returning to the neoclassical business cycle model example. There are several ways in which this can be done in TensorFlow. Two common options are tf-agents, which is a native TensorFlow implementation, and keras-rl2, which makes use of the high-level Keras API in TensorFlow. Since our coverage will be brief and introductory, we'll focus on keras-rl2, which will allow for a simpler implementation with more familiar syntax.

In Listing 10-10, we install the keras-rl2 module and import tensorflow and numpy. We then import three submodules from the newly installed rl module: DQNAgent, which we will use to define a deep Q-learning agent; EpsGreedyQPolicy, which we'll use to set the process that generates policy decisions on the training path; and SequentialMemory, which is used to retain decision paths and outcomes that are then used as inputs to train the deep Q-network. Finally, we import gym, which we will use to define the model environment.

Listing 10-10. Install and import modules to perform deep Q-learning

```
# Install keras-rl2.
!pip install keras-rl2

# Import numpy and tensorflow.
import numpy as np
import tensorflow as tf

# Import reinforcement learning modules from keras.
from rl.agents.dqn import DQNAgent
from rl.policy import EpsGreedyQPolicy
from rl.memory import SequentialMemory

# Import module for comparing RL algorithms.
import gym
```

In Listing 10-11, we'll set the number of capital nodes and define an environment, planner, which is a subclass of gym.Env. This will specify the details of the social planner's reinforcement learning problem.

Our class, planner, is constructed to do the following at initialization: define a discrete capital grid, define action and observation spaces, initialize the number of decisions to zero, set the maximum number of decisions, set the node index of the initial value of capital (500 out of 1000), and set the production function parameter (alpha). For our purposes, the action and observation spaces will both be discrete objects with 1000 nodes, defined using gym.spaces. The observation space in our case is the entire state space: that is, all capital nodes. The action space is also the same.

Listing 10-11. Define custom reinforcement learning environment

```
# Define number of capital nodes.
n_capital = 1000

# Define environment.
class planner(gym.Env):
        def __init__(self):
                self.k = np.linspace(0.01, 1.0, n_capital)
                self.action_space = \
                gym.spaces.Discrete(n_capital)
                self.observation_space = \
                gym.spaces.Discrete(n_capital)
                self.decision_count = 0
                self.decision_max = 100
                self.observation = 500
                self.alpha = 0.33
        def step(self, action):
                assert self.action_space.contains(action)
                self.decision_count += 1
```

```
            done = False
            if(self.observation**self.alpha - action) > 0:
                    reward = \
            np.log(self.k[self.observation]**self.alpha -
            self.k[action])
            else:
                    reward = -1000
            self.observation = action
            if (self.decision_count >= self.decision_max)\
            or reward == -1000:
                    done = True
            return self.observation, reward, done,\
            {"decisions": self.decision_count}
        def reset(self):
            self.decision_count = 0
            self.observation = 500
            return self.observation
```

We next define a step method of the class, which is required to return four outputs: the observation (state), the reward (instantaneous utility), an indicator for whether a training session should be reset (done), and a dictionary object that contains relevant debugging information. Calling this method increments the decision_count attribute, which records the number of decisions an agent has made during a training session. It also initially sets done to False. We then evaluate whether the agent made a valid decision – that is, selected a positive value of consumption. If an agent makes more than decision_max decisions or chooses a non-positive consumption value, the reset() method is called, which reinitializes the state and decision count.

In Listing 10-12, we instantiate a `planner` environment and then define a neural network in TensorFlow. We use the `Sequential` model with one dense layer and a `relu` activation function. Note that the model should have an output layer that contains `n_capital` nodes; however, beyond that, we can choose the architecture that is best suited to our problem.

Listing 10-12. Instantiate environment and define model in TensorFlow

```
# Instantiate planner environment.
env = planner()

# Define model in TensorFlow.
model = tf.keras.models.Sequential()
model.add(tf.keras.layers.Flatten(input_shape=(1,) + env.
        observation_space.shape))
model.add(tf.keras.layers.Dense(32, activation="relu"))
model.add(tf.keras.layers.Dense(n_capital,
activation="linear"))
```

Now that our environment and network have been defined, we need to specify hyperparameters and train the model, which we do in Listing 10-13. We first use `SequentialMemory` to retain a "replay buffer" of 50,000 decision paths, which will be used to train the model. We then set the model to use an epsilon-greedy policy with epsilon = 0.30. During training time, this means that the model will maximize utility 70% of the time and explore with a random decision the remaining 30% of the time. Finally, we set the hyperparameters of the `DQNAgent` model, compile it, and perform training.

Listing 10-13. Set model hyperparameters and train

```
# Specify replay buffer.
memory = SequentialMemory(limit=10000, window_length=1)

# Define policy used to make training-time decisions.
policy = EpsGreedyQPolicy(0.30)

# Define deep Q-learning network (DQN).
dqn = DQNAgent(model=model, nb_actions=n_capital, memory=memory,
         nb_steps_warmup=100, gamma=0.95,
         target_model_update=1e-2, policy=policy)

# Compile and train model.
dqn.compile(tf.keras.optimizers.Adam(0.005), metrics=['mse'])
dqn.fit(env, nb_steps=10000)
```

Monitoring the training process yields two observations. First, the number of decisions per session increases across iteration, suggesting that the agent learns to avoid negative amounts of future periods by not drawing capital down as sharply as a greedy policy might suggest. And second, the loss declines and the average reward begins to rise, suggesting that the agent is moving closer to optimality.

If we wanted to perform a more thorough analysis of the quality of our solution, we could examine the Euler equation residuals, as we discussed in the previous section. This would tell us whether the DQM model yielded something that was approximately optimal.

Summary

TensorFlow not only provides us with a means of training deep learning models but also offers a suite of tools that can be used to solve arbitrary mathematical models. This includes models that are commonly used in economics and finance. In this chapter, we examined how to do this using a toy model (the cake-eating model) and a common benchmark in the computational literature: the neoclassical business cycle model. Both models are trivial to solve using conventional methods in economics, but provide a simple means of demonstrating how TensorFlow can be used to solve theoretical models of relevance for economists.

We also showed how deep reinforcement learning could be used as an alternative to standard methods in computational economics. In particular, using deep Q-learning networks (DQN) in TensorFlow may enable economists to solve higher-dimensional models in a non-linear setting without changing model assumptions or introducing a substantial amount of numerical error.

Bibliography

Athey, S., and G.W. Imbens. 2019. "Machine Learning Methods Economist Should Know About." *Annual Review of Economics* 11: 685–725.

Bellman, R. 1954. "The theory of dynamic programming." *Bulletin of the American Mathematical Society* 60: 503–515.

Brock, W., and L. Mirman. 1972. "Optimal Economic Growth and Uncertainty: The Discounted Case." *Journal of Economic Theory* 4 (3): 479–513.

Hull, I. 2015. "Approximate Dynamic Programming with Post-Decision States as a Solution Method for Dynamic Economic Models." *Journal of Economic Dynamics and Control* 55: 57–70.

Mnih, V. et al. 2015. "Human-level control through deep reinforcement learning." *Nature* 518: 529–533.

Palmer, N.M. 2015. *Individual and Social Learning: An Implementation of Bounded Rationality from First Principles.* Doctoral Dissertation in Computational Social Science, Fairfax, VA: George Mason University.

Sutton, R.S., and A.G. Barto. 1998. *Reinforcement Learning: An Introduction.* Cambridge: MIT Press.

Index

A

Activation function, 173

Adam() optimizer, 124, 164, 228, 240

add() method, 159

Applications in economics and finance, 327, 328

Arbitrary model, 107

Autoencoder loss function, 296

Autoencoder model
actual and OLS-predicted GDP growth, 304
architecture, 297, 301, 304
dimensionality reduction
regression setting, latent state, 303
generative machine learning, 298
noise reduction, 298
functions, 296
latent state time series, 302
loss function, minimizing, 296
neural network, 296
predict() method, 301
reconstructed series for US GDP growth, 302
train, Keras API, 299, 300

Automatic differentiation, 50–53

Autoregressive coefficient, 111

Autoregressive model, 110

B

Bag-of-words (BoW) model
CountVectorizer(), 206, 208
document-term matrix, 204, 205, 208
fit_transform(), 204
inverse document frequencies, 207
sklearn.feature_extraction, 204
submodules, 204
term-frequency inverse-document frequency (tf-idf) metric, 206

Batch matrix multiplication, 33, 34

Batch normalization, 174

Batch size, 224

Bayesian regression methods, 80

Big Data, 62, 63

Binary_crossentropy loss, 164

Binary cross-entropy loss function, 115, 116

BoostedTreesClassifier, 141, 142

Boosted trees regressor, 143, 144

© Isaiah Hull 2021
I. Hull, *Machine Learning for Economics and Finance in TensorFlow 2*,
https://doi.org/10.1007/978-1-4842-6373-0

Printed in the United States
By Bookmasters